Anatomy
of Film

Anatomy of Film

Bernard F. Dick

SECOND EDITON

St. Martin's Press

New York

Senior editor: Mark Gallaher
Development editor: Cathy Pusateri
Project editor: Bruce Glassman
Cover design: Tom McKeveny
Cover photos: (clockwise from top left) *Lady From Shanghai,*
courtesy of MOMA/FSA and Columbia Pictures; *The Wolf
Man,* copyright Universal Pictures, courtesy MCA
Publishing Rights, A division of MCA, Inc.; *Sunset
Boulevard,* courtesy WCFTR, copyright © Paramount
Pictures Corp.; *Casablanca,* courtesy MOMA/FSA; *The
Dead,* courtesy Vestron Pictures; *The Public Enemy,*
courtesy WCFTR.

8 7 6
k j   i h

For information, write:
St. Martin's Press, Inc.
175 Fifth Avenue
New York, NY 10010

ISBN: 0-312-01991-2

Published and distributed outside North America by:

MACMILLAN EDUCATION LTD.
Houndsmills, Basingstoke, Hampshire RG21 2XS and London
Companies and representatives throughout the world.

ISBN: 0-333-55102-8

TO MY STUDENTS
PAST AND PRESENT

Preface to the Second Edition

Since *Anatomy of Film* was first published in 1978, film study has changed significantly. Once regarded as a form of popular culture, film is now a legitimate academic discipline. Colleges and universities that once only offered basic film courses have expanded their offerings to include courses in film genres and individual directors. The public's perception of film has also changed radically over the past decade. The video cassette recorder has made it possible to purchase a video cassette of a film that, in 1978, could only be rented in 16 mm. at a price that was more than ten times the cost of the cassette.

Although the ideal way to view a film is to see it projected on a large screen (in its proper aspect ratio), financial considerations may necessitate other alternatives—the most practical of which is the video cassette. While home video has given students access to films that were often unavailable in the past, it has not solved the perennial problem that film instructors face: the heterogeneous class. There will always be students in an introductory film class who can quote dialogue from *Casablanca* and those to whom "Play it, Sam" has no meaning at all. No teacher can second-guess a class and a textbook writer should not even try. What is important is to provide students with examples they can understand. This does not mean students must have seen all the films in question, that would be impossible. Examples are understood through their context and, thus, *Anatomy of Film* continues to provide a context for every example given. Instructors should feel free to use their own examples; if the examples are clearly presented, students will grasp the principles even if they have not seen the particular films. All of us learned what simile and metaphor were through examples, we did not have to read an entire poem to see how these figures of speech function. Yet once we knew what these figures were, we could appreciate poetry that utilized them.

Just as instructors should be free to add their own examples, so should students. Students should be encouraged to imagine themselves as filmmakers and should be asked how they might frame a particular shot, when they would use a close-up, or how they would plan a long take. If a student has trouble understanding what is meant by a cut, the student should count the number of times a shot changes in the course of a film.

Just as film study has changed in the past decade, so has this author. A book that is ten years old must not only be revised, it must also be rethought. The second edition of *Anatomy of Film* contains as much rethinking as revision and also includes material that is wholly new. Instructors using the book have requested a chapter on film genres, which I have been happy to provide, along with sections on framing, screenwriting, and film adaptation, with *The Color Purple* as a prime example. The Second Edition opens quite differently from the First: it attempts to show how a film begins and ends with a certain image and why the viewer should consider those images integral parts of the film.

The decline in the number of 16 mm distributors has made my original list of rental sources superfluous. Since films change distributors, the best guides to availability are either the latest catalogs or the latest edition of *Feature films on 8 mm, 16 mm, and Videotape,* compiled and edited by James L. Limbacher and published by R. R. Bowker. Bibliographies also tend to become outdated; thus I have substituted a Basic Film Library for the traditional Bibliography that appeared in the First Edition with the purpose of suggesting how a student might start building up a collection of basic works.

No text, much less a film text, can avoid illustrations. Ideally, the illustrations should come from the films in the form of frame enlargements rather than publicity stills that might be inaccurate. Frame enlargements, however, often reproduce poorly and there are some aspects of film that frame enlargements cannot illustrate. A wipe is a *moving* line that "wipes" one image away to make way for another. Even a frame enlargement showing what a wipe might look like on a frame is no substitute for viewing the effect of the wipe in a running film. A film is a *moving* picture; a frame enlargement, however accurate, reduces motion to a still photograph devoid of other elements such as dialogue or sound that might be integral to the shot. Thus, frame enlargements are not the answer; the film is. It is impossible to have a frame enlargement or a still for every point that is made in the book. However, if examples are carefully explained, students will understand them even if there is no corresponding illustration in the text. Film is a wonderfully imaginative medium and should therefore challenge students' imagination in addition to appealing to their visual sense. Visual thinking is an intellectual act, it is not the passive watching of a "flick."

A text is a tool, it is a guide for the instructor, not a substitute. Accordingly, many instructors may prefer their own examples; some might use the blackboard to illustrate film techniques. They might run a piece of chalk horizontally across the blackboard to suggest a wipe or they might mark a spot at the top of the blackboard and one at the bottom to suggest camera placement for high and low angle shots.

More important than the illustrations is seeing a film as a total work of art in which shots, transitions, sound effects, and music are part of a whole. While *Anatomy of Film* anatomizes film, it also restores the parts to their proper place within the whole.

There will always be some disagreement about the way films are cited. Auteurists who maintain the director is the central intelligence behind a film preface their films with the director's name in the possessive: Michael Curtiz's *Casablanca* (1942). Others will either cite the film with its release date in a parenthesis or with its director and release date in a parenthesis. The director-release date parenthesis is the method of citation used in this text. The first citation will follow this method except when a film is mentioned merely to make a point without necessarily providing an example. While directors and release dates could be provided for all films and for all subsequent citations of the same film, a preponderance of parentheses slows the reader down and gives the impression of overloading each sentence unnecessarily.

I would like to thank a few individuals whose contributions to my book were so special that they must be mentioned by name: Alan Alda; John Belton; Jean Chemay; Mary Corliss of the Museum of Modern Art's Film Stills Archive, whom I called "indispensable" in the first edition—an epithet that is now even more applicable; Fairleigh Dickinson University for granting me release time to complete what has amounted to a major revision; Patrick Frank of the Wisconsin Center for Film and Theater Research; Martin Nocente, on whose knowledge of film I continue to draw; and my wife, Katherine M.

Restaino, Dean of St. Peter's College at Englewood Cliffs, who can spot errors that elude the ordinary eye.

An introductory film course should be one of the most enjoyable courses a student can take. I hope *Anatomy of Film* will contribute to that joy.

BERNARD F. DICK
TEANECK, NEW JERSEY

Contents

1

Film, Cinema, or Movie:
Understanding the Medium

Perhaps the most common way of learning the meaning of a word or an idea is through a definition. In grade school, we learn that a square is a rectangle with equal sides, that meter is the regular occurrence of stressed and unstressed syllables, and that a catalyst is a substance that precipitates a chemical reaction without being changed in the process. What is not learned through definition is often learned through experience. After some exposure to art, we discover that paintings are not restricted to watercolors and oils, or sculpture to clay and marble. Yet before we have been exposed to great cinematic art, we have seen some kind of film. Most likely it has been on television: a cartoon, a Three Stooges short, a *Lassie* rerun. By the time we reach college, we have been exposed to a wide range of films— documentaries, promotional films, educational films, TV movies, and, of course, theatrical films (films intended to be shown in movie theaters).

Still, if asked to define film, we might hesitate. Because film is so familiar, we take it for granted. How many of us could come up with scientific definitions of *love, family,* or *car*—words so much a part of our everyday vocabulary that definitions seem superfluous?

Definitions, while useful, are limited. Many are nothing more than etymologies. Anthropology was once defined as the study of humankind (*anthropo* + *logy*). The definition may be etymologically valid in terms of the Greek derivatives (*anthrōpos, logos*) that make up the word; however, other disciplines (e.g., psychology, sociology) study humankind as well, but from different perspectives.

A good definition is also a description. In attempting to define film, John Howard Lawson—the American playwright, screenwriter, and critic—ended up describing it: "A film is an audio-visual conflict; it embodies time-space relationships; it proceeds from a premise, through a progression, to a climax or ultimate term of the action."[1] Lawson has not really described film as such; he has described a particular kind of film: the narrative film, which is the focus of this text. In other words, Lawson has described what is commonly known as a movie.

Many American critics prefer *movie* to *film,* which is an ambiguous word. Film can be a noun (a film, roll film), an adjective (film stock), or a verb (to film on location). An alternative is *cinema,* which some American critics, notably Pauline Kael, disparage because they find it pretentious. However, cinema is perfectly acceptable for categorizing films in terms of their national origins (American cinema, Soviet cinema, French cinema, etc.). *Movie* and *movies* are equally acceptable synonyms for the narrative film.

NARRATIVE FILM

But what is a movie? To Lawson, it is a narrative, told through sound and image, that builds toward a climax and culminates in a resolution. Note that Lawson does not make dialogue part of his definition: He merely says that a movie is audiovisual. A movie does not need spoken dialogue to tell a story. The silent films had no spoken dialogue, but they did have some kind of sound. Piano or organ accompaniment was common, and sound effects were necessary to complement the action on the screen.

Like any narrative, a good movie involves conflict: personalities clash, goals differ, interests diverge, characters are at odds with each other or with society. However, in a movie the conflict is audiovisual; it is heard and seen rather than written and read. A movie "embodies time-space relationships." While a written narrative can suggest that events in two different places are occurring at the same time, a movie can do more than suggest: it can *show* them occurring.

In their accounts of the Passion, the four evangelists imply that Peter's denial of Christ coincided with Christ's interrogation by the Sanhedrin: while Peter was outside in the courtyard denying Christ, Christ was within, being questioned by the chief priests and scribes. A film could make it clear that this was the case by switching back and forth from Peter's denials to the Sanhedrin's questions. In Shakespeare's *Romeo and Juliet* (V, 1), Romeo buys poison from an apothecary and plans to commit suicide because he has not received a crucial letter. In the next scene, Friar John explains to Friar Laurence that he was unable to deliver the letter because he was confined to a house under quarantine. Both actions—the purchase of the poison and the explanation about the letter—seem to be occurring simultaneously. A film could cut from Romeo's buying poison to Friar John's detention; it could even do so without dialogue if the bottle were labeled poison and the house in which Friar John is confined is depicted as plague-ridden.

Frequently, the visuals do the narrating by themselves. *Psycho* (Alfred Hitchcock, 1960) will always be remembered for the shower murder of Marion Crane (Janet Leigh). The episode is completely wordless. There is sound, of course: music that really shrieks, as if anticipating the audience's reaction. As Marion prepares for her shower in her room at the Bates Motel, Norman Bates (Anthony Perkins) is in an adjacent parlor that has a peephole, covered by a picture of Susanna and the Elders. Removing the picture, Norman watches Marion undress. She goes into the shower, luxuriating in the spray of water. Suddenly, a shadow, presumably of an elderly woman, appears against the shower curtain. The "woman" pulls aside the curtain and proceeds to stab Marion repeatedly as blood mingles with the water and swirls down the drain. Although the entire episode lasts less than a minute, a great deal of information has been imparted. Hitchcock's choice of painting was not arbitrary; just as the Elders spied on Susanna as she entered her bath, so does the voyeuristic Norman spy on Marion as she prepares to shower. A shower is a place of privacy, relaxation, and cleansing. Marion's privacy has been invaded. Instead of relaxation, she experiences the repose of death; instead of her body's being cleansed, it is defiled. Actually, it is the shower stall that must be cleansed because it has been splattered with blood.

To write down everything that happens in that episode would take longer than it would to see it. In his *Filmguide to Psycho,* James Naremore devotes five pages to describing these forty-five seconds of film.[2]

This brief discussion of *Psycho* treated the movie as a text, a work to be analyzed and interpreted. A movie is a text and is similar to any text, even a textbook that is used in a classroom. Text comes from the Latin *textus*, meaning something woven. A text weaves the material together in an orderly and coherent fashion. A movie is a text that interweaves sound in any or all of its aspects (noise, music, speech) and image (everything from the printed word to physical action, movement, gaze, and gesture) for the purpose of telling a story.

MOVIE TIME

Since a movie tells a story, it must do so within a certain period of time. Anyone attending movies regularly checks the movie timetable in the newspaper. Television programmers are especially conscious of a movie's running time since films are often cut to fit into a particular time slot. Running time, however, is real time—90 minutes, 105 minutes, and so on. Movie time is not; movie time manipulates real time so that an event can be prolonged or shortened, or an action slowed down or speeded up.

Newspapers and magazines frequently reduce an event to a series of pictures that, when viewed sequentially, enable the reader to reconstruct it. On July 24, 1975, the *New York Times* ran four pictures of a tragedy that had occurred in Boston the previous day when a firefighter attempted to rescue Diana Bryant and her two-year-old goddaughter, Tiare Jones, from a burning building. No sooner had an aerial ladder deposited the firefighter on the balcony than the balcony gave way. The firefighter grasped the ladder, but Diana fell to her death. Tiare was seriously injured but survived.

If a photographer happened to be at the scene of the tragedy, as Stanley Forman was, he would naturally try to get as many pictures of it as he could. The pictures Forman took won him a Pulitzer Prize for spot news photography in 1976. Viewed in succession, the pictures tell a story without words. In the first, Diana grips the railing while the firefighter stands alongside her protectively, his arm raised as if he were acknowledging an ovation. The mood is one of optimism, which changes to shock as the balcony collapses in the second photo, and Diana begins her plunge with the eerie grace of slow-motion death. In the third, Diana moves through space like a swimmer, and Tiare balances herself like a tightrope walker. In the final photo three figures, like the three Fates of mythology, hover over Diana's body.

The images constitute a text that we have read and interpreted; in so doing, we have reconstructed an event that, in real life, was continuous but has been reduced to four separate stages, thereby appearing longer than it actually was. The same would have happened in a movie. In real life, there is no such thing as a slow-motion fall, yet Diana's fall has that effect. In real life, the collapse of the building and the fall of Diana and Tiare would have been concurrent, not separate, incidents. In real life, the tragedy would have been briefer than the pictures (which have been fragmented into stages or "acts") seem to indicate. If we understand what Stanley Forman achieved in these photos, we can understand how fragmentation occurs in film where the time of an event can be made to seem longer or shorter than it actually was.

Movie time is arbitrary. In a movie, a whole day can be compressed into a few minutes or even seconds; likewise, a few minutes or seconds can be prolonged into what seems a whole day. In the famous Odessa Steps sequence in *Potemkin* (1925), Soviet director Sergei Eisenstein distorts real time. He makes the massacre on the steps seem longer than it was because he wants to emphasize the atrocities the czarist troops committed against the people of Odessa. Toward the end of the sequence, a czarist soldier swings his saber, striking a woman with a pince-nez in her right eye. In reality, the soldier would have slashed her eye with one movement of his arm. Eisenstein fragments the act. First we see the soldier, his arm raised with the blade behind his head; then we see his savage face, but not the saber; now his face dominates the screen. Next he shouts something as his raised arm begins to descend. Finally, we see the woman—her mouth gaping, the right lens of her pince-nez shattered, blood spurting from her eye and running down her face.

Conversely, in *Meet John Doe* (Frank Capra, 1941), a cross-country political campaign occurs in a few seconds of screen time. The climax of *Nickelodeon* (Peter Bogdanovich, 1975) is the premiere of *The Birth of a Nation* (D. W. Griffith, 1915). To make the premiere as credible as possible, clips from Griffith's film were used. The premiere is so authentic, and the audience reaction so natural, that we do not immediately realize that Griffith's three-hour epic has been reduced to a few minutes.

While we must observe the laws of time, movies do not; they can expand or contract time and make the result seem believable.

NOTES

[1]John Howard Lawson, *Film: The Creative Process,* 2nd ed. (New York: Hill and Wang, 1967), 292.

[2]James Naremore, *Filmguide to Psycho* (Bloomington: Indiana University Press, 1973), 53–57.

2
The Nature of the Medium, I:
Graphics and Sound

A movie's running time and the rate at which the action progresses are among the many choices that are made before, during, and after production. Who makes these choices is not the point here; often we will not know who was responsible for a particular image or a particular line of dialogue. Dialogue should be the writer's province, but directors like Robert Altman and Martin Brest allow actors to improvise their own dialogue for certain scenes. Brest had Charles Grodin improvise the dialogue in the boxcar scene in *Midnight Run* (1988). If the plot is a flashback, one assumes the screenwriter planned it as such, but it could have been the producer's decision. *Murder, My Sweet* (Edward Dmytryk, 1944) is a flashback movie, not because John Paxton wrote it that way but because producer Adrian Scott wanted it written that way. Thus, in writing about film, we use the general *filmmaker* instead of the specific *director* or *cinematographer* when we are uncertain about the creator of a particular effect.

GRAPHICS
Logos

Although we may never know how all the choices were made in a particular film, we do know a film is intended to begin and end with a certain image. In American films, the first image to appear on the screen is generally the studio's or the distributor's logo.

A logo is an example of graphics, the combination of print and design. It is also a studio's trademark. Although the studios are not what they were during Hollywood's Golden Age of the 1930s and 1940s, the logos of such studios as MGM, Warner Bros., Paramount, Twentieth Century-Fox, Columbia, and Universal have either remained the same or have been slightly modified. Universal's globe still spins in the sky, but it is no longer encircled by an airplane as it was in the 1930s; nor is it made of plexiglass as it was in the 1940s. Columbia's lady with a torch is intact, except that the torch shines more brightly, and the firepoints are visible. If, as Vladimir Nabokov claims in *Transparent Things*, each word contains within it its own history, each logo encapsulates its studio's history. In the 1930s and 1940s, moviegoers knew the differences between the studios. When they heard MGM's lion roar its greeting, they anticipated a well-produced film with an outstanding cast; MGM was Hollywood's largest studio, boasting "more stars than there are in the heavens." When they saw the Republic eagle, they expected a B movie; Republic was known for programmers (for example, Gene Autry and Roy Rogers westerns)—movies that filled out the second half of a double bill. Students of film should be able to distinguish between the studios when studying the films of the past and attending the films of the present.

While it is true that filmmakers have no control over the logo, they often try to integrate it with the film so that it is not merely a trademark. *Indiana Jones and the Temple of Doom* (Steven Spielberg, 1985) opens with Paramount's snow-capped mountain, which appears concurrently with the Indiana Jones theme on the soundtrack. The combination of logo (Paramount's mountain) and music (Indiana Jones theme) says that what follows is both a Paramount picture and an Indiana Jones movie.

Some filmmakers even start the action with the logo. In *That's Life* (Blake Edwards, 1985), the Columbia logo appears simultaneously with background conversation that continues through the credits. We do not know whose voices we are hearing, although they seem to be surgeons performing an operation (they are indeed surgeons, as we

Universal's globe. Universal is now a subsidiary of MCA (Music Corporation of America), a diversified entertainment and leisure company. (Copyright by Universal Pictures, a Division of Universal City Studios, Inc. Courtesy MCA Publishing Rights, a Division of MCA, Inc.)

Vestron Pictures' logo. Vestron, Inc., which began operations in February 1982, is the distributor of such films as Dirty Dancing *(1987),* The Dead *(1987), and* Earth Girls are Easy *(1989). (Courtesy Vestron Pictures)*

discover when the credits are over). The surgeons have just performed a biopsy, the results of which will not be made known until the end.

Blake Edwards clearly expected the audience to be seated at the moment *That's Life* began; it was a Columbia film, and it had to open with the Columbia logo. However, Edwards made an imposition work to his advantage by setting the plot into motion with the appearance of the logo. The moral is simple: one should be in the theater when the movie begins.

Main Titles and End Credits

One should also be in the theater when a movie begins because one never knows exactly *how* it will begin. Take, for example, the main title that is generally the film's title plus the opening credits (although in some cases it is simply the film's title). When the main title consists merely of the film's name, its cast, key personnel, producer, and director, you will not have missed any of the plot if you've missed the main title. But you will have missed a certain part of the movie, a part that is often imaginatively executed. Main titles can be quite creative. In *The Lady Eve* (Preston Sturges, 1941), in which a female cardsharp pursues a timid herpetologist, the main title appears as a snake slithering across the screen; in *The Seven Year Itch* (Billy Wilder, 1955), the main title—designed by Saul Bass, who is renowned for his main titles—consists of credits popping out of a jack-in-the-box. In *Psycho*, the main title was also designed by Saul Bass: the credits intersect as they come onto the screen horizontally and vertically; then the actors' first and last names split apart. The main title prepares the viewer for a movie about a split personality as well as one in which slashing and cutting will figure prominently.

Although its basic function is that of a program or playbill, the main title can establish the mood of the film, especially when it is artistically executed and appropriately orchestrated (as it is in *Psycho*). Missing a main title like that of *Psycho* or *The Last Emperor* (Bernardo Bertolucci, 1987, with credits that appear against exquisite artwork to evocative music) is equivalent to arriving at a performance of Wag-

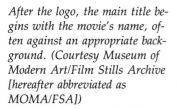

Cry of the City *(Robert Siodmak, 1948) opens with the Twentieth Century-Fox logo. (Courtesy Margaret Herrick Library of the Academy of Motion Picture Arts and Sciences)*

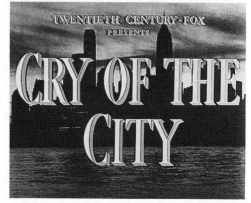

After the logo, the main title begins with the movie's name, often against an appropriate background. (Courtesy Museum of Modern Art/Film Stills Archive [hereafter abbreviated as MOMA/FSA])

ner's opera, *Die Meistersinger,* after the prelude, which is a major piece of music in its own right.

There are some films that dispense with graphic design and begin immediately with a *credits sequence* in which the credits start appearing along with the main action. *That's Life* is such a film, except that the movie starts even before the first credit; it starts with the logo. *The Four Seasons* (Alan Alda, 1981) opens with a credits sequence in which one couple picks up two other couples in their car. During the sequence, the credits start appearing. By the time the sequence is over, and the last credit has disappeared, we have been introduced to the three couples whose trips together constitute the plot.

In *Lady in White* (Frank LaLoggia, 1988), the first image to appear after the logo is that of a plane landing at an airport. A young man disembarks, hails a cab, and asks the driver to stop at a cemetery so that he can visit two graves. The young man is a novelist, and it is only at the end of the film that we realize he is the main character as a boy, that the graves are those of a mother and daughter whose story is told in the film, and that the film we have been watching was the novel he had written. Other films (e.g. *Hustle* [Robert Aldrich, 1975]) open cold, with a *precredits sequence*—a sort of prologue preceding the credits. In a precredits sequence, the title does not appear until *after* the sequence is over.

Missing a credits or precredits sequence is not just missing a part of the film; it is missing a part of the plot.

If important information is lost by arriving after the film has formally begun, significant elements may also be lost by leaving before it has formally ended. It is true that end credits have become longer than they were in the 1930–1950 period, when the end credits were just the cast of characters. Now the end credits acknowledge everyone associated with the film from the accountants to the star's fitness trainer. While comics joke about the end credits being longer than the movie, and mock such job titles as "gaffer" and "best boy," the end credits show the complexity of contemporary filmmaking and prove conclusively that film is a collaborative art in which the gaffer (chief electrician) and best boy (gaffer's first assistant) are among the collaborators.[1]

Since the end credits are prepared by the studio's legal department and must follow a specific order, they do not figure among the filmmaker's choices. Yet, just as filmmakers can use the logo to begin the film, they can use the end titles as epilogue or postlude. In *Sweet Liberty* (Alan Alda, 1986), which depicts the filming of a book about the American Revolution, the end credits are interspersed with scenes from the movie's premiere. Until the very end of the movie, the author, a university professor, is appalled at what is being done to his book. During the end credits, he is interviewed by a reporter who congratulates him on writing history as it should be written. At that moment, a disclaimer appears on the screen to the effect that any similarity between the film and history is purely coincidental. If one leaves during the end credits, one misses the film's main point: in the movies, historical truth may have to be sacrificed for the sake of entertainment. Perhaps the most ingenious use of end credits occurs in *Married to the Mob* (Jonathan Demme, 1988); here, the end credits include outtakes (shots deleted from the film). Whether or not Demme intended it, the end credits have an educational function: they make the audience aware of how much they did not see. Equally educational are the end credits of *Tucker: The Man and His Dream* (Francis Ford Coppola, 1988), which are superimposed over photographs of the real Preston Tucker and his family.

The end credits can also reprise some of the music. The end credits of *Radio Days* (Woody Allen, 1987) are orchestrated with the music of the 1940s, which allows the nostalgic mood of the film to linger.

The end credits are similar to a curtain call except that in the theater, the cast—not the crew—takes the bows; in a movie, everybody does. A serious theatergoer would never leave during a curtain call; a serious moviegoer should not leave during the equivalent. Students who develop this habit will not automatically rise from their seats when they think the film is about to end. Some do this after Tom Joad (Henry Fonda) in *The Grapes of Wrath* (John Ford, 1940) vows to fight for a better world, yet that is only the penultimate scene. The final scene may be anticlimactic by comparison, but it is the one that producer Darryl F. Zanuck decided should end the film. Likewise, *Citizen Kane* (Orson Welles, 1941) does not end with "The End." Welles came from the stage, and it is fitting that in his first film there is a curtain call. Since the cast of *Citizen Kane* was relatively unknown, Welles identified the important members by name as well as by repeating a shot in which each appeared. Peter Bogdanovich did the same at the end of *The Last Picture Show* (1971), and for the same reason: the unfamiliarity of the cast.

One might argue that the curtain calls in *Kane* and *The Last Picture Show* are extraneous to the plot. But they are not extraneous to the films in which they appear. Making a film means making choices. A filmmaker may decide to begin a film with a main title consisting of nothing but the most basic form of graphics: words on a plain background. A director may decide to open with an elaborate main title, with no title, or with a main title that foreshadows the action or includes part of it. A main title like that in *Psycho* is implicitly part of the narrative since it affects how we see what follows. No matter how a film begins, the viewer should be prepared to see it in its entirety, as it was intended to be seen. The student of film will want to make some sense of the main title in the context of the work as a whole.

Opening Titles and End Titles

There are titles other than main titles. A title is simply printed material that appears in a film. Often, after the opening credits there is an opening title that can serve several functions. It can be a time-place designation: "Shanghai, 1935" is the opening title of *Indiana Jones and the Temple of Doom. Psycho* has one of the most specific opening titles in the history of film: "Phoenix, Arizona. Friday, December the Eleventh. Two Forty-Three P.M."

An opening title can be used as a preface or an introduction to a film about an event with which the audience might be unfamiliar. While World War II audiences knew the history of the conflict, contemporary audiences might not be that familiar with it. Thus, in *Empire of the Sun* (Steven Spielberg, 1987), there is an opening title in the form of a preface that briefly explains the significance of December 7, 1941, and, more important, what Japanese aggression meant to British subjects living in Shanghai. An opening title can appear stationary, as in *Empire of the Sun*, or it can roll up or down the screen, in which case it is known as a roll-up title or a crawl. Roll-up titles were common in the serials of the 1930s and 1940s. In an attempt to evoke that era, the Star Wars trilogy (*Star Wars* [George Lucas, 1977]), *The Empire Strikes Back* [Irvin Kershner, 1980], *The Return of the Jedi* [Richard Marquand, 1983]) use elaborate roll-up titles, in which the print moves up the screen.

An epigraph (literary excerpt) or a quotation is another common opening title. *The Picture of Dorian Gray* (Albert Lewin, 1945) opens and closes with the same excerpt from the *Rubaiyat*. George Santayana's "Those who do not remember the past are condemned to relive it" is the epigraph to *Lacombe, Lucien* (Louis Malle, 1974), which shows how a French boy's apathy made him a pawn of the Nazis. Perhaps the most memorable opening title is the "Old Arabian Proverb" about Beauty and the Beast ("And lo the beast looked upon the face of beauty . . .") in *King Kong* (Merian C. Cooper and Ernest B. Schoedsack, 1933), which invites us to consider the film from that point of view.

Opening titles have also been used as disclaimers. *Hennessy* (Don Sharp, 1975), about an attempt to blow up the Houses of Parliament on Guy Fawkes Day, incorporates newsreel footage of the royal fam-

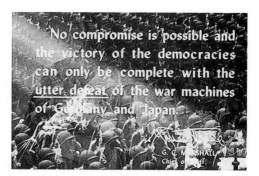

The end title of the World War II documentary Prelude to War *(Frank Capra, 1942). (Courtesy National Archives)*

ily. The opening title states "this motion picture incorporates extracts from a news film of the Queen at a State Opening of Parliament which, when photographed, was not intended for use in a fictional context." Similarly, the opening title of *The Last Temptation of Christ* (Martin Scorsese, 1988) makes it clear that the film is based on a novel and is not a historical interpretation of the life of Christ.

Just as an opening title can serve as a preface or prologue, an end title can function as an epilogue. An end title is particularly useful to inform the audience of the fate of the characters, especially if extending the action would prove anticlimactic or destroy the mood the ending is intended to create. At the end of *The Wrong Man* (Alfred Hitchcock, 1957), which is based on a true story, an end title states that Rose Balestrero (Vera Miles)—who became mentally unbalanced after her husband was falsely convicted of theft—was eventually cured and is now living in Florida. The title is a bald statement of fact and nothing more; when it appears on the screen, it has the effect of a case stamped "Closed." Had Hitchcock shown Rose basking in the Florida sun, he would have shattered the film's somber mood, gratifying only those who want the storm clouds turned inside out to see the silver lining. The title he chose, however, provides neither a happy ending nor a successful resolution.

In *Dog Day Afternoon* (Sidney Lumet, 1975), Sonny Wortzik (Al Pacino), a married Vietnam vet with two children, holds up a Brooklyn bank to finance a transsexual operation for his second wife—a man he married in a wedding ceremony complete with celebrant and bridesmaids. The film ends on a Kennedy Airport runway, a few feet from the jumbo jet Sonny has ordered to fly him to Algeria. Then three titles appear on the screen without any fanfare, as if they were being typed by someone concerned only with the accuracy of the transcription, not with its implications: Sonny is serving twenty years in prison; his first wife Angie is on welfare; his second wife Leon is a woman and living in New York.

In *Shock Corridor* (Samuel Fuller, 1963), the opening and end titles are identical: a quotation from Euripides ("Whom the gods wish to destroy, they first make mad"). The double-duty quotation is appropriate. The film concerns an ambitious reporter who feigns madness to solve a murder. The end title is painfully ironic: the reporter who feigned madness went mad himself.

Tucker: The Man and His Dream ends with Preston Tucker's acquittal. Although the real Tucker lived for six more years, the film did not continue the story of the automobile manufacturer. Thus the end title reminds us that, although only fifty Tuckers were ever manufactured, forty-six exist and are capable of being driven. The title also informs us that, although Tucker died six years after his trial, "his legend lives on."

Intertitles

The silent film made great use of intertitles, printed material that appears periodically on the screen. The intertitle was one of the ways the silent filmmaker supplemented the narrative or clarified the action; it is also a reminder of film's early dependence on the printed word. D. W. Griffith used intertitles for a variety of purposes, not just for reproducing dialogue and identifying characters. He also used intertitles (1) to attest to the accuracy of a particular setting (e.g., the title, "An historical facsimile of Ford's Theater as on that night, exact in size and detail with the recorded incidents, after Nicolay and Hay in *Lincoln, a History*," introduces the Assassination of Lincoln sequence in *The Birth of a Nation*); (2) to comment on the action or play on the audience's emotions (e.g., the title, "Dying, she gives her last little smile to a world that has been so unkind," accompanies the heroine's death in *Broken Blossoms* [1919]); (3) to explain words with which the audience might be unfamiliar (e.g., "Pharisee" and "Sanhedrin" in *Intolerance* [1916]; (4) to reveal a character's thoughts (e.g., the title, "The Inspiration," appears after Ben Cameron sees some white children frighten black children with a sheet in *The Birth of a Nation*; the "inspiration" is the use of bedsheets to make the klansmens' robes for the cross-burning vigilantees). Griffith treated intertitles as images, integrating them with the film so they became part of the narrative.

A Woman of Affairs (Clarence Brown, 1928) shows how silent filmmakers used punctuation, especially the dash, to suggest how the lines would have been spoken:

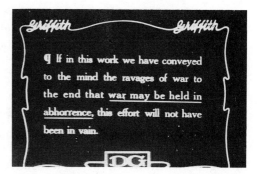

An intertitle from The Birth of a Nation *(D. W. Griffith, 1915). Note the underscoring for emphasis and the DG trademark as a sign of authorship. (Courtesy MOMA/FSA and Epoch Producing Corporation)*

My nerves have gone to pieces—I'm going out—somewhere.
I didn't mean to come here—I started driving—
Why should a man—happy as David was—take his own life?
David died—for decency.

Intertitles did not die with the coming of sound. They are occasionally found in contemporary films such as *Hannah and Her Sisters* (Woody Allen, 1986) and *The Unbearable Lightness of Being* (Philip Kaufman, 1988). Since the directors of both films were responsible for the screenplays, the decision to use intertitles was theirs. Allen may have chosen to use them because, in addition to being an actor, director, and screenwriter, he is also a playwright and short-story writer. Allen's stories are often vignettes, and *Hannah and Her Sisters* is a series of vignettes about three sisters. Thus, Allen segments the film, introducing each vignette with a title that can be (1) a line of dialogue repeated in the segment (the opening title, "God, she's beautiful!," is also the opening line of dialogue, spoken off screen); (2) a character introduction ("The Hypochondriac" introduces the Woody Allen character); (3) a vignette title ("The Abyss" is the title of the episode in which the Allen character believes he has a brain tumor); a quotation ("The only absolute knowledge attained by man is that knowledge is impossible"—Tolstoy). By using titles in so many different ways, Woody Allen not only allies himself with the venerable tradition of the intertitle, but also with the written word.

The Unbearable Lightness of Being opens like a fairy tale. The first title, "In Prague in 1968 there lived a young doctor named Tomas," is followed by a scene showing Tomas in a less than fairy tale situation: making love to a nurse. The second title, "But the woman who understood him best was Sabina," is followed by a love-making scene between Tomas and Sabina. After the third title, "Tomas was sent to a spa town to perform an operation," the film becomes serious, as one might expect of a film about the Soviet-backed invasion of Czechoslovakia in 1968. The titles, with their storybook connotations, run counter to the erotic scenes that succeed them. Once the titles end, the eroticism continues but within a historical, not a storybook, context.

Subtitles

The subtitle shares one of the main functions of the intertitle: the transmission of dialogue. Although subtitles, in which the translation of dialogue appears at the bottom of the screen, are customary in foreign films shown in the United States, they are also used in American films with scenes requiring the characters to speak in a foreign language. For such scenes, filmmakers now prefer to have the actors use the characters' native tongue rather than simulate an accent suggesting the characters' nationality. *Tora! Tora! Tora!* (Richard Fleischer, 1970) is unusual among films about World War II since it was apparently the first one in which the Japanese spoke their own language with subtitles providing the translation. Whenever Sicilian and Spanish were spoken in *The Godfather, Part II* (Francis Ford Coppola, 1974), subtitles were used, as they were for the scenes in which Sioux was spoken in *The Return of a Man Called Horse* (Irvin Kershner, 1976). In *Red Dawn* (John Milius, 1985), which imagined a Soviet invasion of Colorado with the aid of Cuban and Nicaraguan forces, subtitles were used when Russian and Spanish were spoken.

Other Uses of the Printed Word

Printed matter in film is a visual and, as such, it can make a valuable contribution to the narrative. *Citizen Kane* is a quest for the meaning of a man's last word, "Rosebud!" Until the end, the audience does not know the meaning of "Rosebud," nor do any of the characters. At the end, the characters still do not know, but the audience does. Among some of Kane's seemingly useless possessions (being thrown into a blazing furnace) is a sled. As the sled burns, we see that it bears a name: "Rosebud." Thus the film's resolution is a word—a word that must be seen, a word that symbolizes the lost childhood of Charles Foster Kane.

Another example of the symbolic use of print occurs in *Casablanca* (Michael Curtiz, 1942) when Rick (Humphrey Bogart), standing in the rain, reads a letter from Ilsa (Ingrid Bergman) informing him that she cannot leave with him for Marseilles. As Rick reads it, the rain falls on the paper, causing the ink to run, tear-like, down the page. The running ink provides the tears the stoic Rick cannot generate; it also signals the end of an affair that has faded like the words on the letter. In both

The integration of print and plot in Scarface *(Howard Hawks, 1932). (Courtesy Wisconsin Center for Film and Theater Research [hereafter abbreviated as WCFTR])*

Kane and *Casablanca*, print has been dramatically embellished—by flames in one film, by rain in the other.

Naturally, print does not always operate so symbolically. Generally, print is a visual shorthand that enables the filmmaker to identify locales and impart important information without having to resort to awkward exposition. Thus signposts, street signs, newspapers, and plaques are used to pinpoint settings. Since much of *The Grapes of Wrath* consists of a drive from Oklahoma to California along Highway 66, signs along the way tell the audience which state the Joads are in. A San Francisco newspaper, seen at the opening of *The Birds* (Alfred Hitchcock, 1961), immediately identifies the locale.

It is possible to formulate a general rule about the best use of print in film: print should be used as a means of supplying information that can only be imparted in that form. Sometimes the script calls for print. Judith Traherne (Bette Davis) in *Dark Victory* (Edmund Goulding, 1939) learns she is terminally ill by coming upon her medical file and seeing the words "PROGNOSIS NEGATIVE." In a similar film, *An Act of Murder* (Michael Gordon, 1948), a woman learns she is dying from a letter her physician has written to her husband. In *All the*

President's Men (Alan J. Pakula, 1976), Bob Woodward (Robert Redford), realizing that Carl Bernstein's (Dustin Hoffman) apartment is bugged, turns up the stereo and types: "Deep Throat says our lives may be in danger. SURVEILLANCE. BUGGING."

Thus, print can perform an important narrative function in a film. The student of film should determine what that function is.

SOUND

Seeing a narrative film without sound would be an abomination. Even the silent films (which were silent only in the sense that there was no spoken dialogue) had some kind of sound effects as well as musical accompaniment. *Nickelodeon* illustrates the importance of sound in the silent film by showing the world premiere of *The Birth of a Nation*, in which men fire cap pistols backstage to simulate the gunfire in the battle scenes.

Gunfire, a staple in westerns, war films, and crime movies, is one of many sound effects used in films. Under the heading of sound effects come all the sounds heard in a film except dialogue, music, and off-screen narration. Noise is an important sound effect in a film, and can be a legitimate and even a powerful device. *Cat People* (Jacques Tourneur, 1942) would not be the horror classic it is if noise were absent in two crucial scenes. As Alice (Jane Randolph) walks home at night, she hears the ominous sound of footsteps. Just when we think that whatever is following her will catch up with her, we hear the sound of brakes; a bus has pulled up alongside Alice, and she quickly boards it. Later, as she is swimming in an indoor pool, she hears growling sounds, as if a ferocious beast were nearby.

The noise in *Cat People* is atmospheric; it is intended to heighten the suspense. In many films, however, noise is essential to the plot. A scene from *Marnie* (Alfred Hitchcock, 1964), for example, demands noise—a noise that the audience and Marnie must hear, but that another character in the scene cannot hear. After taking money from her employer's safe, Marnie (Tippi Hedren) stealthily leaves the office. In the adjacent area, a cleaning woman is washing the floors. In order not to be heard, Marnie removes her shoes, placing them in the pockets of her jacket. One of her shoes falls to the floor. Anyone in the vicinity would have heard the sound, yet the cleaning woman does not look up from her work. As we wonder whether or not Marnie will be discovered, the janitor calls to the cleaning woman in an unnaturally loud voice, making it clear that she is hard of hearing.

And Now Tomorrow (Irving Pichel, 1946) contains an interesting example of noise that, under ordinary circumstances would be audible, but in the context of the film must be inaudible. When Emily Blair (Loretta Young) wakes one morning, she sees the window panes streaked with rain but does not hear the rainfall. The audience discovers Emily has lost her hearing at the same moment she does: when the rain silently beats upon the window.

Actual and Commentative Sound

As a form of sound, noise can emanate from a source that is either on or off screen. We do not have to see the source of the noise; we only have to know there is a source. We never see the foghorns in *Long Day's Journey into Night* (Sidney Lumet, 1962), but we hear them, and know they are coming from nearby ships. In *A Letter to Three Wives* (Joseph L. Mankiewicz, 1949), everything in the Finney kitchen shakes when the train passes by. We never see the train, but we hear it and witness the results of the vibrations it causes.

Sound, then, can be actual (or natural) in the sense of coming from a real source that we may or may not see. It can also be commentative in that it may come from a source outside the physical setting of the action. Perhaps the most familiar type of commentative sound is background music, the recurring motifs or signature themes that can identify a character (Lara's theme in *Dr. Zhivago* [David Lean, 1965]), a place (the Tara theme in *Gone with the Wind* [Victor Fleming, 1939]), a physical state (the Blindness theme in *Dark Victory*), or an obsession (the Power theme in *Citizen Kane*). In *Dark Victory*, when Judith Traherne discovers she will experience a short period of blindness prior to death, the Blindness theme is heard on the soundtrack. Judith cannot hear the music because it is not coming from a source within the action, but the audience hears it, and having heard it before in various forms, recognizes it as a sign of Judith's fate.

While actual and commentative sound are usually distinct from one another, actual sound can also be commentative if it is used to point out the disparity or similarity between what is happening in a scene and what is being heard. A radio report of the German invasion of Poland on September 1, 1939, has no effect on the guests at a party in *One More Tomorrow* (Peter Godfrey, 1946). Their indifference to the news illustrates the extent to which isolationism prevailed in the United States when World War II broke out in Europe.

Synchronization and Asynchronization

Another way of looking at sound is from the perspective of synchronization and asynchronization. In synchronization, sound and image are properly matched; the sound comes from within the image or from an identifiable source. Synchronization is not just limited to a literal correlation of sound and image. In many films, characters may be in transit (e.g., in a car or a plane) and the audience will see the car on the freeway or the plane in the air, but not see the characters. Yet we hear their conversation. In post production, the dialogue has been added and synchronized with the image.

There are, however, more sophisticated forms of synchronization. For example, a nonhuman sound may be combined with the image of a person. In *Cat People,* Irena (Simone Simon) tactfully tells her husband on their wedding night that she is not ready to consummate their marriage. As they retire to separate rooms, Irena, who is a descendant of a Serbian cat cult and periodically reverts to panther form, falls to her knees, assuming an animal posture. At that moment, the snarl of a panther is heard. The audience knows the source of the sound: the Central Park Zoo, which Irena frequents. However, within the new context of an unconsummated wedding night, the combination of a sound coming from an identifiable source and the image of the crouching Irena adds another dimension to the narrative: her repressed sexuality is given "voice." While sound and image have been synchronized in this instance, we know the sound source and see the image before us; it now seems as if the image is making the sound. Their combination (snarling panther + crouching woman) suggests that within Irena there is something waiting to be unleashed.

Synchronization, then, can be quite imaginative. It can be particularly effective when a character remembers the past. The voice of the person remembering can be combined with the image of what is remembered, or the face of the person remembering can be combined with the sound that is remembered. In *A Streetcar Named Desire* (Elia Kazan, 1951), Blanche du Bois (Vivien Leigh) periodically recalls the music played the night her husband committed suicide. At the end of *Forever Amber* (Otto Preminger, 1947), Amber (Linda Darnell) watches her son go off with his father, never to see either of them again. Earlier, the child's father—Amber's former lover—had said, "May God have mercy on both of us for our sins." In the final scene, Amber standing at the window, recalls his words—her image synchronized with the sound of his voice.

In synchronization, sound and image are related contextually, spatially, and temporally. In asynchronization, sound and image are related symbolically, metaphorically, or ironically. With the latter, the image the viewer expects to see after hearing a particular sound turns out to be something quite different. Asynchronization allows filmmakers to contrast sound and image, substitute a sound for an image, or

Asynchronization in M *(Fritz Lang, 1931). When Mrs. Beckmann calls "Elsie!," the response is not verbal but visual: a place setting never to be used again. (Courtesy MOMA/FSA and Janus Films)*

juxtapose sounds and images that would not normally occur at the same time.

In *M* (Fritz Lang, 1931), Mrs. Beckmann is waiting anxiously for her daughter Elsie to return from school. She leans out the window, calling "Elsie! Elsie!" On the screen we do not see Elsie but rather a series of images: an empty stairwell, an empty attic, Elsie's place at the dinner table, her ball on the grass, and, finally, a balloon that is momentarily caught in some telephone wires and then floats away.

The asynchronization is remarkably subtle. Ironically, Mrs. Beckmann's call is heard but images denoting absence and emptiness answer her. Elsie will never return. Like the balloon that was caught in the wires and then blown skyward by the wind, Elsie was enticed by a child molester and led away to her death.

Voice-over Narration

Voice-over, off-camera narration or commentary, has been a standard feature of film since the beginning of the sound era. It is now so common in film and television that we scarcely notice it. We have become accustomed to the television voices of unseen individuals promoting products, reading labels, or attesting to the miraculous results of a headache remedy. In airports and train stations we continually hear voices announcing arrivals and departures. We seldom inquire about the source or the identity of the voice because we are usually only interested in the information the voice is conveying. Because bodyless voices are everywhere, we tend to give little thought to voice-over narration in film. It is another case of accepting the familiar uncritically.

Voice-over is one of the most abused techniques in film. A gifted filmmaker like Woody Allen will use voice-over intelligently; in *Radio Days*, Allen makes voice-over integral to the film, which is a reminiscence by a narrator whose younger self appears as a character. Unfortunately, voice-over can also be a convenience for writers who cannot think of any other way of imparting information. Voice-over is understandable in a memory film like *Radio Days*, but there are other movies that are not reminiscences in which voice-over is used without any consistency or logic. In *When Willie Comes Marching Home* (John Ford, 1950), the main character's voice keeps intruding even though there is no reason for him to tell his own story.

Historically, when the movies learned to talk, filmmakers seized upon voice-over as a narrative device and attempted to use it as they had used titles. As often happens, the quest for novelty led to eccentricity, and soon voice-over narration was entrusted to everyone—and everything. *The First Time* (Frank Tashlin, 1952), narrated by an unborn baby, dramatizes the disruptions that come with a first child. *Enchantment* (Irving Reis, 1948), narrated by a house, portrays the two generations that have lived in a London house. On the screen, however, baby talk becomes monotonous, and a house that tells of itself and its inhabitants ("I miss my people; in me they live") is a fairy tale house.

Since voice-over has become so widespread, its appropriateness deserves assessment. Is it a convention like a soliloquy in a play? Does it function as an expository prologue? Or is it an emergency cord a filmmaker pulls when he or she is unable to think of another way to convey information? There is no manual a filmmaker can consult to determine whether to use voice-over or titles, or to use neither and work the exposition into the dialogue. Sometimes voice-over needs some kind of aural reinforcement: a few sounds, some chords, a musical theme. Sometimes the necessary information can be incorporated into the dialogue so that both voice-over and titles are unnecessary.

The best filmmakers know intuitively when to use voice-over and when to use some kind of title. They also know that in some instances a combination is required. The 1935 adaptation of Charles Dickens's *A Tale of Two Cities*, directed by Jack Conway, is a good example of the sensible use of print and voice-over. The novel includes two of the most famous lines in English literature: the opening line ("It was the best of times, it was the worst of times") and the closing line ("It is a far, far better thing that I do, than I have ever done: it is a far, far better rest that I go to than I have ever known"). The opening appears as a title without voice-over. This is fitting because these are the words of Dickens, not one of his characters; thus, the text alone is sufficient. At the end, however, voice-over is necessary. The last words of the film, like those of the novel, are the thoughts of Sydney Carton, the main character; they are not Dickens's reflections. Since these are Carton's thoughts, the audience must hear them. Since Carton does not verbalize his thoughts, the audience hears them through voice-over.

The dominant forms of voice-over are the narrating "I" and the Voice of God.

The Narrating "I"

The narrating "I" tells the story, or a portion of the story, that we see on the screen. There can be one "I" or several. Some films are narrated by one character (*Murder, My Sweet*); others by multiple narrators (*Citizen Kane, Sorry, Wrong Number* [Anatole Litvak, 1948]). Since anyone can tell a story in the movies, even a corpse has the opportunity in *Sunset Boulevard* (Billy Wilder, 1950). Narration by a dead person would pose severe problems of credibility in a work of fiction unless it were a tale of the preternatural; yet the narration works in *Sunset Boulevard*, which, for all its realism, is similar to many other films about the old Hollywood that are like tales of the preternatural. In the film, Norma Desmond (Gloria Swanson), a former silent screen star half-crazed by memories of a past that will never return, believes she can make a comeback in a movie about Salome. She hires an out-of-work screenwriter, Joe Gillis (William Holden), to write the script in which she plans to star. When Gillis decides to leave her, Norma kills him. *Sunset Boulevard* begins with Gillis's body floating in a pool; Gillis's voice then proceeds to tell the story of his fatal association with Norma Desmond. The narration is ironically fitting: a corpse talking about the living dead.

Another Billy Wilder film, *Double Indemnity* (1944), is considered a classic of "I narration." It opens with Walter Neff (Fred MacMurray) entering a Los Angeles office building shortly before dawn. Neff describes himself as having "no visible scars"—none, that is, that can be seen *now*. Actually, he has just been shot by his mistress whom he then killed. While Neff still has strength, he recites his whole story into a dictaphone. The film then becomes a flashback in the form of a testimony that is being recorded and dramatized at the same time.

In "I narration," if there is only one narrator, the narrator's voice will recur periodically throughout the course of the film. Narration by one character is the more difficult method since the narration must unify the film, bridging the scenes as the action shifts from present to past. Neff's narration in *Double Indemnity* succeeds because the flashbacks frequently end with a cue line, a line that triggers the next bit of dialogue so the action can return to the present without an awkward

Walter Neff (Fred MacMurray) as the "Narrating I" in Double Indemnity *(Billy Wilder, 1944) is one of the finest examples of first-person narration in film. (Copyright Paramount Pictures, Courtesy of MCA Publishing Rights, a Division of MCA Incorporated)*

transition. When Neff and Phyllis Dietrichson (Barbara Stanwyck) are in a supermarket plotting her husband's murder, Phyllis says, "Remember, we're in it together." "Yes, I remember," Neff answers into the dictaphone.

Sometimes the "I" tells his or her story, hoping to learn from it. *Une Femme Douce* (Robert Bresson, 1969) opens with a suicide. Someone rushes to the veranda, a chair is overturned, a white shawl flutters through the air, and a woman's body falls to the pavement. A man, later revealed to be the woman's husband, begins to speak of her. Bresson keeps returning to her body, which now lies on a bed, to remind us that her husband is narrating the film. The approach is psychologically valid, for the husband is not so much recalling his wife as he is trying to understand why she committed suicide. At the end he knows no more than he did at the beginning.

If the voice of the "I" is flat and dispassionate, the narration will have a distancing effect, which may be desirable in a film in which the characters are not empathetic. "I narration" works well in *Badlands* (Terrence Malick, 1973), whose characters are far from endearing. The heroine is a fifteen-year-old with cornflower eyes that look as if they have lost their physical and moral center; the hero, her boyfriend, can shoot a man in the back and then talk to him as if nothing had happened. Holly (Sissy Spacek), the heroine, narrates *Badlands* in a voice as flat as the western plains she and Kit (Martin Sheen) traverse. She is presumably telling the story to us, but it sounds as if she might be writing it for a pulp magazine. Some of the narration is grimly amusing, particularly when Holly tries to turn a phrase and instead produces a cliché ("Little did I realize that what began in the backways and alleys of this little town would end in the badlands of Montana"), or when she tries to be poetic and succeeds only in being trite ("When the leaves rustled overhead, it was as if the spirits were whispering about all the little things that were bothering them"). Her boyfriend's inclinations cause Holly to remark "Suddenly I was thrown into a state of shock: Kit was the most trigger-happy person I ever met." The line is delivered so apathetically that audiences laugh, perhaps without realizing the implications of their laughter. At any rate, Holly's monotone prevents our sympathizing with her and Kit.

The Voice of God

Between 1945 and the early 1950s, the semidocumentary was a popular type of film. While a documentary is nonfiction, a semidocumentary is fiction based on fact (e.g., *The House on 92nd Street* [Henry Hathaway, 1945], *Boomerang* [Elia Kazan, 1947]). In the semidocumentary the credits often appear in a "typewriter" typeface to give the movie a "case history" look. An authoritative voice delivers the prologue, reminding the audience that the film sprang from today's headlines or the FBI's files and that it was shot on location. Since the voice belongs to no character, it is completely disembodied. Thus it can weave in and out of the action, commenting, reflecting, even questioning. In the semidocumentary the disembodied voice (or voice-of-God technique, as it is sometimes called) has two advantages: it can impart a feeling of objectivity, which is required by a film of this kind, and it can insinuate itself into the characters, noting their moods and emotional states. The voice in *The Naked City* (Jules Dassin, 1948) speaks directly to the characters as if it were an alter ego, confidant, and conscience combined. "How are your feet holding out, Alan?" it asks, or, "Lieutenant Muldoon, what's your hurry?" It even speaks to the audience: "Ever try to catch a murderer?" Since the voice had the first word, it is fitting that it should have the last: "There are eight million stories in the naked city. This has been one of them."

The disembodied voice is not restricted to the semidocumentary. Stanley Kubrick used it ingeniously in his 1975 adaptation of Thack-

This scene from Barry Lyndon *(Stanley Kubrick, 1975) between Barry (Ryan O'Neal) and his son (David Morley) was introduced by the off-camera narrator who said: "Barry had his faults, but no man could say of him that he was not a good and tender father. He loved his son passionately, perhaps with a blind partiality. He denied him nothing." (Courtesy Warner Bros., Inc.)*

eray's novel, *Barry Lyndon*. Both the novel and the film have a narrator; however, in the film, the narrator is not Lyndon—as it was in the novel—but a voice behind the scenes rather like the one in *The Naked City*, although more urbane and much wittier. It is actually the voice of British actor Michael Hordern which, like the traditional voice of God, is omniscient. The voice tells us about something before it happens or informs us of the outcome of an event without dramatizing it for us. When Lyndon is about to die, the voice even reads his obituary. The voice can speak with authority at this moment because it has been speaking with authority since the film began.

Other Kinds of Voice-over

Voice-over is often used in movies that are not narrated by one of the characters but, for purpose of plot, require a character's voice to be heard. Such voices might be labeled the *Epistolary Voice*, the *Subjective Voice*, the *Repetitive Voice*, the *Overlapping Voice*, and the *Voice from the Machine*.

The Epistolary Voice

Advancing the plot through letters is a device common to both fiction and film. The epistolary novel has a long tradition that reaches back to Samuel Richardson's *Pamela* and *Clarissa*, written in the mid-eighteenth century. In film, the letter is a familiar means of setting the plot in motion (*The Letter* [William Wyler, 1940]; *A Letter to Three Wives*, or of bridging the years (*Sea of Grass* [Elia Kazan, 1947]). When an exchange of letters is used to mark the passage of time, voice-over is sufficient. In *The Story of Adele H.* (François Truffaut, 1975), the epistolary voice is put to a variety of uses. We hear Adele's voice as she writes to Lieutenant Pinson, whom she has pursued to Halifax in an attempt to regain his affection. When she writes to her father (later discovered to be Victor Hugo), we hear his reply. In addition to Adele's correspondence, we also hear her diary entries. When Pinson reads the love notes Adele has concealed in his pockets, her voice discloses their contents to us. After following Pinson to Barbados, she collapses in the street. A native woman brings Adele to her home. After learning she is Victor Hugo's daughter, the woman writes a letter to the novelist, informing him of his daughter's pitiful condition.

In an era of film censorship, the epistolary voice was one way of having a character repent by voice-over confession. Robert Anderson's play *Tea and Sympathy* was considered unfilmable in the 1950s because of its subject matter: Tom Lee, a prep school student thought to be homosexual because of his fondness for music and poetry, is initiated sexually by Laura Reynolds, the headmaster's understanding wife. The play is best remembered for the final scene when Laura comes to Tom's room and slowly begins to unbutton her blouse. Pressing his hand against her breast, she makes one request: "Years from now, when you talk about this, and you will, be kind." When MGM decided to film the play in 1956, the Johnston Office* felt that any woman who would offer her body to an adolescent should die. After much wrangling, director Vincente Minnelli decided to make the plot a flashback occasioned by a class reunion at which Tom discovers a letter Laura had written to him. As Tom reads the letter, Laura's repentant voice is heard, urging him to forget what they had done (which was "wrong") and go out in the world and write edifying novels.

What we have been discussing are films in which the letter is a plot device with contents that must be heard. There are few films that are totally epistolary; that is, in which the entire film is a dramatization of a letter or a series of letters. In *A Walk in the Sun* (Lewis Milestone, 1945) and *Platoon* (Oliver Stone, 1986), the narrator is writing letters to his sister and grandmother respectively; however, it does not follow that each film is a dramatization of the letter the character is writing.

If a film is totally epistolary (and such films are rare), it really is an example of the narrating "I," since the epistolary voice is only used to tell the contents of a letter. *Letter from an Unknown Woman* (Max Ophuls, 1948), which revolves entirely around a letter Lisa (Joan Fontaine) has written to her former lover as she lay dying, is totally epistolary. Because the letter is such a personal document, we see

*The Motion Picture Producers and Distributors of America, Hollywood's self-censorship organization, was called the Johnston office when it was headed by Eric Johnston from 1945 to 1963; previously it had been called the Hays Office and the Breen Office.

only its powerful beginning ("By the time you read this letter I may be dead") and its unfinished ending. Otherwise we hear Lisa's voice and experience the visualization of her words. Yet the letter that is being dramatized is also being read by Lisa's lover, who never even bothered to learn her name. Thus, the audience and the lover learn about Lisa at the same time.

The Subjective Voice

Movies abound with examples of the inner voice that literally speaks its mind (called *subjective voice*) because the audience requires access to the character's thoughts. Pip in *Great Expectations* (David Lean, 1947) wonders how Joe Gargery, the blacksmith, will greet him when he returns home dressed as a gentleman. In *The Accused* (William Dieterle, 1948), we hear what a psychology professor, who has killed a student in self-defense, is thinking when she realizes the consequences of her act. During her flight from Phoenix in *Psycho*, Marion Crane imagines what her employer will say on Monday morning when she fails to report for work.

A more sophisticated form of the subjective voice appears in the stream-of-consciousness film. Although *stream of consciousness* has been applied to everything from inarticulate rambling to incoherent prose, it is really the unbroken flow of thoughts, memories, and associations in the waking mind. *Hiroshima Mon Amour* (Alain Resnais, 1959), a stream-of-consciousness film, opens with a man and a woman making love. At first their skin looks charred, like that of the Hiroshima victims; then it becomes dewy, as if cleansed by the act of love. She is a French actor, and he is a Japanese architect she has met in Hiroshima while making a film. As their bodies move toward fulfillment, we hear their voices—his denying that she knows the significance of Hiroshima, hers insisting that she does. But these are not their actual voices; they sound distant, anesthetized. We are hearing the rhythms of poetry, not prose. It is each character's interior that we hear, an interior expressing itself in the language of memory that is made up of both words and images. When the architect's voice says, "You know nothing of Hiroshima," her consciousness replies with pictures of the artifacts she has seen at the museum and newsreel footage of the bombing of Hiroshima. When the woman says, "Who are you?," instead of a verbal reply we see a street in Hiroshima. The man is Hiroshima, the only name she will ever associate with him.

The Repetitive Voice

A character, often the hero or heroine, tosses restlessly in bed while someone's voice reverberates in his or her unconscious, repeating key dialogue from an earlier scene (in case the audience missed its significance). This kind of repetition, called the repetitive voice, occurs in *Rebecca* (Alfred Hitchcock, 1940) when some comments made about Rebecca give Joan Fontaine's character a sleepless night. The same technique appears in *Cat People* when Irena keeps hearing the voice of her psychiatrist as Halloween cats prowl across the screen.

The repetitive voice has become so familiar that it runs the risk of becoming a cliché. Yet at times some kind of recapitulation is necessary, and the filmmaker must decide if the repetition should be aural or visual. If the character's words are important, then it is only necessary to hear what the character has said. At the end of *Gone with the Wind*, Scarlett recalls the words her father had spoken earlier about the value of land and the importance of Tara. Hearing his words is sufficient. On the other hand, in *Murder on the Orient Express* (Sidney Lumet, 1974), the repetition is visual. Since the film is a "whodunit," crucial shots are repeated: guilt is often a question not of what one says but of how one reacts, so the passengers' reactions, not just their words, are recalled for us visually.

The Overlapping Voice

In overlap, sound or dialogue can either carry over from a previous scene or anticipate the next scene. In *Three Days of the Condor* (Sydney Pollack, 1975), a CIA official in Washington is asking questions about an agent, who at that moment is hiding out in a Brooklyn Heights apartment. The official's voice carries into the next scene with the agent. The overlapping voice gives the impression that the CIA is everywhere, including Brooklyn Heights.

At the end of *Medium Cool* (1969), which is set in Chicago during the 1968 Democratic convention, director Haskell Wexler lets the audience hear of an event before it happens. As a TV cameraperson and an Appalachian schoolteacher are driving away from a bloody confrontation between the police and antiwar protestors, a newscaster's voice describes the smash-up of their car before it is actually shown. Like the film, the untimely newscast is disturbing, for it is not merely a matter of overlap but of omniscience. It is as if the cool medium, as Marshall McLuhan referred to television, knows our destiny and therefore can compose our obituary before we die.

These two examples illustrate intelligent use of overlapping sound. It is ordinarily designed only to bridge two scenes by carrying dialogue or sound (e.g., music, noise) from one scene to another or by having sound that properly belongs to the second scene begin at the end of the first.

The Voice from the Machine

Some filmmakers regard voice-over as the modern equivalent of the *deus ex machina* (god from the machine) from the Greek theater. In certain Greek tragedies, a god would descend from a crane to resolve the action and bring the play to a conclusion. Some movies feature a "voice from the machine"; it belongs to none of the characters and materializes near the end to tie up any loose plot points or offer some commentary on the action. The voice from the machine is not the voice of God, which is consistent throughout the film; the voice from the machine is heard only at the end. At the end of *The Lady and the Monster* (George Sherman, 1944), a voice intrudes to remind us that Patrick Cory (Richard Arlen) has been sent to prison for his role in an experiment to keep a dead man's brain alive. The voice also reminds us that this is to be a film with a happy ending, and that Cory will emerge from jail to find his beloved waiting for him. Since no voice had been heard up to this point, we wonder whose it is. It must belong to a supernatural power that knows more about the script than the screenwriter.

Despite its title, *I Walked with a Zombie* (Jacques Tourneur, 1943) is a superior horror film. Initially, the movie is narrated by the "I" of the title—a Canadian nurse who has come to the West Indies to tend a woman who turns out to be a zombie. At the end, the zombie is killed by her brother-in-law, who then commits suicide. Suddenly, a male voice asks God to pardon the unholy couple. The switch from the nurse's voice to the voice from beyond imparts a moralistic tone to a film that otherwise has remained aloof from moral issues. Perhaps the coda was a sop to the Legion of Decency, which frowned on suicide. Still, it vitiates the artistry of an unusually intelligent B movie.

Voice-over, then, is not just faceless sound; it is a narrative device that can serve different purposes. It can be personal (the narrating "I") or impersonal (voice of God); it can reveal the contents of a letter or the contents of the unconscious; it can refresh a character's memory or our own. Because of its versatility, voice-over is often abused; thus one should always be sure to approach its use critically.

NOTES

[1]For a readable guide to all the individuals involved in the making of a movie, see Eric Taub, *Gaffers, Grips and Best Boys* (New York: St. Martin's Press, 1987).

3

The Nature of
the Medium, II:
Film Space
and Image

As discussed in Chapter 1, film can manipulate time. But it can also manipulate space. The subject can be near or far, partial or full, stationary or moving. How we see the image, and how much of it we see, are the result of the filmmaker's choice of shot.

TYPES OF SHOTS

A shot is simply what is recorded by a single operation of the camera. Shots can be defined in terms of distance. Does the camera appear to be close to the subject? If so, the shot is a close-up (CU)—in terms of human anatomy, a shot of the head, for example. Perhaps it is a head-and-shoulders shot; then it is a close shot (CS). It may be a specific part of the body—an eye, a mouth—such a shot is an extreme close-up (ECU). A shot of the complete human figure, with some of the background visible, is a full shot (FS) or a long shot (LS). If the camera is so far away that the result is a broad panoramic view, it is an extreme long shot (ELS). A shot that is neither a close shot nor a long shot, but something in between, is a medium shot (MS), showing, for example, the subject head-to-waist or waist-to-knees.

Perhaps the shot defines an area—a room, for example, with all its appointments; such a shot is an establishing shot (ES), a type of long shot that is often broken down into its components. Establishing shot can also mean a shot that establishes location (e.g., the Golden Gate Bridge in San Francisco; the Eiffel Tower in Paris), so that the viewer knows the setting and where the action takes place.

Shots can also be defined by what they contain. A two-shot includes two characters; a three shot includes three characters. "Shot/reverse shot" is the principle of alternating shots of characters in a conversation so that first one character is seen, then the other.

CLOSE-UPS AND LONG SHOTS

Jean-Luc Godard is fond of saying that the close-up was invented for tragedy, the long shot for comedy. This is something of an oversimplification, since long shots and extreme long shots are staples of the western. But at least Godard is suggesting that filmmakers have reasons for choosing one shot over another depending on the kind of movie they are making or the kind of scene they are shooting. A close-up can reveal a particular emotion for which, under the circumstances, a long shot would have been inappropriate. When Lucy (Lillian Gish) is denounced by her father in *Broken Blossoms*, Griffith uses a close-up to express her fear.

The close-up is also a means of emphasis. Hitchcock found the close-up ideal for objects like a suspicious glass of milk (*Suspicion*, 1943), an envelope dropped by a Nazi agent (*Saboteur*, 1942), and a wine bottle filled with uranium ore (*Notorious*, 1946). These objects are so crucial to the plot that Hitchcock was unwilling to assume they would be noticed unless their presence was emphasized.

Hitchcock also used the extreme close-up for reasons having to do with genre. *Psycho* is a horror film; audiences expect the proverbial chill up the spine, and Hitchcock does not fail them: the extreme close-ups of Marion Crane's screaming mouth and staring eye in the shower sequence stay in the memory. Extreme close-ups of the eye are, in fact, standard in horror films, especially if it is the eye of the killer spying on a prospective victim through a peephole, as is the case in *Psycho* and *The Spiral Staircase* (Robert Siodmak, 1946).

The extreme close-up is not just an embellishment; like any shot, it can have a direct bearing on the plot. The words, "Prognosis Negative," that confirm Judith Traherne's terminal condition in *Dark Vic-*

tory must be visible, and that can only be done in extreme close-up. If a scar identifies a murderer, as it does in *A Stranger Knocks* (Johan Jacobsen, 1963), the scar would need to be photographed in ECU.

The ECU should be used sparingly, however; too many such shots create an imbalance in the film. They are such an extreme form of emphasis that a preponderance of them is like the speech pattern of someone who gives equal emphasis to every word, including "a" and "the."

While the close-up is useful to point up the intense emotion of tragedy, the long shot—despite Godard's assertion—can be ideal for tragedy as well, since it makes death less painful to watch. The death of Santiago (Arthur Kennedy) in *The Naked Dawn* (Edgar G. Ulmer, 1955) is photographed in long shot. Santiago is on horseback when the bullet strikes him; we see neither stunned eyes nor spurting blood. The shot has a formalized beauty about it reminiscent of a painting like Breughel's *Fall of Icarus,* in which the death of Icarus is made part of the setting.

Western filmmakers favor long shots and extreme long shots because these shots make the subject part of the environment in addition to conveying the vastness and awesomeness of nature. In *Shane* (George Stevens, 1953) a deer laps water from a stream with snow-fringed mountains in the background. A man bids farewell to a woman who merges with the landscape as he rides off in *My Darling Clementine* (John Ford, 1946). Many of Ford's long shots have an intensely pictorial quality. In *Clementine,* we see a stretch of sky brooding over the dusty main street of Tombstone, a bar thronged by men—sometimes in silhouette, sometimes illuminated by the kerosene lamps hanging overhead—and Monument Valley with its cliffs and mesas rising skyward from a flat plain and dwarfing all who pass beneath them.

HIGH-ANGLE AND LOW-ANGLE SHOTS

Shots are also defined by the position of the camera in relation to the subject. When Lillian (Jane Fonda) looks out of her hotel window in *Julia* (Fred Zinnemann, 1977), what she sees on the street below is rendered as a high-angle shot. In a high-angle shot, the camera is positioned above (sometimes "high above") the subject. This is occasionally referred to as a *God's eye view,* a type of shot favored by Hitchcock because it suggests an unseen presence looking down on the subject. If the camera shoots up at the subject from below, it is a low-angle shot.

A low-angle shot makes the subject loom larger than it actually is.

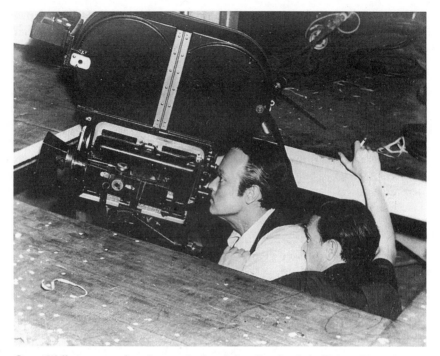

Orson Welles prepares for a low-angle shot, below floor level, in Citizen Kane *(1941).*
(Courtesy MOMA/FSA and RKO)

Such a shot can suggest dominance or power, as it does in *Citizen Kane* when Kane's guardian hovers over him as he presents the young Kane with a sled. Conversely, a high-angle shot makes the subject seem smaller than it is. When a member of the French underground interrogates the title character in *When Willie Comes Marching Home,* the high angle from which Willie is photographed suggests the feeling of helplessness that the intense cross-examination produces.

The high angle shot of the president pacing the floor in *Abraham Lincoln* (D. W. Griffith, 1930) reminds us that the burdens of the office dwarf even the great. In *All the President's Men,* as reporters Bob Woodward and Carl Bernstein are sorting out library slips, the camera watches them from above; indeed, they seem to grow smaller as they realize the enormity of their task. The scene ends with the camera's peering down at the reading room of the Library of Congress, which looks like a magnified snowflake.

Sometimes the script requires a high- or low-angle shot for reasons that have nothing to do with symbolism or imagery. In *Julia,* the shot following Lillian at the window had to be a high-angle shot; an eye-level shot would have made no sense. If a man is waiting at the foot of a staircase for a woman to descend, as Gabriel (Donal McCann) waits for Gretta (Anjelica Huston) near the end of *The Dead* (John Huston, 1987), the woman must be photographed in a low-angle shot to match the man's angle of vision.

In *The Blue Dahlia* (George Marshall, 1946), Mrs. Harwood (Veronica Lake) is on the mezzanine of a hotel where she phones down to Johnny Morrison (Alan Ladd) at the registration desk in the lobby; the camera had to shoot *down* at Morrison to match the angle from which Mrs. Harwood saw him. The context of the action determines the nature of the shot.

The same holds true of other types of shots as well; the screenplay and the filmmaker's intentions regarding the screenplay dictate the nature of the shots.

SUBJECTIVE CAMERA

An objective shot represents what the camera sees; a subjective shot (sometimes referred to as a subjective camera) represents what

Robert Redford and Dustin Hoffman prepare for the Library of Congress scene in All the President's Men *(Alan J. Pakula, 1976). The camera is set for a high shot. (Courtesy Warner Bros., Inc)*

A low-angle shot of Gretta (Anjelica Huston) descending the stairs in The Dead *(John Huston, 1987). (Frame enlargement courtesy Vestron Pictures)*

the character sees. As the Joads drive into a Hooverville in *The Grapes of Wrath*, the residents are looking straight ahead as they step aside for the truck. At whom are they staring, one might ask? They are looking at the Joads, who are not to be seen. Thus, they are looking at *us:* we have been put behind the wheel in order to see poverty and squalor through the Joads' eyes.

Sometimes in a film we experience sheer motion without a corresponding image. In *Marnie*, for example, Mark (Sean Connery) is seated at his desk when Marnie enters the room. Mark looks straight into the camera, acknowledging Marnie's presence. However, we do not see Marnie, we only experience some sense of movement toward the desk. For a moment we have become Marnie, but we cease to be Marnie when she reaches the desk.

Because subjective camera offers a one-sided view of reality, it should never dominate a film as it did in *Lady in the Lake* (Robert Montgomery, 1946)—the textbook case of how not to make the audience a participant in the action. The main character in the film, Philip Marlowe (Montgomery), is never seen except in a mirror. Thus there are scenes in which the other characters, supposedly looking at him, stare straight into the camera, which represents Marlowe and, by extension, the audience. When a woman kisses Marlowe, she has to purse her lips into the lens. Thus it seems as if she is kissing the

A low-angle shot from Suddenly, Last Summer *(Joseph L. Mankiewicz, 1959), showing Violet Venable (Katharine Hepburn) ascending in her private elevator. (Courtesy Margaret Herrick Library of the Academy of Motion Picture Arts and Sciences)*

audience. When she lights Marlowe's cigarette, she thrusts the lighter into the lens as if she is about to ignite the viewer.

Subjective camera should be restricted to specific scenes or sequences as is the case in *Dark Passage* (Delmer Daves, 1947), in which the plot requires subjective shots. Unjustly convicted of his wife's murder, Vincent Parry (Humphrey Bogart) escapes from San Quentin to track down the real killer. He cannot solve the murder looking as he does because his picture is in every newspaper, so he chooses to undergo plastic surgery. Daves, who also wrote the screenplay, had two options. He could use another actor in the early scenes, and after the operation, introduce Bogart, or he could use a combination of subjective camera and Bogart's voice for the first thirty minutes, and then drop subjective camera after Bogart finally appears. Daves was pretty much forced to do the latter: in 1947, Humphrey Bogart was too big a star to make his initial appearance thirty minutes into the picture.

Parry escapes by concealing himself in a barrel that has been loaded on a prison truck. The camera is totally subjective, jostling us as Parry maneuvers the barrel from the truck, and making us reel with dizziness as it rolls down a hill. When the barrel comes to rest, we peer out of it cautiously but get nothing more than a tunnellike view

Philip Marlowe's (Robert Montgomery) reflection in Lady in the Lake *(Robert Montgomery, 1946), the subjective camera film in which Marlowe is only visible when a mirror catches his image. (Courtesy WCFTR)*

of the outside. Parry is now a presence. When he hitches a ride, the driver speaks to the presence, who answers but is still unseen. When the driver recognizes him, the presence knocks him unconscious. Later, the presence scans the highway and climbs into Irene Jansen's (Lauren Bacall) waiting car.

When the presence showers, a hand adjusts the shower head and a jet of water sprays the camera lens. Camera movements express the presence's emotional state. When the presence is wary, the camera darts in the same direction as his apprehensive eyes. A telephone rings, and the camera swings around the way a tense person does at an unexpected sound. Gradually, Daves begins to switch from subjective to objective camera, from Parry as a presence to Parry as a character. The transition begins in a cab at night so that Bogart's face is kept in shadow. The sympathetic cab driver recommends plastic surgery and refers Parry to a reliable doctor. After the operation, Bogart's voice returns to Bogart's body, and the camera ceases being subjective.

Related to subjective camera is the point-of-view shot. A point-of-view shot (POV) represents the point of view of the character, or what the character sees. A famous POV shot occurs at the end of *Spellbound* (Alfred Hitchcock, 1945) when Dr. Murchison (Leo G. Carroll) is unmasked as the murderer of the former director of a mental institution. Murchison aims a gun at his accuser and then turns it around to fire at himself. The close-up of the gun with which Murchison commits suicide is a POV shot, representing the way he saw it when he turned it on himself.

SHOTS AS PARTS OF A WHOLE

It is easy to become enamored of particular shots, especially ones that are strikingly photographed. The close up of the burning crucifix in *Amadeus* (Milos Forman, 1986) is a powerful moment in the film. It would still have an impact, although not perhaps the same kind, if one saw a still or a frame enlargement of it without having seen the film. However, it is the context that makes the shot not only powerful but chilling: Salieri, realizing Mozart's superiority, is so angry with God for giving him a rival that he destroys a symbol of his faith. The clock without hands that the main character sees in his dream in *Wild Strawberries* (Ingmar Bergman, 1957) is a shot that would still have an effect out of context. If one were shown a still or a frame enlargement of it and asked what it meant, the reply would be something like "time has stopped" or even "death." A good answer, and not all that different from what it means in the film. But in *Wild Strawberries*, the clock without hands is one of many death symbols; thus, it takes on its deepest meaning within the context of the film, which is a death odyssey.

At the end of *Radio Days*, a father holds his son lovingly on his lap. Anyone seeing a still of that scene and knowing nothing of the film would assume that the character was a caring father. Throughout the film, however, the father has not been especially affectionate toward his son. The reason the boy is on his father's lap is that the boy is getting a spanking. As he is being spanked, a report comes over the radio that a child who had fallen into a well has died. Suddenly the father's attitude changes, and instead of punishing his son, he caresses him. The death of someone else's child has made the father feel warmer toward his own.

Shots are like excerpts; just as some excerpts communicate more information than others, so too do shots. The excerpt is part of the work, just as the shot is part of the total film in which its meaning resides.

Tight framing in Detour *(Edgar G. Ulmer, 1946). The camera tracks in for a close-up of Roberts (Tom Neal), who looks imprisoned within the frame. (Frame enlargement courtesy of John Belton)*

FRAMING THE SHOT

The concept of framing is easily understood by anyone who has either studied painting or has actually painted. Framing is the act, and sometimes the art, of composing a shot, reflecting the choices similar to those painters make about how their canvas will ultimately look. The filmmaker's canvas is the frame, the strip of celluloid on which the image is captured. Like a painter, the filmmaker must arrange the details of the frame in terms of the visual or dramatic points being made, or the ideas being expressed.

While there are no ironclad rules of framing, certain principles are widely followed.

1. Tight framing gives a feeling of oppression. In tight framing, the subject appears confined within the horizontal and vertical borders of the frame so that there is not even a hint of off-screen space. To create an atmosphere of fatalism, Edgar G. Ulmer chose tight framing for several shots of Roberts (Tom Neal) in *Detour* (1946). When Roberts' face is trapped within the frame, destiny seems to be closing in on him.

2. The frame should be slightly asymmetrical. Whatever is to be emphasized should occupy a position of prominence, but not in the center of the frame. If the image were dead center, a sense of depth would be lost because the subject would seem to be stamped on the frame. If a disorienting or unusual effect is sought, the extremity of the frame might be used. For example, in *Detour,* when Roberts discovers that Vera (Ann Savage) has accidentally strangled herself with a telephone cord, her body is seen right of frame, head hanging over the bed.

3. Vertical and horizontal compositions denote solidarity; diagonals and oblique compositions denote tension. In *Potemkin,* the masts of the ships, the raised arms of the sailors, and the waving arms of the

The shadows cast by the Cossacks create ominous diagonals on the steps in Potemkin *(Sergei Eisenstein, 1925). (Courtesy MOMA/FSA and Janus Films)*

The juxtaposition of strong verticals (the soldiers' legs) and stable horizontals (steps) with broken lines (sprawled bodies and hands raised in supplication) suggest the dominance of the Cossacks and the helplessness of the people in Potemkin.

people suggest a solidarity that is destroyed when the Cossacks appear at the top of the Odessa steps. Their shadows falling on the steps create a diagonal that breaks the unity. A canted shot (also known as a Dutch angle shot) results in an oblique composition in which the frame looks lopsided. Edgar G. Ulmer uses canted shots in *Bluebeard* (1944) to emphasize the madness of the central character; the canted shots in *The Third Man* (Sir Carol Reed, 1949) imply a world in which things are askew. In the violent argument between the title character and her mother in *Carrie* (Brian De Palma, 1976), the frame looks as if it will tip over.

Sometimes vertical framing is intentionally ironic. In *Address Unknown* (William Cameron Menzies, 1944), Griselle (K. T. Stevens) flees from a mob that has discovered she is Jewish. She hopes to find refuge in the home of a family friend. Framed by trees, she looks hopefully into the distance where the friend lives. Ordinarily, such a composition with its strong verticals would imply hope. However, Griselle is a Jew in Nazi Germany, and the man she assumes is a friend has become a Nazi.

CANTED SHOTS

A canted shot of Orson Welles as Harry Lime in The Third Man *(Sir Carol Reed, 1949). (Courtesy MOMA/FSA)*

Vertical bars across the face, on the other hand, have another connotation: mystery, imprisonment, exclusion. When Carmen (Rita Hayworth) appears behind a beaded curtain in *The Loves of Carmen* (Charles Vidor, 1948), the verticals give her face an exotic yet dangerous look. When Griselle in *Address Unknown* finally arrives at the friend's house and stands before the gate, the composition recalls the earlier one in which she was framed by trees. However, here the gate is a barrier, and even though she reaches it, she still does not gain access to the house. The use of verticals in this different composition, as bars across the face, suggests exclusion: prevented from entering, Griselle is killed by the Gestapo.

. 4. Geometrical compositions can be symbolic as well as visually interesting. In Jungian psychology, the circle is a symbol of wholeness, suggesting unity and commonality. Such is the case in *Sahara*

Griselle (K. T. Stevens) in Address Unknown *(William Cameron Menzies, 1944) is framed between two trees, expecting to be saved from the mob pursuing her. Here the verticals are a support, but only a temporary one. (Courtesy Columbia Pictures)*

*Griselle before the gate leading to the home of a family friend who will not receive her (*Address Unknown*). (Courtesy Columbia Pictures)*

TRIANGULAR COMPOSITIONS IN *JULES AND JIM* (FRANÇOIS TRUFFAUT, 1961) SHOWING CATHERINE (JEANNE MOREAU), JULES (OSCAR WERNER), AND JIM (HENRI SERRE), WHO BECOME A *MÉNAGE À TROIS.*

The ménage *running. (Courtesy MOMA/FSA and Janus Films)*

The ménage *shot from below. (Courtesy MOMA/FSA and Janus Films)*

(Zoltan Korda, 1943) when Sergeant Joe Gunn (Humphrey Bogart) passes a cup of water around to his thirsty men who stand in a circle. If a composition involves three characters, triangular arrangements can make a statement about their relationship, as is the case in *Jules and Jim* (François Truffaut, 1961), in which two men share the affections of the same woman.

5. Iconography should be unobtrusive. If the filmmaker is imitating a painting or a sculpture, the composition should look natural even though it is a replica of, or an homage to, a favorite work of art. The beggars' banquet in *Viridiana* (Luis Buñuel, 1961) is an obvious parody of *The Last Supper*, made even more so by the use of the "Hallelujah Chorus" as background music. A less blatant parody of *The Last Supper* occurs in *M*A*S*H* (Robert Altman, 1970) when the medics stage a literal last supper for the dentist who plans to commit suicide because he thinks he is impotent. Christ imagery with crucifixion and "way of the cross" motifs tends to call attention to itself: When the bloodied Terry Malloy (Marlon Brando) staggers along the dock at the end of *On the Waterfront* (Elia Kazan, 1954), one might recall Christ on his way to Calvary. A more subtle "way of the cross"

A different triangular composition from Citizen Kane *(Orson Welles, 1941), showing Kane (center) flanked by Thatcher (left) and Bernstein (right) as he is about to relinquish control of his enterprises after the crash of 1929. The position of Kane at the apex of the triangle makes him both the focus of attention and an object of defeat since he is dwarfed by the more prominent figures of Thatcher and Bernstein. (Courtesy MOMA/FSA)*

appears in *Meet John Doe* (Frank Capra, 1941) when the title character makes his lonely way through a crowd that reviles him.

6. The angle at which the subject is viewed is determined by two factors: narrative logic and symbolic implications. As we have seen, if a character is looking out of a hotel window onto the street below, the shot that follows must be a high-angle shot. Similarly, if a character is on the ground looking up at someone, the person at whom the character is looking must be photographed at a low angle, with the camera shooting upward. Since subjects photographed from a high angle look small and those photographed from a low angle look large, high angle shots can imply inferiority, defeat, or oppression; low angle shots, power, dominance, superiority. Susan Alexander Kane is often photographed at a high angle in *Citizen Kane* because she is dominated by her husband, who is often photographed from a low angle.

7. The focus within the frame depends on how much or how little is to be seen. If the filmmaker decides that in a particular shot, foreground, middle ground, and background should be equally visible, the shot will have a deep focus. In *Citizen Kane*, Orson Welles used deep focus for several reasons: to convey a greater sense of depth, to minimize the need to cut from one shot to another, and to bring out meanings that might not otherwise be apparent. The classic

deep focus shot in *Kane* shows Mary Kane making arrangements with a banker who is to raise her son as a gentleman because she and her husband cannot. The position of the mother (foreground), banker and father (middle ground), and son (background, seen through the window blissfully playing in the snow) says infinitely more about the way young Kane's life is being signed away without his knowledge than if the action were broken down into four separate shots: mother, father, banker, son.

Sometimes shallow focus is preferred, for example, when the background should not be as distinct as the foreground because it would detract from the foreground. At other times, the background must remain indistinct until the time for it to be clear. In such a case, the filmmaker will pull focus: first, the background will be a blur and the foreground sharp; then the background will be sharp and the foreground blurry. This technique, known as *rack focus*, is used in *Time after Time* (Nicholas Meyer, 1976). Someone is behind the heroine, but the person's face is a blur. Then the face comes into focus, and we realize it is Jack the Ripper's.

Focus may be deliberately erratic, with the image going in and out of focus, as might happen if a character is hallucinating, disoriented, or drunk. In *Detour*, when Roberts realizes that Vera has accidentally strangled herself, objects go in and out of focus as he looks around the room in a state of shock.

Iconographic Framing: The Last Supper *parody in* Viridiana *(Luis Buñuel, 1961). (Courtesy MOMA/FSA and Janus Films)*

Another Last Supper *parody in* M*A*S*H *(Robert Altman, 1970). (Courtesy Margaret Herrick Library of the Academy of Motion Picture Arts and Sciences)*

8. If the frame is to be masked—that is, if its shape is to be altered—the same considerations that govern other framing techniques apply: narrative logic and symbolic value. If a character is peering through a pair of binoculars, a telescope, a microscope, or a keyhole, the next shot should assume the appropriate configuration.

9. If a character is positioned in a doorway, the result is a frame-within-a-frame or double framing; within the film frame is another frame—the frame created by the doorway. Double framing may reveal something about the character so framed. John Ford often uses the frame within the frame, especially in *The Searchers* (1956). When Ethan (John Wayne), who will always be a loner and a searcher, returns with Debbie, the object of his search, he remains in a doorway while the others go inside the house.

Because doorways and archways resemble the proscenium arch of a theater, they have a dramatic effect. In *The Quiet Man* (John Ford, 1952) Mary Kate (Maureen O'Hara) is framed in the doorway as Sean (John Wayne) pulls her toward him. In *The Little Foxes* (William Wyler, 1941), the Hubbards do their plotting in the archway of the drawing room, thus seeming like the stage villains they were in Lillian Hellman's play.

10. The long take—a shot lasting more than a minute—can also be framed. Recall the definition of a shot: a single run of the camera. The camera can accommodate ten minutes worth of film, although few filmmakers would allow it to run for that length (Hitchcock did so in *Rope* [1948], an eighty-minute film consisting of eight ten-minute takes. *Rope*, however, was an experiment—and not an especially successful one.) The average shot lasts between ten and twenty seconds, but many shots are often longer, and even a three-minute shot can be framed.

The most famous long take in American film is the three-minute credits sequence in *Touch of Evil* (Orson Welles, 1958). Someone puts a time bomb in the trunk of a car. Two people get into the car and proceed down the street of a Mexican border town, past Mr. and Mrs. Vargas (Charlton Heston and Janet Leigh). The Vargases reach the customs booth before the couple. In their conversation with the customs officer, we learn that Mrs. Vargas is American and that Mr. Vargas, soon revealed to be Mexican, is a narcotics agent. Then the car with the couple pulls up to the booth. The driver, Mr. Linnekar, is known to the customs officer. The woman with him, who admits she is not an American citizen, complains about a "ticking noise," but the customs officer does not take it seriously. The Vargases, who behave like newlyweds, are more interested in each other than in the occupants of the car. The car crosses the border, continues a short distance, and then explodes into flames. Within three minutes of uninter-rupted camera movement, we have had the credits, been introduced to two of the main characters, discovered that the drug trade will be an important element of the plot, learned that Mrs. Vargas is Ameri-can while her husband is Mexican, witnessed a car bombing that will have to be explained, and entered a world where the unpredictable and the incalculable are the norm. Welles chose to make the credits sequence of *Touch of Evil* a long take and framed it accordingly, creat-ing an atmosphere of restlessness by a camera that is continually moving.

Shots can be framed graphically in terms of lines (horizontals, verticals, diagonals); they can be framed geometrically or icono-graphically; in deep or shallow focus; from a high or a low angle; in a frame that has been masked or doubled. A shot can last a second or run ten minutes. Guided by a script that requires a scene to be filmed in a particular way and by aesthetic considerations that will enhance the script and enrich the narrative, the filmmaker makes his or her decisions. These decisions, however, should not be accepted on faith; rather, the viewer should ask if the decisions were the right ones.

THE MOVING SHOT

Movement in film can be deceptive. In the three-minute long take in *Touch of Evil*, the camera was literally moving. However, when the camera rotates horizontally on a fixed axis (pan shot) or vertically (tilt shot), it is not, strictly speaking, moving. The camera head—but not the camera itself, which is probably on a tripod—is moving. For mo-bile camera shots, the camera is on a moving vehicle such as a dolly, a truck, or a crane, or on specially built tracks. The mobile camera has the advantage of being able to add to the narrative by opening up more space, thereby augmenting what is seen. The pan and the tilt can add to our knowledge, too.

Pan shots generally move left to right in imitation of the reading eye, but they also can go from right to left. In *The Thin Man* (Woody Van Dyke, 1934), it does both in the same shot. As Nora Charles (Myrna Loy) opens a door on the right, the camera pans right to left, from the doorway to the interior where her husband is comforting a weeping girl. When the husband catches sight of his wife, the camera pans left to right, back to Nora in the doorway, as if the camera is also embarrassed at what it has discovered. Through panning, a film-maker can have the camera comment on a situation, thus making the camera almost a character. As David Locke (Jack Nicholson) in *The Passenger* (Michelangelo Antonioni, 1975) cries aloud in desperation because his Land Rover is stalled in the sand, the camera answers by panning the indifferent desert. A swish pan (unusually rapid panning that produces a momentary blur) can suggest a sudden change or a transformation. In *Dr. Jekyll and Mr. Hyde* (Rouben Mamoulian, 1932), there is a swish pan immediately after Dr. Jekyll drinks the potion and becomes Mr. Hyde.

When the camera pivots vertically, the result is a tilt shot (sometimes called a vertical pan; hence the expression *pan up/down*). Tilting also mimics eye movement: in this case the eye's tendency to move up the face of a building to take in its height, or down a column of names. In *Jane Eyre* (Robert Stevenson, 1944), the camera tilts down from a plaque that reads "Lowood Institution" to the figure of the sleeping Jane Eyre, who is being carried into it. In *Citizen Kane*, the camera tilts up to the entrance gate of Kane's estate, Xanadu, past the No Trespassing sign, reminding us that the warning applies to everyone but itself. At the end of the film, the camera tilts *down* the gate to the No Trespassing sign as it returns to its starting point.

Like the pan, the tilt shot can be a silent spectator, commenting visually on a situation. As the vampire is about to sink her teeth into a victim's neck in *Dracula's Daughter* (Lambert Hillyer, 1936), the camera begins tilting up the wall, leaving the rest to the viewer's imagination. A tilt shot can even suggest the actual or potential fate of a character. When Phillip Vandamm (James Mason) in *North by Northwest* (Alfred Hitchcock, 1959) discovers his mistress is an American agent, he decides to kill her aboard a plane: "This matter is something that is disposed of at a great height—over the water," he remarks. At the mention of "height," the camera tilts up—to nothing but empty space.

As it pans or tilts, the camera guides the eye horizontally or vertically, determining both the direction and the object of the audience's vision. Tilt-pan and pan-tilt combinations are also possible, to direct the viewer's or the character's gaze across one surface and up or down another. In *The Passenger*, the camera is in the process of tracing the curve of a surface wire up the wall of a hotel room when a sudden knock at the door interrupts its ascent, causing it to backtrack over to the door to see who is there.

A combination of panning and tilting occurs in the notorious flashback in *Stage Fright* (Alfred Hitchcock, 1950), which is later revealed to have been a total lie. Jonathan Cooper (Richard Todd) is explaining to his bewildered girlfriend how Charlotte Inwood (Marlene Dietrich) begged him to go to her flat and bring her a new dress; it seems the one she was wearing is stained with her husband's blood. As Cooper enters the flat, the camera pans across the room to Mr.

Inwood's body and then tilts up a closet door. At first the camera's tilting up a clothes closet seems odd; yet it is part of Hitchcock's plan to make Cooper's story believable. Thus, Hitchcock has the camera guide Cooper to the clothes closet, from which he removes the dress, as if Cooper did not know where the closet was. If Cooper headed straight for the closet, the audience would sense he was more familiar with Charlotte's flat than he should be and would therefore not accept his story.

As we have seen, in panning and tilting the camera itself does not move. Strictly speaking, then, a pan or a tilt is not a moving shot since the camera merely rotates on a tripod. In a moving shot, the camera moves with, toward, or alongside or away from its subjects. There are several kinds of moving shots, depending on the way in which the camera moves. If it moves on tracks, it is a tracking shot; if it is mounted on a dolly, a dolly shot; if it moves up and down, in and out of a scene on a crane, it is a crane shot, which is easily identified by its ascending or descending motion, although a crane can move laterally as well.

Some writers use the terms *dolly shot* and *tracking shot* interchangeably; the camera dollies in (tracks in) when it moves toward the subject, dollies out (tracks out) when it moves away from the subject. Other writers simply call any shot in which the camera is moving on a vehicle (a truck, a dolly, a bicycle) a tracking shot, which is identified by the direction of the camera: forward tracking shot, vertical tracking shot, diagonal tracking shot.

Tracking shots have distinct advantages over other types because they can encompass a greater area and supply more detail; thus, they can sustain a mood for a longer period of time. While the pan and tilt can act as a silent commentator, the track can be a character's alter ego or unseen companion. Max Ophuls was a master of the moving shot. In his films, the camera seems to waltz and glide; it can rush up the stairs with the breathless lovers or accompany them on a stroll, occasionally slipping behind a fountain so as not to be conspicuous. In *Letter from an Unknown Woman*, Ophuls makes the camera almost human. As a provincial band ruins Wagner's "Song to the Evening Star," the camera, unable to stand the tinny sound, rises up fastidiously and leaves the square. In the same film, the camera accompanies the operagoers up the grand staircase as if it were escorting them.

The moving camera can draw viewers physically into the action, and it can even lure them into a character's consciousness, as it does in the film's version of Eugene O'Neill's *Long Day's Journey into Night*. The crane shot that ends the film is one of the great feats of moviemaking; in it, Lumet manages to incorporate almost all of Mary

Tyrone's great monologue. Mary (Katharine Hepburn) is in her parlor with her husband and two sons. She recalls how a nun had dissuaded her from entering the convent because she claimed to have visions of Our Lady of Lourdes. If regression could be visualized, it would consist of gradual diminution. Almost as soon as Mary begins her monologue, the camera starts pulling back from her; then it rises up as her thoughts leave this world. As Mary grows smaller, so do her husband and sons. As the monologue draws to a close, Mary appears in close-up as she speaks the final lines: "That was in the winter of senior year. Then in the spring something happened to me. Yes, I remember. I fell in love with James Tyrone and was so happy for a time." Mary's close-up is followed by close-ups of the other Tyrones; then there is one last close-up of Mary's face, now strangely peaceful.

ZOOMS AND FREEZES

Many contemporary filmmakers prefer the zoom to the moving shot because, for one reason, it is more economical. Technically, the zoom is not a moving shot because the camera does not move; rather, an adjustable lens gives the impression of its moving close to, or far away from, the subject (hence, the terms *zoom in/zoom out*). There are occasions when a zoom is useful: to single out someone in a crowd, to pinpoint the criminal's hiding place in the woods, to capture a facial expression without the person's being aware of the camera's presence. On the debit side, zooming flattens the image and creates an unreal sense of depth. It is one thing if a two-dimensional effect is desired, as it is in *Barry Lyndon* where Kubrick zooms out of close-ups to reveal scenes that resemble paintings. But this is not the case in most films where zooming is an inexpensive alternative to tracking.

The opposite of the zoom, which represents deceptive motion, is the freeze, which is a form of stopped motion. In a freeze, all movement suddenly halts, and the image "freezes" as it turns into a still photograph. The most famous freeze occurs at the end of *The 400 Blows* (François Truffaut, 1959). Antoine Doinel (Jean-Pierre Léaud) escapes from a reformatory and heads toward the ocean. When he reaches the water's edge, he walks into the shallows; then he turns and faces the shore. At that instant Truffaut freezes the frame, trapping Antoine between the reformatory and the ocean, between the past and the present. The freeze implies immobility, helplessness, or indecison.

The zoom and the freeze are similar in that they can call attention to details more dramatically than other devices. Because of their strong underscoring power, they are as easily misused as italics are by inexperienced writers. Since many contemporary films end with a

The most famous freeze frame in film: the final shot in The 400 Blows *(François Truffaut, 1959). (Courtesy MOMA/FSA and Janus Films)*

freeze frame which then becomes the background for the end credits, examples of an intelligent use of the freeze frame are hard to come by. A great filmmaker will freeze for a reason; a mediocre one will freeze for effect. The freeze at the end of *Women in Love* (Ken Russell, 1970), the film version of D. H. Lawrence's novel, is perfectly motivated. The novel comes to no real resolution. The film duplicates the unresolved ending by repeating Lawrence's dialogue, which leads to a natural freeze. When Birkin (Alan Bates) tells Ursula (Jennie Linden) that he wants an "eternal" relationship with another man, Ursula, who cannot conceive of such a relationship, says, "You can't have it, because it's false, impossible." "I don't believe that," Birkin replies, and with these words the novel ends. The same dialogue appears in the film, but when Birkin says, "I don't believe that," Ursula's face freezes into utter bafflement. His words have left her speechless, and what conveys speechlessness better than a freeze?

COMBINING SHOTS: THE SEQUENCE

In film, shots combine to form sequences, or what we generally think of as scenes. Note that some writers prefer to distinguish between a scene and a sequence. A scene, they would say, is a unit of the action taking place in the same location and made up of one shot (e.g., a long take) or many shots. A sequence is a group of shots forming a self-contained segment of the film that is by and large intelligible in itself.

From the above definitions, scene and sequence appear to be virtually synonymous, and for all practical purposes they are. The chief difference is that there can be scenes within a sequence, but not sequences within scenes. In the "Key" sequence in *Notorious*, as we will see (below), there are several scenes. The sequence begins in the bedroom with Alicia's removing the key to the wine cellar from Alex's key chain (scene 1); next, she gives the key to Devlin downstairs (scene 2); finally, Devlin and Alicia go down to the wine cellar (scene three).

There are several kinds of sequences, two of which have already been discussed: credits and precredits sequences (Chapter 2). Someone who has not seen *The Wild Bunch* (Sam Peckinpah, 1969) and is shown only the credits sequence would still be able to make some sense of it. What appears to be a detachment of cavalry troops rides into a small town. Some children are feeding a pair of scorpions to a horde of ants. The soldiers ride past the children and proceed up the main street toward the payroll office. On the rooftops of the buildings flanking the street is a band of armed men crouching behind the parapets. The soldiers dismount at the payroll office, enter it, flash their .45s, and pistol-whip the employees. By the time all the credits have appeared, a drama in miniature has unfolded in the form of a sequence. The peaceful tenor of the town has been established and threatened. We now know that the troops are bandits; the rooftop crowd, bounty hunters in the employ of the railroad; the townspeople and children, unsuspecting victims of the crossfire that will certainly erupt.

Sequences can also be identified as linear, associative, and montage. Note that these types of sequences are not mutually exclusive. Credits and precredits sequences can be linear (with a beginning, middle, and end); they can also be a montage of various shots (like the New York montage that accompanies the credits of *Manhattan* [Woody Allen, 1979]). Similarly, an associative sequence can be linear (although a linear sequence is not associative). When a sequence is designated as associative, it means that the links between beginning, middle, and end are not so much narrative as visual.

The Linear Sequence

In a linear sequence, one action links up with another, creating a miniature drama with a beginning, a middle, and an end. Let us look again at the "Key" sequence in *Notorious*. Alicia Huberman (Ingrid

Bergman) is an American intelligence agent whose mission required her to marry Alexander Sebastian (Claude Rains), a top-ranking Nazi residing in post–World War II Brazil. Since Sebastian has given Alicia a key to every room in the house except the wine cellar, she suspects it may contain more than wine. Gaining access to the cellar poses a problem, however, because Sebastian carries his key ring with him most of the time. On the evening of a party the couple are giving, Alicia notes her husband has left the key ring on his dressing table. While he is in the bathroom, she removes the wine-cellar key.

The beginning of the sequence initiates the action: Alicia removes the key. The middle adds something to the action: Alicia slips the key to her coworker Harry Devlin (Cary Grant) during the party; they proceed to the wine cellar, where they discover that some of the bottles contain uranium ore; meanwhile, the champagne supply dwindles, and Sebastian and the wine steward go down to the cellar. The end follows and completes the action: Sebastian discovers his wife and Devlin together. In a linear sequence, then, the connections between the incidents are like links in a chain.

In some linear sequences, however, a few links may be missing; thus, the sequence is *elliptical*. A linear sequence is designated as elliptical when certain details have been omitted because the viewers are expected to make the connections for themselves. The "Wedding of Angharad" sequence in *How Green Was My Valley* (John Ford, 1941) comprises three episodes that appear, on the surface, to be loosely related: "The Courting of Angharad," "The Visit to Gruffydd," and "The Wedding." In the first episode, Evans, a mine owner's son, comes to court Angharad (Maureen O'Hara) after his pompous father has made the initial arrangements. Since Angharad appears to have a mind of her own, there is little likelihood that Evans will win her despite his wealth. Thus, we do not take the courting seriously. In the second episode, Angharad calls on Mr. Gruffydd (Walter Pidgeon), the minister, whom she really loves. There is something disturbing about this episode—it hints at love never to be consummated. Angharad speaks of her affection for the minister to discover if he feels the same toward her. But his only concern is his low salary, which makes marriage impossible. In the third episode, Angharad steps wraithlike into a carriage, her bridal veil billowing in the breeze.

The three episodes become linked by the impressions they create in the audience's mind. Initially, there seems to be no connection between the courting and Angharad's visit to Gruffydd, but the link becomes clear with the final episode: *money*, which means nothing to Angharad but means a great deal to the minister. In choosing Evans, she chose what Gruffydd considered the prerequisite for marriage.

The folly of her choice is a mirthless wedding where the wind makes sport of her veil as if it were a kite. The tragedy of her choice is mirrored in the minister's face as he watches the wedding party drive away.

The Associative Sequence

In an associative sequence, the scenes are linked together by an object or a series of objects. In another sequence in *Notorious*, Alicia, who has fallen in love with Devlin, plans an intimate dinner for the two of them. As Devlin leaves for headquarters, Alicia asks him to pick up some wine. In the next scene, Devlin enters his supervisor's office with a bottle of champagne, which he leaves on the desk. When he discovers that Alicia's assignment requires her to seduce Sebastian, he is so disturbed that he forgets the champagne. Scene 2 ends with a close-up of the bottle. In the third scene, Devlin is back in Alicia's apartment, where the dinner is burned and there is not even any wine to salvage the evening. Devlin looks around for the champagne: "I guess I left it somewhere," he mutters. These three episodes coalesce into a sequence that might be entitled "The Ruined Dinner," whose three scenes might be called "The Bottle Suggested," "The Bottle Purchased," and "The Bottle Forgotten." It is an object that unifies the sequence: the close-up of the bottle in scene 2 links scenes 1 and 3, bringing them into dramatic focus.

A similar sequence occurs in Hitchcock's *Rebecca*. Maxim de Winter's new bride lives in the shadow of her husband's first wife, Rebecca, whose presence is everywhere. In a sequence that might be called "The Ubiquitous Rebecca,"we first see a shot of Rebecca's room, closed since her death and guarded by her dog; then a napkin with Rebecca's initials; finally, Maxim de Winter (Laurence Olivier) and his young bride (Joan Fontaine) at opposite ends of a long table. What separates them is not just distance but the spirit of Rebecca, who is present even in the napkins on the table. Hitchcock has fashioned a sequence out of three different shots, each dominated by an object associated with the late Rebecca de Winter: a bedroom door, an embroidered napkin, and a dining room table.

In the sequence that ends another Hitchcock film, *North by Northwest*, Eve Kendall (Eva Marie Saint) is holding on to the hand of Roger Thornhill (Cary Grant) to keep from sliding off Mt. Rushmore. Thornhill encourages her to "hang in there," and, as an added incentive, proposes marriage. In one of the smoothest transitions in film, the hand to which Eve was just clinging is now helping her climb to the upper berth of a compartment on the Twentieth Century Limited.

Harry Devlin (Cary Grant) on the verge of forgetting the champagne in Notorious *(Alfred Hitchcock, 1946). Hitchcock ends the scene with a close-up of the bottle, the object that unifies the entire sequence. (Courtesy ABC Picture Holdings, Inc.)*

Without the audience's suspecting it, the scene changed from Mt. Rushmore to the train compartment. Thornhill's hand was the unifying image; it rescued Eve from death and saved her for marriage.

The Montage Sequence

Montage is a word that has many meanings. When used to describe a sequence, *montage* can be defined as a series of shots arranged in a particular order for a particular purpose. In a montage sequence, the shots are so arranged that they follow each other in rapid succession, telescoping an event or several events of some duration into a couple of seconds of screen time. *A New Life* (Alan Alda, 1988) contains a dating montage that shows a newly divorced woman trying to resume a form of socializing she has not done in twenty-five years. Another kind of montage, called *American montage* because it was so prominent in American films of the 1930s and 1940s, works from the same principle: time is collapsed as shots blend together, wipe each other away, or are superimposed on each other. A typical American montage might consist of calendar pages blowing away as one month yields to another, then one year to another, while over the blowing pages are superimposed headlines giving the main events that happened during that time period. Finally, the montage ends, and the action resumes.

Just as an associative sequence can also be linear, a montage sequence can have features of the linear and the associative sequence. A montage sequence compressing a decade into ten seconds could be linear in its chronological arrangement. The World War II montage was common in films of the 1940s. First, one would see a headline announcing the Japanese attack on Pearl Harbor, then subsequent headlines would enumerate key battles, and the last headline would proclaim the Japanese surrender.

A montage can also be unified by images. For example, the tour of Washington montage in *Mr. Smith Goes to Washington* (Frank Capra, 1939) combines shots of the Capitol, the White House, the Washington Monument, the Lincoln Memorial, and excerpts from Lincoln's Second Inaugural Address and the Gettysburg Address, all of which are associated with the spirit of American democracy.

FROM SHOT TO SHOT

Cuts

Cut is one of the most commonly used terms in film. It can be a verb a director shouts to terminate a shot ("Cut!"), or a noun meaning a strip of film or a joint between two separate shots. It can also be a version of a movie in its various stages (rough cut, director's cut, final cut). In the context of this chapter, a cut is the joining of two separate shots so that the first is instantaneously replaced by the second, showing something the preceding shot did not. There are five basic kinds of cuts: straight, contrast, parallel (cross), jump, and form.

In a straight cut, one image instantaneously replaces another. Straight cuts are the most common kind: shot B replaces shot A. In *The Lady Eve* (1941), Preston Sturges cuts from Charlie Pike (Henry Fonda) sitting at a table in a ship's dining room (shot A) to a group of women staring in his direction (shot B). In a contrast cut, the images replacing each other are dissimilar in nature; for example, the cut from the manacled feet of slaves to the galloping hooves of horses in *Slaves* (Herbert J. Biberman, 1969) contrasts the enslaved and the free.

The parallel cut, or crosscut, presents two actions occurring simultaneously. In *Saboteur,* an attempt to sabotage a battleship at a christening in the Brooklyn Navy Yard is crosscut with the ceremony itself. In *Moonstruck* (Norman Jewison, 1987), a mother is having dinner with a university professor, while her daughter is at the Metropolitan Opera with her lover. *King and Country* (Joseph Losey, 1964) includes two actions that are crosscut: the mock trial of a rat the soldiers are staging in the rain, and the actual trial of a deserter that is being conducted in the barracks. Thus, the plight of the soldier is equated with the plight of the rat. Both the soldier and the rat are victims—the deserter of a dubious military code, the rat of the soldiers' cruelty that stems from boredom.

A break in continuity that leaves a gap in the action constitutes a jump cut. In *Darling* (John Schlesinger, 1965), a shot of a couple about twenty yards from the entrance to a building is followed by a shot of them going through the door to the interior of the building. Obviously, not everything has to be shown in a particular scene or sequence, but excessive jump cutting can give a film the continuity of a comic strip. On the other hand, when a knowledgeable director jump cuts, there probably is a reason. In *Breathless* (Jean-Luc Godard, 1959), the main character shoots a police officer in Marseilles, runs across a field, and emerges in Paris. Godard is too talented a filmmaker to break continuity without a reason. *Breathless* is the kind of movie that calls attention to itself as a movie: it is dedicated to Monogram Pictures, which produced low-budget films during the 1930s and 1940s, and recreates, in a more intellectual way, the style of the low-budget American film where a character can move from one location to the other without being seen in transit.

A form cut is a cut from one object to another that is similarly shaped. In *Detour* there is a cut from a record in a juke box to a drumhead—one circular object replaces another. Similar in principle to the form cut is the match cut, in which one shot "matches" the other, following it so smoothly that there is no break in continuity. Often a match cut is similar in shape to the shot it matches, although it need not be. Probably the most famous match in film is the one in *2001: A Space Odyssey* (Stanley Kubrick, 1968) when an ape hurls a bone into the air in one shot, and a space station in orbit appears in the next. The match condenses the history of evolution into two images.

Transitions

In a cut there is no bridge between shots; one shot simply replaces another. Just as writers use transitional phrases (however, moreover, in fact) to bridge ideas, filmmakers use transitional devices to bridge scenes. And just as one can spot transitional phrases, one can also spot transitional devices in film because they are more notice-able than cuts. The following are the chief transitional devices in film.

The Fade

The fade-out is the simplest kind of transition: the light de-creases, and the screen goes dark. The opposite is the fade-in, where the light increases as the picture gradually appears on the screen. (The term *fade* generally refers to a fade-out.) Most fade-outs are no more profound than a blank screen. Yet some fade-outs can bring an action to an artful close in the way a gifted orator rounds out a sen-tence. A good illustration is the first fade-out in *Mrs. Miniver* (William Wyler, 1942). The first sequence covers a day in the lives of the Minivers. Husband and wife feel guilty for having purchased some-thing the other might find frivolous: Kay (Greer Garson) has bought a new hat, and Clem (Walter Pidgeon) a new car. At the close of the day, the camera pans the bedroom, pausing at the hat smartly perched on the bedpost. The scene fades out with the hat in silhou-ette. Fading out on the hat brings the sequence full circle: it began with Kay's buying the hat and ends with its being displayed. We smile at the fade because it provides the same pleasure of recognition we receive when a speech begins and ends with the same image. But we also smile at its wisdom, for it represents one of those little domes-tic triumphs that seems more meaningful at the end of the day than at the beginning.

In the theater, the curtain sometimes descends between the scenes of an act to mark the passage of time. In film, a fade can function in the same way. The first fade in *Notorious* occurs at a particu-larly dramatic moment. There is an unidentified guest at Alicia's party, sitting with his back to the camera. Curiously, he remains after everyone leaves. Hitchcock fades out on the back of the man and fades in on his face, which is none other than Cary Grant's. Hitchcock interrupts the party with a fade to indicate a lapse of time; but the fade is also a clever way of introducing the male lead by linking two scenes in which he appears—one ending with his back to the camera, the other beginning with his face coming into view. The fade produces a more natural rhythm than if Hitchcock had cut from the back of Grant's head to a close-up of his face.

A fade can also be commentative. In *Mr. Skeffington* (Vincent Sher-man, 1944), the aging Fanny Skeffington (Bette Davis) reassembles her former suitors, who are now either married or balding. The scene fades out as the men enter the dining room and fades in on a gentle-man's hat and gloves. A cut would spoil the mood, which is one of genteel hypocrisy. The hat and gloves belong to Edward (Jerome

Harry Devlin as the uninvited guest at Alicia's (Ingrid Bergman) party in Notorious. *Hitchcock will fade out on the back of Grant's head and fade in on his face. (Courtesy ABC Picture Holdings, Inc.)*

Cowan), an impoverished suitor who has returned to court Fanny. The fade-out allows us to see a connection between the two scenes. In the first, Fanny has invited her suitors to dinner to reassure herself that she is still beautiful. However, Edward is not interested in her beauty, which is nonexistent, but only in her money, also nonexistent although he does not know it. One charade fades out and another fades in. A cut would have been too abrupt, and it would also not have conveyed the idea of one farce rising out of another.

The Dissolve

A fade denotes demarcation—it indicates the end of a narrative sequence. A dissolve denotes continuity by the gradual replacement of one shot by another. This kind of transition, in which the outgoing and incoming shots merge, serves a variety of functions. Sometimes a dissolve simply has the force of "in the meantime" or "later." In *North by Northwest*, Hitchcock dissolves a shot of Roger Thornhill bribing his mother to get a key from the desk clerk at a hotel to a shot of the two of them walking down the corridor toward the room Thornhill was so anxious to enter.

A dissolve can also mean "no sooner said than done." The Mother Superior in *The Song of Bernadette* (Henry King, 1943) no sooner asks to see Bernadette than the shot dissolves into Bernadette's room. In *Caught* (Max Ophuls, 1948), a shot of a woman gazing at a picture of a model in a mink coat dissolves into a shot of the woman, who has become a model herself, wearing a mink.

When is a dissolve a transition and when is it more than a transition? This is like asking when a word is simply a conventional sign and when a word is a symbol. Water can simply be a liquid, or it can be a sign of birth, rebirth, or fertility. It depends on the context: in T. S. Eliot's poems, water is never just water. It is the same with a dissolve. What a dissolve means—if, in fact, it means anything—is determined by the context. The dissolve in *North by Northwest* was just a way of getting two characters from the hotel lobby to one of the floors.

However, when two images blend in such a way that their union constitutes a symbolic equation, the result is a metaphorical dissolve. This is a visual form of synecdoche (or metonymy, to which synecdoche is very similar), a species of metaphor in which the part is substituted for the whole (roofs for houses, sail for ships) or a sign for the thing signified (green = Go, crown = royalty). We often use this figure of speech without knowing it: "Give us this day our daily *bread*" (bread = food); "All *hands* on deck" (hands = crew); "He addressed his comments to the *chair*" (chair = chairperson).

In *The Two Mrs. Carrolls* (Peter Godfrey, 1947), Geoffrey Carroll (Humphrey Bogart) is a wife poisoner. Early in the film, Sally (Barbara Stanwyck) discovers a letter he dropped, addressed to his wife. Because Sally is in love with Geoffrey, she questions him about his marriage. He replies that he is getting a divorce. The letter dissolves into a neatly wrapped package of poison Geoffrey has just purchased from a pharmacist. The merging of the two images, the letter and the package, results in the equation: Mrs. Carroll + package = death. Dissolving an envelope bearing a woman's name into the means that will make her only a name is an ingenious touch.

The dissolves in George Stevens's films have an effect similar to the homogenization of cream and milk. In *Shane,* when Starrett (Van Heflin) and Shane (Alan Ladd) succeed in uprooting a stubborn tree trunk, Stevens slowly merges their triumphant faces into the landscape, making the men one with nature. Later, when Starrett watches a homeowner's property go up in flames, Stevens dissolves his vengeful face into the burning house. The resulting equation—man + nature = natural man; face + burning house = consuming rage—do not advance the plot; their purpose is rather to illustrate one of the film's main themes: the pioneer's oneness with nature, which enables him to become part of everything he sees or does.

A dissolve can sometimes have the effect of dramatic foreshadowing if the filmmaker prepares the audience for subsequent events by hinting at their outcome earlier. In *King and Country,* a skull mired in mud dissolves into the face of a soldier playing a harmonica. The dissolve prefigures the fate of the soldier, who later dies in the mud, his voice silenced by a pistol shot in the mouth.

Just as they can foreshadow, so dissolves can recapitulate. At the end of *The Last Picture Show,* Sonny (Timothy Bottoms) returns to the house of Ruth Popper (Cloris Leachman), the coach's wife, with whom he had been having an affair. The movie house has closed its doors forever; Sam the Lion and Billy are dead; Duane is on his way to Korea. All that remain are Ruth and the dreary Texas town where the tumbleweed rolls down the main street. As Sonny and Ruth look at each other, their eyes forge the only bond that can unite them— loneliness. At that moment, Sonny and Ruth dissolve into the town and the vast Texas flatlands. There is no difference between a young man without prospects, a middle-aged woman without hope, and a town without a future. Their destinies have become one.

At the end of *Colorado Territory* (1949), Raoul Walsh's western remake of his earlier success *High Sierra* (1941), the hands of Wes (Joel McCrea) and Colorado (Virginia Mayo), touching in death, dissolve into a shot of a ringing bell. The dissolve does not so much connect two images as two events that the lovers' hands and the bell represent. Earlier in the film, Wes had hidden some stolen money in an abandoned church. After the deaths of Wes and Colorado, a priest discovers the money and uses it to restore the church bell, telling the villagers it was the gift of two lovers who passed by.

The Form Dissolve

A filmmaker can merge two images with the same shape or contours through a form dissolve. Often a form dissolve is merely easy on the eyes. For example, in *Jane Eyre,* the figure of a ballerina on top of a music box dissolves into a little girl dressed in the same costume. A form dissolve can also be directly related to the plot. In *The Wrong Man,* a jazz musician is falsely accused of a holdup. As the musician (Henry Fonda) prays in front of a picture of Jesus Christ, the scene gradually changes to one of a man walking down a dark street. Then the man's head merges with the musician's, which in turn becomes hollow enough to accommodate the other's face. The man whose head fits into the musician's is the real criminal. The dissolve shows how easy it is to mistake the innocent for the guilty; it is just a matter of superimposing one face upon another.

The Wipe

Some television news programs change news items by means of a line traveling vertically across the screen. That traveling line is a wipe, and in the 1930s and the 1940s, this device was the most stylish of the transitions. Since the screen is rectangular, the wipe can move vertically, horizontally, or diagonally; it can create a theatrical effect by rising or falling like a drop curtain, as it does in a scene in *The Thin Man*, where it moves from the bottom of the screen to the top, revealing a stage full of dancers.

Sometimes wipes complement each other: One shot ends with a wipe that travels from left to right; the next with a wipe that moves across the screen from right to left. The best example of complementary wipes can be found in the opening of *The Petty Girl* (Henry Levin, 1950).

More fluid than a cut and faster than a dissolve, the wipe is ideal for presenting a series of events in quick succession. Frank Capra, a frequent user of the wipe, employed it in the opening sequences of *It Happened One Night* (1934), *Mr. Deeds Goes to Town* (1936), and *Mr. Smith Goes to Washington*. In the handwriting sequence in *Mr. Smith Goes to Washington*, for example, one expert after another testifies to the authenticity of Jeff Smith's signature. After each expert speaks, Capra simply "wipes" him off the screen, thereby showing the inanity of the investigation.

Rouben Mamoulian's excellent use of the wipe is apparent in *Dr. Jekyll and Mr. Hyde*. After Jekyll (Fredric March) becomes Hyde, he goes off into the night, deserting Muriel Carew (Rose Hobart), his fiancée, who expects him at her dinner party. A wipe opens like a fan, dividing the screen diagonally: On the left is the departing Jekyll; on the right, the party in progress. When Jekyll leaves the Carew estate, Mamoulian wipes him out of the frame, which expands to disclose the dinner guests and the worried Muriel. At that point, the frame divides diagonally again: On the right is Ivy (Miriam Hopkins) sipping champagne, the woman Hyde will kill; on the left is Muriel, the woman Jekyll yearns to marry. The wipe acts as a parallel cut, informing us that while Muriel was at her party, Ivy was at home. But the split screen also represents the protagonist's ideal woman, who is similarly halved. It is only fitting that for a double man (Jekyll/Hyde) there should be a double woman (Ivy/Muriel).

When Muriel's father, furious at Jekyll's absence, cries, "Muriel, you will have nothing more to do with that man," a wipe begins to move him from the left of the screen to the center, revealing the "man" himself. However, it is not Jekyll but Hyde whom we see. The wipe is an ironic commentary on the father's outburst; clearly, he did not mean that Muriel should have nothing to do with Hyde (whom he cannot know) but with Jekyll. However, at this point Jekyll is Hyde.

Some writers compare the wipe to a windshield wiper. Hitchcock uses it as such in *Rebecca,* when the second Mrs. de Winter sees Manderley for the first time through the windshield as the wipers clear away the rain. He repeats the technique in *Psycho:* as Marion drives in the rain, the sign for the Bates Motel materializes on her windshield. In each film, the wipe introduces a new phase of the character's life by bringing the future before the character's eyes. In Mrs. de Winter's case, it was the house where she learned the truth about Rebecca, her husband's first wife; in Marion's, it was the motel where she met her death.

The Iris

Mt. Rushmore as seen through a telescope in *North by Northwest* appears inside a circle in the middle of the darkened screen. This is a masking shot, or to be more accurate, an iris shot, in which everything is blacked out except for what is to be seen telescopically. The frame can also be altered to simulate other shapes (e.g., the view from a keyhole, a crack in a door, binoculars, a submarine periscope) depending upon the form in which the director wants the audience to see the image.

In addition to the iris shot, there is what is known as irising in and irising out. Irising in consists of opening up the darkened frame with a circle of light that keeps expanding until the picture fills the frame. Irising out is the opposite; it is as if darkness is seeping into the frame from all sides, forcing the diminishing picture into some part of the frame until it becomes a speck and disappears.

A director can dolly in or out of a scene, or today, zoom in or out of one; but there is nothing quite like an iris to open the frame. Griffith used the iris breathtakingly in Sherman's March to the Sea in *The Birth of a Nation.* The frame opens from the upper lefthand corner to reveal a mother and her children on a hill; at first we do not know why they are huddled in fear, but as the frame opens, we see Sherman's soldiers in the valley below. In *Intolerance,* Griffith gradually disclosed the splendor of Babylon by expanding the frame, starting at the lower right-hand corner.

The iris is especially effective in death scenes. Lucy of *Broken Blossoms* and the Mountain Girl of *Intolerance* both die in iris. Irising out can suggest death because of the way in which darkness creeps into the frame, reducing the size of the image to a pinpoint and then annihilating it. Orson Welles chose the iris to symbolize both the death of Wilbur Minafer and the end of the horse and buggy era in *The Magnificent Ambersons* (1942). A horseless carriage moves in long shot across the snow. The passengers sing merrily, but their song is in sharp contrast to the landscape, which is dominated by a dead tree with wiry branches. As the motor buggy moves out of frame, Welles starts irising out until it disappears in the darkness that floods the screen. Welles irises out into a fade. One would have expected him to iris out of one scene and into another; but the shot that follows the fade is of a black wreath on the door of the Amberson house. The iris and the fade imply finality in different ways—the iris gradually and poetically, the fade irrevocably.

The principle of the iris unifies the flashbacks in George Stevens's *Penny Serenade* (1941). Julie (Irene Dunne) recalls incidents from her marriage by playing recordings of popular songs that had meaning for herself and her husband. Each flashback begins with a close-up of the center of the disc, which then opens up, irislike, to reveal the scene.

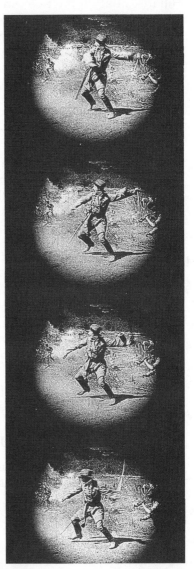

A frame enlargement of an iris shot from The Birth of a Nation. *In an iris shot, the image appears within a circle on an otherwise dark screen. (Courtesy MOMA/FSA and Epoch Producing Corporation)*

Because of their fondness for the movies of the past, both François Truffaut and Jean-Luc Godard use the iris more readily than did many of their peers. Truffaut irises out repeatedly in *The Wild Child* to make the scenes resemble the stages of a scientific experiment conducted as dispassionately as possible. Godard uses the iris for sheer nostalgia in *Breathless*. In one scene he irises out on Michel gazing idolatrously at a poster of Humphrey Bogart in his last film. One is tempted to say that Godard is irising out on the old Hollywood—except that irising is still being practiced, although not as regularly as it was in Griffith's day or during the 1930s and the 1940s. However, we do find irising on certain television programs and in movies where techniques of the past function as period touches. When George Roy Hill irises out on the two con men at the close of *The Sting* (1973), it gives the ending a deliberately old-fashioned look. Similarly, Peter Bogdanovich's use of irising in *Nickelodeon* lends an air of authenticity to the film, set in the early days of the movie industry.

Contemporary filmmakers such as Steven Spielberg, Francis Ford Coppola, and Martin Scorsese, who are also immersed in films of the past, understandably use the techniques of the past. They use wipes, irises, and fades both because they respect those techniques as vestiges of a past they admire, and also because those techniques can still be effective narrative devices. Brian De Palma uses the fade as a sign of demarcation at the beginning of *Dressed to Kill* (1980) when he fades to white after Kate's sexual fantasy. Steven Spielberg fades to black in *Empire of the Sun* to indicate that the first part of the action is over. Francis Ford Coppola uses a wipe in *Peggy Sue Got Married* (1986) to take Peggy Sue (Kathleen Turner) from high school where she is talking with a male student to her bedroom where she is talking with her girl friends. Martin Scorsese irises frequently in "Life Studies," the first of three short films that make up *New York Stories* (1989). Wipes and irises abound in the Star Wars trilogy, which evoke the old movie serials where wipes and irises were common. Here they have the double function of evoking nostalgia and promoting the narrative. Alan Alda ends *Sweet Liberty* with a variation on the iris out; the image does not narrow into a circle but into a rectangle that grows progressively smaller until it disappears. As more film disciples go on to become filmmakers, their work will reflect what they have learned and what they have seen.

ASSEMBLING THE SHOTS

When Alfred Hitchcock said that a film must be edited, he meant that the shots making up the movie had to be assembled and arranged in such a way that the action proceeds in a logical and coherent manner. Editing involves selecting and arranging the shots based on the following considerations: their place within the narrative, their contribution to the mood of a particular scene or to the film as a whole, their enhancement of the film's rhythm, their elucidation of the film's deeper meaning, and their fulfillment of the filmmaker's purpose.

The most common form of editing in the narrative film is continuity editing, which entails assembling shots so that they follow each other smoothly and without interruption, as opposed to the piecemeal way in which a movie is filmed. Although movies are shot out of sequence (with location filming usually done before soundstage filming, and scenes involving actors with other commitments shot when the actors are available), filmgoers do not care which scenes were shot first or that the climax in the Grand Canyon was shot on the second day of shooting because the weather happened to be ideal. Continuity editing preserves the illusion of an ongoing narrative.

Eisenstein's Theory of Montage

While *montage* is sometimes used as a synonym for editing (e.g., montage and American montage sequences), it had deeper implications for the great Soviet filmmaker Sergei Eisenstein, who believed that shots should not so much connect as collide, and that the viewer should be affected by their collision. Thus, montage calls attention to itself, unlike continuity editing which is supposed to be unobtrusive. If a man postures like a peacock, cut from the man to the peacock; if he is figuratively a horse's ass, pair him with a real one. If the purpose of a scene is to show people being killed like animals, cut from workers being massacred to an ox being slaughtered. If one wishes to state visually that all wars waged in the name of God are immoral, arrange a series of shots starting with a baroque Christ and ending with an idol, thereby making militarism a form of regression. This is the kind of montage that Eisenstein practiced.

Eisensteinian montage is based on contrast and conflict, which can exist both within the film as a whole and within a particular shot or scene. In the Odessa Steps massacre in Eisenstein's *Potemkin*, a body lies diagonally across the steps; the Cossacks cast shadows that fall menacingly at oblique angles to the steps; the steps form three contrasting planes, with the Cossacks at the top firing at a woman on a landing behind which lies a trail of bodies.

Eisenstein discovered how ideas could arise from the contrast and conflict of images. Without creating an actual series of cause and effect, Eisenstein opened *Potemkin* with a shot of breaking waves and followed this image of turbulence with shots of men sleeping in hammocks that formed a shroudlike tangle, mess tables swinging back and forth, meat crawling with maggots—each image jarring us, disquieting us, but ultimately preparing us for the sailors' revolt.

Eisenstein's influence was enormous, but not always beneficial. Instead of producing an artistic effect, sometimes the collision of images produced only pretentiousness. There is an embarrassing scene in Mamoulian's otherwise excellent *Dr. Jekyll and Mr. Hyde* when Jekyll, exulting over his impending marriage to Muriel, cries, "If music be the food of love, play on!" as he sits down at the organ and pounds away. Five shots appear in rapid succession commenting on his rapture: a lighted candelabra, an illuminated art object, a smiling statue, the butler's beaming countenance, and a blazing hearth. Jekyll's rapture is evident from the way he plays the organ; the accompanying montage is superfluous.

To Eisenstein, montage meant the visual conflict of images. On the Continent, *montage* means editing: selecting and editing the shots that will form the scenes and sequences of the film. In England, the same process is called *editing* or *cutting,* but with a slight difference: *editing* means the step-by-step assembling of the shots in the cutting room while *montage* refers to the process considered as a whole. A further complication is that, during the 1930s and 1940s, American films employed what has become known as *American montage* which, as we have already seen, is a convenient way of collapsing time. In a typical American montage scene, newspapers would spin across the screen announcing a murder trial as one headline obliterates the other. The face of the judge would dissolve into the defendant's; during the trial, one shot would wipe away another. Superimposed over the defendant's face would be his anguished wife's, and over hers, the face of the real murderer who is hiding out in a sleazy room above a bar. Although this form of montage in which time is telescoped through a blend of dissolves, wipes, and superimposures is not in vogue today, in its time it was highly effective and was regarded as sufficiently important to warrant screen credit for the montage editor. Slavko Vorkapich was especially adept at montage (*Mr. Deeds Goes to Town, Mr. Smith Goes to Washington*), and Don Siegel began in montage at Warner Brothers before going on to become a well-known director (*Invasion of the Body Snatchers* [1956], *Dirty Harry* [1971], *Escape from Alcatraz* [1979], etc.)

Continuity Editing

While montage may seem to be more exciting intellectually than continuity editing, it would be a mistake to dismiss continuity editing as merely the sequential arrangement of shots. Continuity editing is based on other editing principles that affect a film's rhythm, time, space, tone, and theme.

Rhythm

No great film is rhythmically uniform. Some shots remain on the screen longer than others; some sequences move more rapidly than others. One sequence may be uncommonly slow, while another may be unusually fast. The best filmmakers vary speed, movement, and pace, knowing that long strips of film produce a slower rhythm, short strips a more rapid rhythm. The process itself is not the issue here; the effects are, as one can see in the first two sequences of *Citizen Kane*, "The Death of Kane" and "News on the March."

The film begins with the camera ascending the gate of Xanadu, defying the No Trespassing sign. A series of dreamlike dissolves culminates in a shot of a lighted window that suddenly goes dark. A mouth utters "Rosebud!" through a veil of falling snow, and a glass paperweight with a snow-covered house inside it smashes without making a sound. A nurse enters a room and folds a dead man's arms on his breast. The mood of the first part of "The Death of Kane" is slow and languid. As the camera draws nearer to the window, the rhythm accelerates. Snow falls to the sound of crystal-pure music evoking Kane's Colorado boyhood. The paperweight breaks, and the nurse enters. Then the rhythm decelerates, and the mood becomes solemn as she places Kane's arms on his chest.

Without warning, a voice bellows "News on the march!" as a newsreel of Kane's life unfolds. In the second scene the pace is frenetic; fifty years of a man's life are compressed into a few minutes.

FROM THE DEATH OF KANE IN *CITIZEN KANE*
Frame enlargement of the glass paperweight that falls from Kane's hand. The lighted window of Kane's bedroom goes dark. Suddenly snow begins to fall; it is the artificial snow in the glass paperweight that falls from Kane's hand as he utters his last word, "Rosebud!" (Courtesy MOMA/FSA and RKO)

As the nurse enters Kane's room, her image is refracted through a piece of the shattered paperweight. (Courtesy MOMA/FSA and RKO)

The pace builds inexorably until the "News on the March" is over and the camera sputters out, as if in exhaustion.

Time

Parallel cutting makes it possible for two concurrent actions to be depicted on the screen without one's being completed before the other begins—the filmmaker simply cuts back and forth between them. Most novelists would never narrate two simultaneous episodes by completing the first before going on to the second; the novelist would bring the first to a certain point and, leaving the reader in suspense, proceed to the second. The novelist would then gradually add to each episode until the episodes are resolved either separately or jointly. D. W. Griffith understood this principle when he made *The Lonely Villa* (1909), in which he cut back and forth between a mother and her daughters being terrorized by thieves who have broken into their home, and the father en route to rescue them. The action is resolved by the last-minute rescue.

Space

Film's ability to alter our perception of space is well known. A filmmaker can combine a shot of a tractor trailer that has jackknifed on the New England Thruway with a shot of a girl who had just gotten off the Cyclone at Coney Island, looking appropriately dazed. The combination could lead one to conclude that the girl witnessed the jackknifing even though the one event occurred outside of Boston, the other in Brooklyn.

D. W. Griffith's *Intolerance* is a four-plot film about the theme of injustice as seen in four different periods: the early twentieth century, the time of Cyrus the Great (sixth century B.C.), the time of Christ, and the St. Bartholomew's Day massacre of the Huguenots in 1572. Although the film depicts events in four different parts of the world, at the climax everything seems to be occurring within the same location. By alternating between shots of Christ proceeding toward Calvary, the mountain girl in her chariot on her way to warn Cyrus, the car's attempt to catch up with a train to prevent an innocent man from being executed, and Prosper the Huguenot rushing through the streets of sixteenth-century Paris to rescue his beloved, Griffith makes it seem that all of these events are occurring not only at the same time but also in the same general area. The parallel cutting has affected our sense of space as well as time. It also suits the film's theme: the existence of intolerance at all times and in all places.

Tone

Just as tempo should vary in a film, so too should tone, which is primarily light, shade, and color. Again *Kane* is an excellent example. The first sequence, "The Death of Kane," is dark and eerie. The second sequence, "News on the March," is the exact opposite; it is a newsreel and looks as grainy as any newsreel ever made.

Theme

A filmmaker might deepen a film's theme by juxtaposing contrasting shots. As we have seen, there is a cut in *Slaves* from the manacled feet of slaves to the galloping hooves of horses. Whether the horses are in the same vicinity as the slaves is irrelevant; the point of the cut is the contrast between the enslaved and the free. In *A Doll's House* (Patrick Garland, 1973), there is a cut from Nora's upper-middle-class home to Krogstad's hovel; seeing how Krogstad lives makes it easier to understand his blackmailing Nora.

The Role of the Editor

Since it is a common fallacy that films are made in the editing room, students often have difficulty distinguishing between the editor's role and the filmmaker's. We have seen that editing involves selecting and arranging the shots in a particular order. But who does the arranging, the editor or the filmmaker?

Let us use an analogy from student life. After you have written an essay or a term paper, you submit it to your instructor. Even before submitting it, you have edited it: removed superfluous words, substituted the right words for the wrong ones, corrected spelling and grammar. Still, your essay may not be perfect. You have been too close to it to catch all the mistakes. Since your instructor has not written it, he or she can be more objective. You may have sentences, or even paragraphs, that should be transposed. What you thought was an introduction might work better if you made it your conclusion. Perhaps you did not prune the paper of all its excesses; your instructor will note that. A good instructor can take what you have submitted and, by making the proper corrections and suggestions, show you how it can be improved. Your instructor did not write the paper, yet has done something for it that you could not do: your instructor has made it better.

An editor performs a similar task: an editor takes what has been shot and improves upon it. The ideal film editor is the director's alter ego, carrying out what the director would do if the director had the time to be all things to the film. Thus, an editor may select the shots or decide what portion of a shot should be used. An editor can give an action scene its distinctive rhythm by alternating tempo and varying directional movement. If a sequence needs greater momentum, an editor can cut it in such a way that it acquires it. If a scene is especially violent, an editor can cut it so rapidly that the movie will receive a PG instead of an R rating. If shot A shows the cavalry pursuing the Indians left to right, shot B must show the Indians fleeing left to right; otherwise, it would look as if the cavalry and the Indians collided. If a character exits shot A from the left, the character must enter shot B from the right.

Because all films require some form of editing, the importance of editors has often been exaggerated and their role sometimes equated with that of directors. Lee Bobker compares editors with painters, working in isolation to create the movie's pace, mood, and rhythm. Yet despite Bobker's respect for the editor's function, he is forced to admit it is a subservient one: "The editor should always enjoy a wide creative latitude, but he should never fall prey to the illusion that he is creating a new film from scratch. His primary purpose is to bring to completion an artistic work already in progress."[1]

In the first edition of *The Technique of Film Editing*, Karel Reisz dubbed the editor "the interpreter of the small details rather than the prime creator of the continuity."[2] For the second edition, Professor Thorold Dickinson provided an introduction to the second part of the book in which he stated that "the modern editor is the executant for the film-maker and no longer his equal on any self-respecting film."[3]

Most good editors would agree. The best answer to the question "What is film editing?" was given by British editor Anthony Gibbs: "Film editing is putting into dramatic form the basic filmed material given to the editor by the director."[4] However, just as there are average, good, and great directors, there are average, good, and great editors. Gibbs would call a good editor someone who can achieve "the total interpretation of the director's and the writer's intentions," and a great editor as someone capable of "taking their intentions even farther, showing them a dimension to their project which even they may not have imagined to be there."[5]

True greatness is rare in any profession; thus, great editors are probably at a premium. It is not unlikely that an editor capable of bringing to the surface what the filmmaker did not even know was there would go on to become a director. The motto of Edward Dmytryk, who began his career as an editor and then went on to direct some fifty films between 1935 and 1975, is relevant: "Substance first—then form."[6] The filmmaker must provide the substance if the editor is to provide the form.

COLORING THE IMAGE
The Black-and-White Film

Film theorist Rudolph Arnheim has argued that color is accidental to film, and that audiences can accept the absence of color in black-and-white movies. The history of film proves that a movie photographed in black and white can render all of the important plot details without loss of verisimilitude. Just as sound films cannot be considered superior to silent films simply because the dialogue can be heard, color films cannot be considered superior to black and white because all the colors can be seen. Nor are black and white films that include references to color less effective because the color cannot be seen; the color can be imagined. In *Jezebel* (William Wyler, 1938), a black-and-white film, Julie (Bette Davis) arrives at a ball in a red dress that she had been forbidden to wear. The dress photographs as non-white, and white was the color Julie was expected to wear. Juliet's act of rebellion is as effective today, when color films are the norm, as it was in 1938 when color films were the exception.

One should always remember that it has only been since the late 1960s that color has been the norm. Yet even when black and white was the norm, filmmakers could work within the parameters of monochrome and achieve something akin to color. In *Twelve O'Clock High* (Henry King, 1949), Gregory Peck plays an Air Force general whose inflexibility results in a nervous breakdown. He tolerates no deviation from the rules—he might even be termed a person who thinks in "black and white." When the general breaks down, the blackness of his hair and leather jacket and the stark whiteness of his face set against a translucent grey background imply that the grey area in

The creative use of black and white in The Merry Widow *(Ernst Lubitsch, 1934). (Courtesy MOMA/FSA)*

human affairs that lies between the extremes of black and white was something the general had relegated to the background. It was his inability to perceive shades of difference that led to his breakdown.

In *The Merry Widow* (Ernst Lubitsch, 1934), the black-and-white photography produces a color scheme that even the most advanced form of color technology would find hard to rival. Since the film is based on a Viennese operetta, everything looks as if it has come from a confectionary. It is impossible not to think of chocolate, icing, and whipped cream when watching the film: the widow's mansion looks like a tiered wedding cake; her boudoir is like a pastry shell; the walls of her boudoir are creamy and incandescent. When the widow wears a black negligee, the dramatic contrast of her attire and the appointments of her boudoir satisfy whatever craving for color a viewer might have.

Although *Citizen Kane* was photographed in black and white, it is rich in color symbolism. Throughout the film, white is an ambivalent symbol. It suggests innocence as well as the loss of innocence; it is the color of the real snow that Kane knew as a boy in Colorado, and the color of the artificial snow in the glass paperweight he keeps as a memento of that happy time. White is also a symbol of freedom; when Susan leaves Kane, a white cockatoo screeches and flies away. But white also evokes sterility and death. Xanadu, Kane's palatial home, is adorned with useless statues and white marble; the nurse who enters Kane's room at the moment of his death wears a white uniform. The symbolic values of white can be rendered so artfully by black and white that color is not missed.

The Color Film

If black-and-white photography can achieve such art, it would seem that color can go even further. Color can be simply part of the way a film is made, or it can be used creatively by those who think creatively. There are, also, some outstanding uses of color as a means of deepening the narrative. Although the heroine of *Marnie* has suppressed all memory of a murder she committed as a child, the guilt persists in the form of an intense aversion to red. Instinctively, she removes red gladioli from a vase and replaces them with white mums. A drop of red ink on her white blouse sends her rushing to the washroom; the red polka dots on a jockey's uniform petrify her. Not until the end of the film do we learn that Marnie's aversion to red was the result of her having killed a sailor with a poker to protect her prostitute mother from possible harm.

The title character in *Juliet of the Spirits* (Federico Fellini, 1965) is a housewife whose fantasies are dominated by erotic reds. When we first see Juliet, she is trying on a red wig; then she sets the table with red candles. When she visits a clairvoyant, she wears a red scarf. Yet red is not her color; it is the color of the women of her fantasies. At the end of the film Juliet reverts to white, the color that typfies the ordinary person that she is.

The title character in *Carrie* is a high-school senior with telekinetic powers. Her mother is a religious fanatic, and both have reddish hair. When Carrie menstruates for the first time, she thinks she is bleeding to death. Her naiveté makes her an object of derision to her classmates, who humiliate her publicly at the senior prom by dropping a bucket of pig's blood on her. The blood reddens Carrie's pink dress, and Carrie literally sees red. Her revenge, as one might suspect, is appropriately bloody.

The Godfather, Part II integrates the lives of Vito Corleone and his son Michael by contrasting the immigrant world of Little Italy where Vito grew to manhood with the world of modern Lake Tahoe where Michael lives. Michael's world has a dark mahogany look; everything about it is forbidding and austere. Vito's world is one of pastels; the colors are soft, delicate, warm. Not only are father and son con-trasted, but their respective eras as well: a sunlit past as opposed to a somber present. A similar contrast occurs in *The Wizard of Oz* (Victor Fleming, 1939). To convey the disparity between the colorless real world and the colorful world of the imagination, the Kansas scenes were photographed in sepia, and the Oz scenes in color.

Color can embellish, suggest, characterize, and forge symbolic connections; so can black and white. An astute filmgoer will know when color is decorative or functional and when monochrome is per-functory or motivated.

Colorization

Colorization, a practice that began in 1985, is the use of a computer-aided process to apply color to black-and-white movies. Colorization requires the film to be analyzed shot by shot and scene by scene, so that the colorization is consistent. The colors of the open-ing frames must be determined first by consulting sketches, memos, and set designs if they are available. Once the colors for the opening frames are selected, a computer applies the same colors throughout, varying the hues in terms of the lighting pattern in the original. Still, there is no guarantee that a color sketch provided for a black-and-white film would be valid if the studio had decided to shoot the film in color. Thus, the claim that a colorized version of a black-and-white film would have proved satisfactory if the filmmaker had the opportu-nity to shoot it in color is false.

The foes of colorization—and there are many, including James Stewart, Burt Lancaster, Woody Allen, Frank Capra, Martin Ritt—contend that colorization vitiates the principle of creative choice that is essential to art. When a studio chose to film a movie in black and white rather than color, that choice entailed several factors, the chief one being, no doubt, the cost. During Hollywood's Golden Age, there was no aesthetic policy that dictated what kinds of movies should be made in black and white, and what kinds in color. One cannot say, for example, that color is more suited to westerns than black and white since some of John Ford's classic westerns were photographed in black and white: *Stagecoach* (1939), *My Darling Clementine, Fort Apache* (1948), *Wagonmaster* (1950), *The Man Who Shot Liberty Valance* (1962). Nor was color considered mandatory for musicals; the great musicals of the 1930s, notably those starring Fred Astaire and Ginger Rogers, were black and white. Color was expensive and was not lavished on every film, only on films that the studio deemed important enough to warrant it or on films that needed color to realize their dramatic potential to the fullest. *Gone with the Wind* was intended to be in color; another film set in the South and released the previous year, *Jezebel*, was not.

When the decision is made to shoot a film in color, everything—costumes, lighting, makeup, settings—is planned and executed in terms of that choice. That choice, however, was to shoot the film in a color *process* such as Technicolor, Trucolor, Warnercolor, and so on. Colorization is not a *color* process; it is a *computer-aided* process that, in the absence of any guiding intelligence, allows a computer to make the choices that should be the prerogative of the filmmaker.

LIGHTING THE IMAGE

The classic Hollywood film is an example of three-point lighting—key, fill, and back lights used in combination to light the subject. These are not the only lights; still, three-point lighting is a standard lighting scheme, and if understood properly, explains how lighting can affect one's perception of a character or a setting.

The key light, the principal source of illumination, leaves shadows if it is used alone. Thus, another light is necessary to fill in the areas the key light has left unlit and to soften the shadows it has cast: the fill light, an auxiliary light of slightly less intensity placed at eye level. But even a combination of key and fill light is not sufficient if a sense of depth is desired. Hence, a back light, placed above and behind the subject, is required. The back light alone would produce merely a silhouette. But in combination with the key and fill lights, the back light separates the subject from its environment, thereby creating a feeling of depth.

In terms of effect, lighting can be categorized as high key and low key. A low-contrast ratio of key and fill light will result in an image of almost uniform brightness, or what is called *high-key lighting*, the kind used in musicals, comedies, and for scenes of tranquility and peace. Conversely, a high-contrast ratio of key and fill light will result in *low-key lighting* and create a shadowy effect and a nighttime aura, often with intensely white faces against an onyx-black background. Directors of horror films, melodramas, and *film noir* (a type of melodrama where passions run high in urban settings that are grimy and often fogbound and where streets are dark, mean, and continually rain-slick) prefer low-key lighting for its shadows and its strong contrast of light and darkness.

In addition to these two general categories of lighting, there are five other types distinguished by the angle from which the light source illuminates the subject: front, back, top, side, and bottom.

High-key lighting in Meet Me in St. Louis *(Vincente Minnelli, 1944). (Courtesy MOMA/FSA and MGM)*

Front lighting has a softening effect that makes whatever we are viewing seem more attractive than it actually is. Front lighting of the face creates an ageless look, but it also robs the face of character. Back lighting, as we have seen, adds depth and brings out subtleties of design and pattern. When a character is backlit, as Esther (Barbra Streisand) is when she sings "Evergreen" at the end of *A Star Is Born* (Frank Pierson, 1976), a halo-like aura is produced that gives an ethereal quality. Similarly, top lighting creates an atmosphere of youthfulness or spirituality, as it does in *The Song of Bernadette,* where it emphasizes Bernadette's saintliness. Side lighting leaves the subject half in

Low-key lighting in Crossfire *(Edward Dmytryk, 1947). (Courtesy WCFTR)*

light, half in shadow; thus, it can denote a split personality, a morally ambiguous character, or a *femme fatale.* Greta Garbo and Marlene Dietrich were often photographed in this fashion. Bottom lighting gives the subject a sinister air; it was the kind of lighting D. W. Griffith employed in *Dream Street* (1921) to bring out the villainy of Sway Wan.

In a black and white film, the interplay of light and darkness can produce visual symbolism. Throughout *Citizen Kane,* Thompson, the reporter trying to decipher the meaning of Kane's dying word ("Rosebud!") is always seen in shadow. He is literally in the dark and remains in that state throughout the film. Just as darkness can denote ignorance, so light can intimate knowledge. When Thompson enters the Thatcher Memorial Library to read the memoirs of Kane's guardian, shafts of light illuminate the mausoleum-like room. Perhaps the memoirs will explain the meaning of "Rosebud." But the light is deceptive, and Thompson leaves the library as much in the dark as ever.

Thompson is not the only character who suffers from ignorance. Although Thompson is ignorant of the meaning of "Rosebud," Kane is ignorant of himself. When Kane delivers his Declaration of Principles, promising to be a "fighting and tireless champion" of the peo-

Back lighting in Sunset Boulevard *(Billy Wilder, 1950). The back light is coming from a projector during the screening of a silent film starring Norma Desmond (Gloria Swanson), who, in the middle of it, stands up and with arm raised vows to return to the screen. (Courtesy WCFTR. Copyright © 1949, Paramount Pictures Corporations. All rights reserved.)*

ple, his face is in darkness. Kane does not know that he will never live up to his declaration, and the lighting states as much.

Lighting is also used effectively in *Sullivan's Travels* (Preston Sturgis, 1941). In that film, some black parishioners invite the white prisoners of a local chain gang to their church to watch a movie. When we see the prisoners making their way to the church, they are in darkness; for a moment they look like black men. The lighting establishes a bond between the black congregation and the prisoners; it also reinforces the film's theme that moviegoing is a form of brotherhood that erases all distinctions, including racial ones. Movies are the great leveler; in the dark everyone is equal.

NOTES

[1]Lee R. Bobker, with Louise Marinis, *Making Movies: From Script to Screen* (New York: Harcourt Brace Jovanovich, 1973), 209.

[2]Karl Reisz and Gavin Miller, *The Technique of Film Editing*, 2nd ed. (New York: Focal Press, 1968), 84.

[3]Ibid., 277.

[4]"Film Editors Forum," *Film Comment* 13 (March–April 1977): 24.

[5]*Ibid.*

[6]Edward Dmytryk, *On Film Editing: An Introduction to the Art of Film Construction* (Boston: Focal Press, 1984), 145.

4
Film Genres

Thus far we have been talking about techniques, using examples from such films as *My Darling Clementine, Detour,* and *Carrie.* While these films illustrate certain principles of moviemaking, they also illustrate certain types of films. Each of these films represents a particular genre: *Clementine,* the western; *Detour, film noir;* and *Carrie,* the horror film.

When English professors speak of a genre, they mean a literary form with certain conventions and patterns that, through repetition, have become so familiar that readers expect similar elements in works of the same type. In Greece of the fifth century B.C. and Elizabethan England, the two great ages of tragedy, audiences attending a performance of *Oedipus the King* or *Hamlet* were not witnessing a wholly new dramatic form. The protagonist embarking on a quest that will result in his or her undoing was already a familiar one. Equally well established was the tragic progression from ignorance to self-knowledge, and from prosperity to catastrophe.

The conventions of tragedy (protagonist with a tragic flaw, fatal mistake, reversal of fortune, etc.) appear in all tragedies; they do not always, however, appear in the same way. The Elizabethan tragic heroes, for example, exercise their free will to a greater degree than did their Greek counterparts. Modern tragedy, on the other hand, seems to be deterministic, with characters such as Blanche du Bois of Tennessee Williams's *A Streetcar Named Desire* and Willy Loman of Arthur Miller's *Death of a Salesman* destroyed by forces over which they have no control. Yet *Death of a Salesman* is as much a tragedy as *Oedipus* or *Hamlet,* even though it may not be written in verse, and the protagonist may not be from royalty. The same basic elements that make *Hamlet* a tragedy also make *Salesman* one.

Thus, a genre is not monolithic. Just as a genus admits of species, so a genre has subcategories. There are various kinds of tragedy: Greek, Elizabethan, French neoclassical, historical, modern. There are also tragedies that blur into melodrama, where chance occurrences seem more important than causality. Genres are never simple. Even comedy admits of various kinds: slapstick, bedroom farce, romantic comedy, drawing room comedy, and Chekhovian comedy (which blends pathos and humor in a unique way). Similarly, mystery fiction can be subdivided into crime fiction, detective fiction (softboiled and hardboiled), gothic fiction, espionage fiction, and the police procedural.

Thus it is not easy to pigeonhole a work of literature. While a long work of prose fiction can be classified as a novel, the crucial question is what kind of novel. Film genres are equally complex. While some literary genres reappear in film, not all do. Comedy is itself a genre in literature, but not in film, where genres tend to be more specific. Not all kinds of comedy have succeeded on the screen. While a book can be written about theatrical drawing room comedy or comedy of manners, neither has produced enough examples in film to warrant study of film drawing room comedy or film comedy of manners. On the other hand, screwball comedy, which is not a literary genre, is a well-established film genre. But perhaps the greatest difference between literary and film genres is that literary genres represent a hierarchy created by critics, while film genres represent the response of the studios to the marketplace. By the sixteenth century, a hierarchy of literary forms had been established, beginning with the lowly pastoral and culminating in the lofty epic. While this particular hierarchy no longer exists, the mentality behind it does. There are still many literary scholars who rank poetry above fiction and drama below it; there are also some who would relegate the essay to the category of expositional or informal prose and deny it literary status. In film, on the other hand, there is no hierarchy of genres: there are only types of movies that succeed and types that do not. (Traditionally, for example, sports films do not succeed, while horror films do.) Furthermore, genres that succeed in one era may not in another unless they can adapt to the changing times. The woman's film was popular in the 1930s and especially in the 1940s, when women constituted the majority of the moviegoing public. The woman's film still exists, as we shall see, but it is not what it was when stars like Bette Davis and Joan Crawford reigned supreme.

Finally, while the best examples of a genre may be pure (e.g.,

Stagecoach and *My Darling Clementine* are pure westerns), there are also films that cross genres. *Pursued* (Raoul Walsh, 1947) is a western that crosses over into the "whodunit"; *Easy Living* (Mitchell Leisen, 1937) is a screwball comedy that is implicitly critical of "easy living" during the Great Depression and thus takes on overtones of the social-consciousness film; the musicals *A Star Is Born* (the 1954 and 1975 versions) and *New York, New York* (Martin Scorsese, 1977) end unhappily.

The point is not to come up with a definitive classification of a particular movie; categorizing a movie is not like categorizing a biological species. Nominally, *Pursued* is a western, *Easy Living* screwball comedy, and *New York, New York* a musical. What gives each an added distinction is that it embodies elements of another genre besides its own. Rather, the point is to see how various kinds of movies have survived over the years by repeating, varying, or altering their conventions.

THE MUSICAL

The musical is a good genre with which to begin because its plot conventions are relatively simple. It is axiomatic that in a musical, emotions are expressed, and the plot is advanced, through song and dance. Although this may seem self-evident, there are still moviegoers who look down on the musical for its unreality. Historically, there is some justification for this view: the frequent lack of integration of song and action in many musicals results in an interruption of the plot for a production number. For example, in *Lady Be Good* (Norman Z. McLeod, 1941), there is no motivation for Eleanor Powell's tap dance except that Powell was a superb tap dancer whose role in the movie was minor, but whose fans expected her to dance—which she did in a show-stopping number.

Ideally, Eleanor Powell's tap dance should have been a natural outgrowth of the action, not a diversion. However, the seamless blending of song and narrative is rare in film musicals. Indeed, in early movie musicals, integration did not exist. The plots were thin; rather, what is memorable about the musicals of the thirties are the chic dancing of Fred Astaire and Ginger Rogers and the production numbers in which the chorus formed intricate geometric patterns. We may have vivid memories of Astaire and Rogers dancing the Carioca in *Flying down to Rio* (Thornton Freeland, 1933), but few of us can reconstruct the plot.

Whether the first integrated musical was *On the Town* (Gene Kelly and Stanley Donen, 1949) or *Singin' in the Rain* (Kelly and Donen,

1952) is a matter of debate. *On the Town* was based on a Broadway musical that was itself superbly integrated with music by Leonard Bernstein and book by Betty Comden and Adolph Green. *Singin' in the Rain*, which was neither a Broadway show nor a play set to music, is something of a rarity: an original screenplay with songs that flow out of the action. While the film is remembered for the title song danced in the rain by Gene Kelly, the sequence is related to the plot: the boy is so in love with the girl that he dances out his joy despite the elements.

If we recall that genres are not simple, we can better appreciate the diversity of the movie musical. Here are some familiar types.

1. The revue. While the stage revue was a popular musical form from the 1920s through the mid-1950s, its amorphous nature (sketches interspersed with song and dance) did not lend itself to the movies, whose audiences require some kind of plot. When the Broadway revue *New Faces of 1952* was filmed, a wisp of a plot was added, but not enough to conceal the fact that the film was a photographed stage show. Some movie musicals (e.g., *Star Spangled Rhythm* [George Marshall, 1942], *Ziegfeld Follies* [Vincente Minnelli, 1946]) were disguised revues that offered a number of stars an opportunity to do their specialty within a loosely plotted format.

2. The operetta. Most movie operettas have been adaptations of stage operettas (*Naughty Marietta* [Woody Van Dyke, 1935], *Bittersweet* [Van Dyke, 1940], *The Student Prince* [Richard Thorpe, 1954], *The Vagabond King* [Michael Curtiz, 1956], etc.). Occasionally, one comes upon an operetta-like film such as *The Emperor Waltz* (Billy Wilder, 1948) with a fairy-tale plot shored up by music, or *The Umbrellas of Cherbourg* (Jacques Demy, 1964) in which everything is sung including the dialogue, but operettas are rarely written for the screen.

3. The comedy with music. One of Paramount's most successful series was the Road movies of the 1940s and early 1950s featuring Bing Crosby, Bob Hope, and Dorothy Lamour in zany adventures that took them across the world. Since all three could sing, musical numbers were inserted into the plot, most of which had no relation to the narrative—which itself had no relation to reality. Many of the so-called Elvis Presley musicals were really comedies and, in a few cases, dramas with music.

4. The drama with music. Neither a dramatic musical nor a musical drama, the drama with music is rarer than the comedy with music because it provides a true fusion of music and a serious plot. In *A Star Is Born* (George Cukor, 1954), a musical version of the 1937 nonmusical film about the price of Hollywood fame, the basic plot remained intact: a fading male star marries an unknown talent, whose career

skyrockets while his plummets. This remake, with Judy Garland and James Mason, includes some excellent musical numbers, all of which fit neatly into the action. The third version of *A Star Is Born* (1975) also had no choice but to feature music, but of a different sort: rock, because the main characters had been changed to rock stars. The same plot device of the heroine's career eclipsing the hero's was used in another drama with music, *New York, New York*, in which the songs (the title song as well as standards of the 1940s) were expertly interwoven with the plot.

5. The show business musical. Sometimes called *backstage musicals*, musicals of this kind chronicle the joys and heartaches of show business. The backstage musical has five common plot pegs: the "overnight sensation," breaking up the act, writing the song, the crucial song, and career versus marriage.

The overnight sensation is the "unknown" who substitutes for the star and, on the basis of his or her initial exposure to the public, achieves instant stardom. The best known overnight sensation is the understudy (Ruby Keeler) in *42nd Street* (Lloyd Bacon, 1933) who is told by the director (Warner Baxter): "Sawyer, you're going out a youngster, but you've got to come back a *star*." She did, and a Hollywood cliché was born. The "Born in a Trunk" sequence in the 1954 *A Star Is Born* parodies the overnight sensation theme.

The break-up theme often gets underway when a producer hires one of the members of an act for a Broadway show but not the other(s). In *The Jolson Story* (Alfred E. Green, 1946), Steve Martin stays in vaudeville while his protégé, Al Jolson, goes on to become a star. A family act breaks up when the children go their separate ways in *There's No Business Like Show Business* (Walter Lang, 1954); a husband-and-wife team breaks up when the wife wants to do serious drama instead of musical comedy in *The Barkleys of Broadway* (Charles Walters, 1949); a marriage breaks up when a husband prefers an adoring audience to his wife in *The Jolson Story*.

Several backstage musicals revolve around finding the right lyrics to the right melody. This kind of situation assumes that the audience knows the right lyrics and will therefore be amused by all the difficulties the lyricists are having: the songwriters working out the lyrics to "Lady Be Good" for *Lady Be Good*, the lyricist trying to find the "three little words" for the title song in *Three Little Words* (Richard Thorpe, 1950).

Some musicals feature a crucial song that is heard so often during the film and acquires such associative properties that it becomes inseparable from the plot (e.g., "You'll Never Know" in *Hello, Frisco, Hello* [H. Bruce Humberstone, 1943]). Sometimes the crucial song is either sung incorrectly or at the wrong tempo until the singer is forced to sing it correctly. In *Coney Island* (Walter Lang, 1943), Betty Grable is ruining "Cuddle Up a Little Closer" with her flamboyant gestures until George Montgomery handcuffs her, thereby forcing her to tone down her delivery and sing the song as a ballad.

The backstage musical generally climaxes in a big production number, which illustrates a convention of the genre: the stage on which the number is performed would never be found in a Broadway theater because it is a large Hollywood soundstage doubling as a Broadway stage. No Broadway theater could ever accommodate the winding ramp down which Rita Hayworth rushes in *Cover Girl* (Charles Vidor, 1944) or the gigantic platform on which Frank Sinatra sings "Ol' Man River" at the end of *Till the Clouds Roll By* (Richard Whorf, 1946). A movie musical that is an adaptation of a stage musical clearly shows the difference between a soundstage and a theater stage. The movie version of Lerner and Loewe's *Brigadoon* (Vincente Minnelli, 1954) was shot entirely on an MGM soundstage. In both the stage and screen versions, the lovers walk through the heather on the hill as they sing the duet, "The Heather on the Hill." No stage designer could have created such spectacular heather, nor could there ever have been so much of it on the stage as there is in the movie.

6. The dance musical. In the theatre, *dance musical* refers to a type of musical in which the cast functions as a kind of chorus that both sings and dances. *A Chorus Line* and *Cats* are both dance musicals in the sense of having no real stars and giving the appearance of having been choreographed rather than staged. In film, a dance musical is one in which dance is a means of furthering the action as well as of expressing the characters' emotions and psychological states. Since dance is as central to the action as song, such a film is really a *song and dance musical*, for unlike a stage dance musical like *Cats*, which has no real plot, the movie dance musical does.

Of the various kinds of dancing in the dance musical, the courting dance is the most famous. Its effectiveness depends on star chemistry. In the Astaire-Rogers musicals, the chemistry is complementary. Astaire courted an aloof Rogers, who gradually responded as he encircled her, wooing her with every step. Their dancing was the epitome of Art Deco, stylized and sleek. When Astaire appeared later in his career with the long-legged Cyd Charisse, the dancing became more erotic, since Astaire had a more sensuous partner. When Gene Kelly and Rita Hayworth danced to the music of "Long Ago and Far Away" in *Cover Girl*, their dancing took on elements of yearning, as if each were looking for the dream lover suggested by the lyrics ("I dreamed a dream one day").

Fred Astaire (in his signature clothes) and Ginger Rogers, the musical film's most popular dancing team, in Swing Time *(George Stevens, 1936) with a score by Jerome Kern. (Courtesy MOMA/FSA and RKO)*

The two great exponents of the dance musical, Fred Astaire and Gene Kelly, had diametrically opposed styles. Astaire was cool and aristocratic; he was born for top hat, white tie, and tails. Gene Kelly, on the other hand, who once played ice hockey and taught gymnastics, is more athletic. Yet Kelly could work aspects of ballet into his dancing, which Astaire could not. While each represents a different style, together they epitomize the golden age of the Hollywood musical.

THE WESTERN

The American western is more complex than the overworked and often misleading distinction between the black-hatted villain and the white-clothed hero suggests. In fact, some westerns totally disregard that color code. In *My Darling Clementine*, Doc Holliday (Victor Mature), who is far from evil, dresses in black, but so does the true villain, Old Man Clanton (Walter Brennan). In *High Noon* (Fred Zinnemann, 1952), the marshal (Gary Cooper) wears a black hat; so does Ethan (John Wayne) in *The Searchers*.

As James Kitses has demonstrated in his study of the western, *Horizons West*,[1] the western is not so much a matter of good vs. evil as wilderness vs. civilization. Within these extremes are three others: the individual vs. the community, nature vs. culture, West vs. East. The tension between the wilderness and civilization is evident in *Clementine* when the civilizing institutions of the church and the school begin to encroach on the frontier, bringing order and stability into lives that have neither. As the film shows, the frontier is changing: the one-street town of Tombstone sports a barber shop where a haircut is capped by spray of cologne; a church is being dedicated; an actor gives a Shakespeare reading; Clementine (Cathy Downs) becomes Tombstone's first teacher.

In the western, opposites continually confront each other: freedom/responsibility, self-concern/commitment, ignorance/education, the desert/the garden. The western hero is a loner, often fiercely independent. If he is to develop as a person, he must assume a sense of responsibility—for example, by marrying or by serving the community as peace officer, educator, wagon train leader. Nor can retirement stand in his way if he is needed, as Captain Brittles (John Wayne) is needed in *She Wore a Yellow Ribbon* (John Ford, 1949).

Initially, the western hero avoids marriage because it is an institution that curtails freedom. Thus, the hero can only be comfortable with a woman who is his alter ego or his complement. If the hero has a criminal past, he may be drawn to a social outcast, as Ringo (John Wayne) is to the prostitute Dallas (Claire Trevor) in *Stagecoach* or as Link (Gary Cooper) is to Billie (Julie London) in *Man of the West* (Anthony Mann, 1958). If he is an upright man like Wyatt Earp (Henry Fonda) in *Clementine*, he will be attracted to a virtuous woman.

The frontier encourages a survival instinct that is so strong it can cause a community to abandon its lawman, as the townspeople do in *High Noon* when they refuse to come to the aid of their marshal. The frontier is also parochial: Easterners are regarded with suspicion be-

John Wayne as the black-hatted but hardly villainous Ethan in The Searchers *(John Ford, 1956). (Courtesy MOMA/FSA and Warner Bros., Inc)*

cause they bring with them education and a knowledge of the law. In *The Man Who Shot Liberty Valance*, an eastern lawyer is an object of ridicule; in *The Man from Laramie* (Anthony Mann, 1955), a frontier woman dismisses her rival as "a piece of fluff from the East." The East, however, is necessary to the West; it can bring the garden to the desert in the form of irrigation. In *Liberty Valance*, the cactus rose is all that can bloom in the desert until the arrival of irrigation—the result of legislation initiated by the eastern lawyer who was dismissed as a "dude."

Still, there are those who cannot adapt to the wilderness turned garden: outlaws, uncompromising individualists, romantic idealists. For the unassimilated there are two choices: flight or a return to the wilderness. In *Stagecoach*, Ringo and Dallas are "saved from the blessings of civilization," as one of the characters observes—they head for Mexico, bringing the individualism of the frontier with them. In *The Searchers*, Ethan spends five years trying to find Debbie, who had been abducted as a child by Indians. When he brings her back at the end, he stands momentarily in the doorway as the others enter the house. He does not enter because home and community are not meant for him; instead, he returns to the wilderness like the gods of myth who descend to earth to help humankind and leave when their job is done.

In *Beyond Formula*, Stanley Solomon offers a single explanation for the plots, characters, and locales of the western: the landscape, which not only determines setting but also the kind of people who would be attracted to it and the kinds of situations they would encounter there.[2] Because the West is rugged, only the hardy can survive there. But even they need protection from unscrupulous bankers, cattle barons, crooked lawyers, and land speculators. Hence, they need the cavalry, lawmen, crusading newspaper editors, honest lawyers, fearless clergymen—the traditional heroes of the western.

The landscape also explains a certain sameness of setting: plains, valleys, mesas, deserts, ranches, trading posts, forts, and towns with a single street that features a combination saloon, gambling house, and brothel and, if civilization has made any incursions, a barber shop and a newspaper office. The landscape also accounts for modes of travel—stagecoach, horseback, wagon train, railroad—and helps to explain recurring plot devices and rituals. The western plot often revolves around a quest or a journey: a search for a loved one in *The Searchers*, or for a loved one's killers in *The Bravados* (Henry King, 1957) and *Last Train from Gun Hill* (John Sturges, 1956). It can also include a trek across inhospitable terrain: the trip through Apache territory in *Stagecoach*, the cattle drive in *Red River* (Howard Hawks, 1948), the Mormons' journey across the mountains in *Wagonmaster*.

Those embarking on the quest or making the journey are a varied lot, usually a mix of individualists and traditionalists, the educated and uneducated, moral people and amoral ones, romantics and realists. The passengers in *Stagecoach* are representative: the loner hero with a criminal past, the prostitute, the good woman, the drunken doctor, a Southern gambler, a whiskey salesman, an embezzling banker, a kindly lawman, and a driver with a Mexican wife. Other films broadened the list to include homesteaders, cavalry officers, miners, trappers, prospectors, 'geezers, bullies, and matriarchal and patriarchal figures. As the genre matured, unusual variations on traditional character types were introduced: the sheriff turned bounty hunter in *The Tin Star* (Anthony Mann, 1956), bilingual and trilingual Indians (*Fort Apache* and *She Wore a Yellow Ribbon*); the white men who marry Indian women in *Broken Arrow* (Delmer Daves, 1950) and *Broken Lance* (Edward Dmytryk, 1954), and the loner heroine in *Johnny Guitar* (Nicholas Ray, 1954).

Despite its realistic nature, the western is also ritualistic. Certain acts are invested with a ceremonial quality, as if they are being performed according to a rite or a liturgy. Such rituals include gunplay, confrontations, dress, returns, departures, and burials. In a western, one does not just reach for a gun and shoot; one draws from the hip, with style. The gun is more than a weapon; it is an extension of one's personality. Sometimes, a character will remove it slowly from the holster with a cool gracefulness; at other times, the character will whip it out and fire it by thumbing or fanning. A character might even fire two guns, standing defiantly with legs apart and holding the guns at different angles. The gun is also an icon—an image that inspires awe—to be held as one might hold a talisman or a sacred object.

In a western, clothes make the character. The virtuous woman is dressed primly and simply, covered up to her neck. The prostitute is usually dressed provocatively in an off-the-shoulder blouse and ruffled skirt, plumes and feathers, or a low-cut gown with a rhinestone bodice. In symbolic westerns like *Shane* and *The Searchers*, the hero's dress is so striking that it gives him the aura of a medieval knight or an epic warrior. Shane, who materializes like a god descended to earth to aid a homesteader and his family, wears white buckskins that set him apart from the others. Ethan in *The Searchers* makes his first appearance wearing a black neckerchief and a Confederate cloak, and carrying a saber. His rifle is in a fringed buckskin cover that resembles an aegis. His dress, a vestige of his Civil War days, marks him as an anachronism in postbellum Texas, but it also gives him heroic stature.

Ever since the first western, *The Great Train Robbery* (E. S. Porter, 1903), the shoot-out has been a dramatic, sometimes an operatic, event. In *The Great Train Robbery*, when one of the outlaws is shot, he does a ballet-like twirl, firing his gun as he falls. Sam Peckinpah's westerns continue the tradition of choreographed death, often in slow motion, that adds a macabre quality to the bloody climax. Perhaps the most operatic death occurs in *Duel in the Sun* (King Vidor, 1947) in which Pearl and Lewt (Jennifer Jones and Gregory Peck) are firing away at each other when suddenly they realize they are in love; thereupon Pearl crawls up rocks and boulders to die, blood-splattered, in Lewt's arms.

Most shoot-outs, while less bizarre, are still theatrical. Even those that seem to be conventional usually have a theatrical touch: Doc Halliday's handkerchief fluttering in the wind after he has been killed at the O.K. Corral in *Clementine*, McCabe's solitary death in the snow in *McCabe and Mrs. Miller* (Robert Altman, 1971). Sometimes the shoot-out takes the form of a long walk: the hero walks down a street that the townspeople have cleared or deserted to confront the villain or the villain's gang, as in *High Noon*. A variation on the shoot-out is the climax of *Red River* when Tom Dunson (John Wayne) strides down a street intending to challenge his surrogate son, Matt (Montgomery Clift), only to discover that Matt has too much respect for him to retaliate.

Homecomings, departures, and burials in the western are also

Alan Ladd in his white buck-skins in Shane *(George Stevens, 1953). (Courtesy MOMA/FSA and Paramount Pictures)*

acts of ritual. The homecoming is often a *nostos*, a return in the epic sense. When Ethan returns from the Civil War at the beginning of *The Searchers*, it is as a hero; he walks toward his brother's house as if in a one-person processional, with each member of the family looking at him with awe. When Wyatt Earp takes leave of Clementine, and Shane of Marion, each behaves like a knight bidding farewell to his lady. In John Ford's cavalry films, the cavalry does not merely leave the fort; it troops out in the grand manner to the music of "The Girl I Left Behind Me" or "She Wore a Yellow Ribbon." Burials are strikingly framed, with the mourners set against the horizon as if they are figures in a painting. Occasionally a touch of pathos is added. In *Shane*, the dead man's dog stretches out a paw to touch his master's casket as it is lowered into the ground; in *She Wore a Yellow Ribbon*, a woman uses part of her red petticoat to make a flag for an officer's burial.

The western, then, is far from a gathering of the good, the bad, and the ugly; it is a complex genre that, in its own way, records the history of America.

THE CRIME FILM

Filmmakers have always been intrigued by the gangster and the criminal. The gangster era coincided with the beginning of Hollywood's Golden Age in the late 1920s, thereby providing screenwriters with fresh plot material. The plots often came straight from the headlines—and with Al Capone, Bonnie Parker and Clyde Barrow, John Dillinger, and "Lucky" Luciano making headlines, there was no dearth of subject matter. Filmmakers were not the only ones attracted to criminals—the public was also. Gangsters were colorful figures amidst the bleak Great Depression, doing what moviegoers could not do, even if they wished. Gangsters did not so much break the law as flaunt it. But they flaunted it in accordance with the American success scenario. They practiced their own form of upward mobility, beginning with holdups and graduating to bank heists. They started as lackeys and ended up as heads of syndicates. As they advanced, they acquired the trappings of success—overcoats, fedoras, and dark or pin-striped suits. But most of all, gangsters exercised their freedom, the quality Americans prize most dearly. Unrestrained by conventional mores, they gloried in their independence, achieving an emancipation that moviegoers might envy but could never experience because the price was too high.

Thus, the crime film portrays gangsters and criminals with a combination of fascination and compassion, stopping just short of exoneration. As the Production Code insisted, crime could not pay; but this stricture did not stop Hollywood from giving gangsters a sinister charisma and making their lives high drama until the last few minutes when it came time for retribution. And even then, the gangster died in a grand manner, whether in the street or on a sidewalk, the surface of which was always elegantly black as if specially prepared for those who revealed their dark side.

In addition to being gunned down in the streets (*Scarface* [Howard Hawks, 1932]) and on sidewalks (*He Ran All the Way* [John Berry, 1951]), gangsters often met their ends on steps and cliffs, symbolizing their fall from power. Eddie Bartlett (James Cagney) dies on the steps of a church in *The Roaring Twenties* (Raoul Walsh, 1939), cradled in the arms of his mistress. When a police officer asks Eddie's identity, his mistress replies, "He used to be a big shot." Roy Earle (Humphrey Bogart) in *High Sierra* plunges from the top of a cliff. His death is a literal fall from the heights as opposed to the figurative fall in classical tragedy. Sometimes when a criminal and his beloved die, one body folds over the other (*Criss Cross* [Robert Siodmak, 1948]). If physical union is impossible, their hands attempt to touch (*Bonnie and Clyde* [Arthur Penn, 1967]).

Like the western, the crime film has inspired theatrical death scenes. Two of the best occur in James Cagney films. In *Angels with Dirty Faces* (Michael Curtiz, 1938), Rocky Sullivan (Cagney) agrees to

Stylized death in the classic crime film as seen in The Public Enemy *(William Wellman, 1931). (Courtesy WCFTR)*

feign cowardice to discourage the teenagers who idolize him from turning to a life of crime. Walking cockily to the electric chair, Rocky suddenly turns craven and begs hysterically for his life. In *White Heat* (Raoul Walsh, 1949), Cody Jarett (Cagney) dies amid an apocalyptic explosion of chemical tanks, yelling "Top of the world, ma!" Cody Jarett made it to the top, only to go up in flames.

The crime film has other features in common with the western. In both, the gun is an icon. Just as the gun in the western can be a reflection of the user's personality, the gun in the crime film is a projection of the user's neurosis or sexuality. Cody Jarett brandishes a gun as a child would who fancies himself an adult. Jarett's behavior is understandable: he has a relationship with his mother that is so oedipal that he sits on her lap. In *Bonnie and Clyde*, the gun is sexual. For the impotent Clyde, it is a substitute for potency; for Bonnie, who fondles Clyde's gun provocatively, it is the equivalent of a sexual thrill.

The crime film unfolds within a world of back rooms, bars, diners, sleek cars, mean streets, sleazy hotel rooms, speakeasies, nightclubs, tenements, gaudy apartments, and mausoleum-like homes. Unlike the western, which allows the loner—even if he or she had been on the wrong side of the law—to find a mate and live happily ever after, the crime film cannot. Usually, the gangster finds the true mate (another criminal or a person like Marie in *High Sierra*), only to die in his or her arms.

The classic American crime film depended for its effectiveness upon performers who were themselves icons: James Cagney, Humphrey Bogart, Edward G. Robinson, John Garfield. With actors who were able to ignite a human spark in characters that could be otherwise flat or unlikable, the gangster and the criminal become both lower and higher versions of ourselves. They are our dark side, doing what we would never dare, and yet achieving the American dream of success, wealth, and fame. While we are glad we are not they, at the same time we cannot help but envy their daring because, as one film scholar has noted, the gangster is "the archetypal American dreamer whose actions and behavior involve a living out of the dream common to most everyone who exists in the particular configurations and contradictions of American society, a dream in conflict with the society."[3]

FILM NOIR

While *film noir* has its roots in hardboiled detective fiction, it can take the form of either a private-eye story or a crime film without a private eye. Note, however, that neither a private-eye film nor a crime film is necessarily *film noir*. *Murder, My Sweet* is a private eye film that is also a classic *film noir; Meet Nero Wolfe* (Herbert Biberman, 1936) is just a private-eye movie. *Criss Cross* and *Gun Crazy* (Joseph H. Lewis, 1950) are crime films and *films noirs; Angels with Dirty Faces* and *The Roaring Twenties* are just crime films.

Film noir is virtually impossible to define, yet its characteristics are among the most recognizable of any genre. Literally, the term means "dark film"; film that is both dark in its look, with the look of nighttime rather than daylight, and dark in the sense of revealing the dark side of humankind and society. In *film noir,* the interplay of light and dark is accomplished by high-contrast photography and low-key lighting, which create a monolinear world of white and black. Street lamps shed circles of light on glistening black pavements; neon signs illuminate dark skies; blondes wear black gowns decorated with silver stripes; the hoods of dark cars look glazed by the moonlight. Murders are committed in darkness or in shadow, but during the struggle a table lamp is often knocked over so that when the body is discovered the victim's face is illuminated by the overturned lamp.

The world of *film noir* is one of paranoia and entrapment, of

THE NOIR NIGHT AND THE NOIR CORPSE IN *MILDRED PIERCE* (MICHAEL CURTIZ, 1945). (SEE PAGE 98.)

Wally (Jack Carson) and Mildred Pierce (Joan Crawford) on the pier. (Courtesy WCFTR)

forces bearing down on the individual that are too overwhelming to resist. Tight framing encloses characters within a universe from which there is no escape. Slow tracking shots create a mood of uncertainty; long backward tracks suggest continuous movement, pursuit, life on the run. Canted shots imply a world gone haywire. That world is often enshrouded in fog. Riverside Drive in New York is seldom fog-bound, but when Roberts and Sue walk down it in *Detour*, they seem to be walking through a fogbank. The fog is not so much real as symbolic of a universe whose workings are impenetrable and whose design, if there is any, can never be known. The stock characters of *film noir*—private detectives, insurance salesmen, prostitutes, murderous housewives, two-time losers, ex-convicts, or gamblers—are essentially reducible to two: a man and a woman caught up in a chain of circumstances from which only the death of one—or both—can extricate them. When the woman is a *femme fatale*, the man can either follow her to his—or their—fate, or free himself from her snares. In either case the end is violent, sometimes dramatically so. While

O'Hara (Orson Welles) does free himself from Elsa Bannister (Rita Hayworth) in *The Lady from Shanghai* (Orson Welles, 1948), Elsa dies in a hall of mirrors where she shoots it out with her husband as their images, reflected in the mirrors, shatter with the glass. (Mirrors are a favorite prop of *film noir* because the characters are often mirror images of one another.) Before he fires at his wife, Bannister, appropriately, tells Elsa that in killing her, he is killing himself.

Sometimes the climax of a *film noir* is a "Liebestod" (love death). Common to *film noir* is the theme of *amour fou* or "mad love," love generated by a combination of passion and infatuation that takes a perverse turn, causing one lover to kill or attempt to kill the other. At the end of *Double Indemnity*, the adulterous lovers plan to kill each other. Phyllis fires at Neff, wounding him; then suddenly regretting what she has done, she moves toward him. Neff takes her in his arms and embraces her while at the same time firing a bullet into her heart.

Wally discovering Monty Berrigan's (Zachary Scott) body. Note the overturned lamp, a typical noir prop in a typical noir framing. (Courtesy WCFTR)

ANATOMY OF FILM

The hall of mirrors in The Lady from Shanghai *(Orson Welles, 1948). (Courtesy MOMA/FSA and Columbia Pictures)*

Film noir plots are convoluted, reflecting the intricacies of fate. Voice-over narration and flashbacks are common; in *The Locket* (John Brahm, 1946) there are flashbacks within flashbacks. Chance—in the sense of a character's being in the wrong place at the wrong time—is more significant in *film noir* than in most other genres. In *Gun Crazy,* a young man whose fascination with guns landed him in reform school wanders into a carnival featuring a female sharpshooter; the chance encounter changes both of their lives as they become bank robbers in the tradition of Bonnie and Clyde and end up dying in a foggy swamp. In *Detour,* Roberts, hitchhiking from New York to Los Angeles, is picked up by a man with a heart condition who dies en route. Thinking the man's death will be misconstrued as murder, Roberts adopts the dead man's identity. He later makes the mistake of picking up a woman who knew the dead man and who therefore knows that Roberts is not the owner of the car. The woman, Vera, makes Roberts her prisoner and dies in a manner that is bizarre even by *film noir* standards. Drunk, Vera grabs the phone, rushes into the bedroom, and locks the door behind her. Falling on the bed, she becomes entangled in the telephone cord which is coiled around her neck. Outside,

Robert pulls at the part of the cord that is under the door, not knowing the rest of it is around Vera's neck. When he finally breaks the door open, he bursts into the bedroom as we see the reflection of the prostrate Vera in the mirror. This is Roberts's second brush with fate; he is now a two-time loser.

To most scholars, the era of *film noir* was the period from the mid-1940s to the mid-1950s. Yet contemporary films such as *Body Heat* (Lawrence Kasdan, 1981), *Mona Lisa* (Neil Jordan, 1986), and *Angel Heart* (Alan Parker, 1987) are considered *film noir* by some critics. Purists argue that true *film noir* is shot in black and white, but a film shot in color can simulate the nighttime look of *film noir* and even approximate the black/white dichotomy. Kasdan does so in *Body Heat* by dressing the *femme fatale* in white which, when set against the black night, becomes a study in high contrast.

Perhaps *postmodern noir* is a better designation for films of the genre shot in color. At any rate, the conventions of *film noir* are still being used, and it is the perpetuation of a genre's conventions and themes that ensures its longevity.

SCREWBALL COMEDY

Like tragedy, comedy has its own conventions: mistaken identity, lovers' quarrels and reconciliations, marital mixups, the deflation of the pompous, trickery, deception, and masquerade. It also has its own gallery of stock characters—irate fathers, errant husbands, clever servants, fops, foundlings, and amorous wives—all of whom speak in maxims, non sequiturs, puns, double entendres, and malapropisms—the traditional sources of verbal humor.

Although film comedy draws on the same sources of humor as stage comedy, it has a genre peculiar to itself: screwball comedy. While screwball comedy may have overtones of drawing room comedy or romantic comedy because of its witty and sophisticated dialogue, screwball comedy also contains elements of farce and slapstick that are alien to the comedy of the drawing room: a food riot in an automat (*Easy Living*), a leopard on the loose (*Bringing Up Baby* [Howard Hawks, 1938]), destruction of property for comic effect (the shooting spree that leaves a club car in shambles in *The Palm Beach Story* [Preston Sturges, 1942]).

The special place screwball comedy occupies in film history proves that film genres are fluid; they are not bound by canons and hierarchies as literature is. A film genre comes into existence when a particular type of movie becomes so popular that its form is repeated and imitated. Screwball comedy was a dominant type of comedy in the 1930s and 1940s; its influence is still felt in such films as *Moonstruck* and *Crossing Delancy* (Joan Micklin Silver, 1988).

Like *film noir*, screwball is better described than defined. One or both of the leading characters is a "screwball"—an oddball whose unconventional nature is responsible for the equally unconventional situations in which the characters find themselves. In *It Happened One Night*, an heiress rebels against her father, ends up hitchhiking with a reporter, masquerading as his wife, and finally discarding the masquerade for marriage. In *Easy Living*, a young working woman is riding on the top deck of a double-decker bus at the very moment an irate husband hurls his wife's sable coat from their penthouse terrace. The coat lands on the young woman, who is then mistaken for the husband's mistress, and ensconced in a luxury hotel. She later falls in love with a worker at an automat who turns out to be the son of the man who threw the coat from the terrace. A socialite and a paleontologist become involved with a leopard who responds to the song, "I Can't Give You Anything But Love, Baby" in *Bringing Up Baby*. A couple in the process of divorcing vie for custody of their dog and vie to sabotage each other's prospects for remarriage in *The Awful Truth* (Leo McCarey, 1937).

The hero in screwball is usually a professional: a reporter in *It Happened One Night* and *Nothing Sacred* (William Wellman, 1937); an editor in *His Girl Friday* (Howard Hawks, 1940); a herpetologist in *The Lady Eve*; a film director in *Sullivan's Travels*; a professor in *Ball of Fire* (Howard Hawks, 1941). The heroine can be a socialite as in *It Happened One Night, Bringing Up Baby*, and *My Man Godfrey* (Gregory LaCava, 1936); a Cinderella figure, as in *Easy Living*; a reporter as in *His Girl Friday*; a gold digger as in *Midnight* (Mitchell Leisen, 1939) and *The Palm Beach Story*. Rarely are hero and heroine from the same social class. Sometimes the heroine is from the higher class (*It Happened One Night, My Man Godfrey*); at other times the hero is (*The Lady Eve, Easy Living*). In any event, class barriers never stand in the way of a happy ending.

One distinguishing feature of screwball comedy is dialogue that is sharp, fast, and witty. One character picks up on what another says to put the other down and score a point. In *Sullivan's Travels*, Sullivan (Joel McCrea) is trying to convince a studio executive of the importance of making social-consciousness films. When he is told that one such film failed in Pittsburgh, he scoffs: "What do they know in Pittsburgh?" "They know what they like," the executive replies. "If they knew what they liked, they wouldn't live in Pittsburgh" is Sullivan's capping retort. Later, he is making the same appeal to an unemployed actor, extolling a somber movie called *Hold Back Tomorrow*.

Cinderella (Jean Arthur) in the automat in the classic screwball comedy Easy Living *(Mitchell Leisen, 1937). (Copyright by Paramount Pictures, Courtesy of MCA Publishing Rights, a Division of MCA Incorporated)*

"You take a picture like *Hold Back Tomorrow*," he begins. "You hold it," she replies drily.

Screwball comedy delights in non sequiturs. In an attempt to fend off Susan's (Katharine Hepburn) advances in *Bringing Up Baby,* Henry (Cary Grant) informs her he is engaged to be married. Susan replies with screwball logic: "Then she [his fiancée] won't mind waiting. If I was engaged to be married to you, I wouldn't mind waiting. I'd wait forever."

Double entendre is common in screwball. Since the Production Code frowned on suggestiveness in dialogue and situations, writers encoded the dialogue with double meanings with the expectation that audiences would choose the right meaning; most did. In *The Palm Beach Story*, a millionaire tells the fortune-hunting heroine that he admires women who can cook. "You should taste my popovers," she says playfully. "I'd love to," he replies. Somewhat more subtle but also more suggestive is a character's slip of the tongue in referring to a boys' magazine in *Easy Living*; instead of calling it by its correct name,

The Boy's Constant Companion, the character calls it *The Boy's Constant Reminder.*

Although the great age of screwball comedy was the period between 1930 and 1950, its influence has continued in later films that pair a sedate male and a madcap female (*What's Up Doc?* [Peter Bogdanovich, 1972]) or an oddball male with an inhibited woman who blossoms as a result of their relationship (*Moonstruck*). As long as there are screwballs, there will be screwball comedy.

THE REFLEXIVE FILM

Reflexive literature calls attention to itself as literature: a reader, for example, may sense that the novel he or she is reading is really a novel about the art of the novel or about the act of writing a novel, and not just a work of prose purporting to tell a story. Iris Murdoch's *Under the Net* is such a novel; it is both about the nature of fiction as well as an implicit criticism of existential fiction, which the author feels has sacrificed the personal for the philosophical. Robert Frost's "The Wood Pile" seems to be about a wood pile but is really about the way poetry transforms the ordinary. An extreme example of reflexivity is Jean Anouilh's *Number One,* in which the play a dramatist is trying to write turns out to be the play we have been watching.

A reflexive film calls attention to itself as a film. Reflexivity appears in varying degrees in the following kinds of films:

1. Films about the nature of film. *The Purple Rose of Cairo* (Woody Allen, 1985) explores the consequences of mistaking the illusion of the screen for the reality of life. During a movie, which also has the same title, a character steps off the screen and into the audience, leaving the other characters stranded in mid-plot. The other characters then become autonomous, refusing to continue with the plot until he returns. The character's adventures in the real world point up the difference between life and art: one cannot live art, only life.

2. Films that refer to specific films. Sometimes called "movie movies," such films depend for their effectiveness upon an audience's knowledge of film. It is true that one can enjoy *The Last Picture Show* for its plot alone; however, anyone who is knowledgeable about film will have a deeper appreciation of Bogdanovich's movie. "The last picture show" of the title is *Red River,* which serves two purposes: it allows the movie theater to close with a bang rather than a whimper—with an epic western and not, as was the case in the original novel, with a minor one. *Red River* is also a metaphor for the film itself. In *Red River,* the John Wayne character befriends a fatherless boy with whom he develops a close relationship. In *The Last Picture Show,* Sam the

Lion (Ben Johnson) befriends two boys who might as well be father-less. With its references to *Red River*, *The Last Picture Show* establishes itself as a film that, at least on one level, is about America's film heritage, reflecting not only the way generations of Americans be-haved but also the way generations of filmmakers portrayed America.

Likewise, to appreciate—rather than merely enjoy—*Raiders of the Lost Ark* (Steven Spielberg, 1981), some knowledge of the old movie serials is essential, especially *Nyoka and the Lost Tablets of Hippocrates* (1942) which, along with the anti-Nazi films of the 1940s, inspired *Raiders*.

3. Films about the filmmaking process, including a behind-the-scenes look at the movie world and those who work in it. Such movies depict with some accuracy the way movies were made at a particular time. *Nickelodeon* and *The Perils of Pauline* (George Marshall, 1947) are historically accurate in their portrayal of silent filmmaking; *Two Weeks in Another Town* (Vincente Minnelli, 1962) and *Sweet Liberty* are valid depictions of contemporary on-location filming.

4. "What price Hollywood" films that demythologize the indus-try by stripping away the glamor and exposing the grim reality be-neath the painted surface. All three versions of *A Star Is Born*, even though the third is about the rock scene, show how stars are con-stantly being replaced in the pantheon. *Sunset Boulevard* dramatizes a silent star's descent into madness because she cannot adjust to a Hollywood that is not the one she remembers.

There is always the danger that a reflexive film will become so obscure in its illusions and quotations that it will appeal only to film buffs. No one enjoys being trapped in a conversation that has become so specialized that only experts can participate in it. The films men-tioned in this section can be appreciated by anyone regardless of his or her knowledge of movies or lack of it. On the other hand, a film like *Detective* (Jean-Luc Godard, 1985), which expects the viewer to be familiar with all of the incongruities of the private-eye movie that Godard renders even more incongruous, is a parody of reflexivity; by its elitism, it alienates moviegoers who can accept the incongruous but not the incomprehensible.

THE WOMAN'S FILM

While "woman's film" is an accepted term in film criticism as well as a legitimate film genre, "man's film" is neither. The woman's film developed into a genre for two main reasons: the film industry's early attempts to woo female audiences, and the emergence of female stars with personalities capable of elevating them to the level of icons.

Female audiences were always special to the industry either because it was assumed that women had more time for moviegoing than men or that women were more inclined to be movie fans than men. Thus in the early days of film, some nickelodeon owners attempted to attract middle-class women to their theaters by offering them free admission for prenoon shows. Others, less generous, allowed women in for half price.

Theater owners used a different tactic in the 1930s and 1940s: they sponsored "dish nights." Once or twice a week, a free piece of dishware was included in the ticket price and, in the course of time, a complete set of dishware could be acquired. With women comprising such an important—and during World War II, a major—segment of the audience, Hollywood responded by giving women their own genre with stars such as Bette Davis, Joan Crawford, and Barbara Stanwyck—stars who became so inseparable from their personas that one often speaks of a "Bette Davis movie" or a "Joan Crawford movie."

Bette Davis and Joan Crawford could not play subservient women. Rather, they played women who were the equals, and at times, the superiors of men. In *Mildred Pierce* (Michael Curtiz, 1945), Mildred (Joan Crawford) goes from being a housewife to owning a restaurant chain; in *The Corn Is Green* (Irving Rapper, 1944), Miss Moffat (Bette Davis) establishes a school for Welsh coal miners and sends her prize student to Oxford.

In a woman's film, the plot revolves around the woman, and her only limitations are those imposed by her mortality. Yet even when faced with death, the woman dies nobly. In *Dark Victory*, Judith Traherne (Bette Davis), dying of a brain tumor, not only manages to conceal her imminent death from her husband; she also chooses to die alone. In *No Sad Songs for Me* (Rudolph Maté, 1950) a wife faces terminal illness with a spirit of resignation that puts her husband to shame.

The woman's film of the 1930s and 1940s promoted self-sacrifice. When a daughter decides to marry above her class, her mother disappears from her life, but reappears to watch the wedding ceremony through the window (*Stella Dallas* [King Vidor, 1937]). Women struggled to provide a better life for their children (*Mildred Pierce*) or raise a friend's illegitimate child (*The Great Lie* [Edmund Goulding, 1941]). They even give up their own illegitimate children (*The Old Maid* [Edmund Goulding, 1938]) and stand by watching the child address someone else as mother.

While women suffered nobly in many films throughout the 1930s and 1940s, they also succeeded in male-dominated professions. The woman's film of the period portrayed women in a variety of occupa-

Bette Davis as Judith Traherne and George Brent as Dr. Steele in Dark Victory *(Edmund Goulding, 1939), a major "woman's film" (Courtesy Movie Star News)*

tions: lawyers, copywriters, reporters, actors, surgeons, nurses. However, by the 1960s, there was nothing unusual about a successful woman lawyer or entrepreneur. Terminal illnesses had become standard television fare and they were no longer special. The cancer victim had become the cancer patient and resignation to the inevitable was no longer the noble gesture it was in *Dark Victory,* but rather, the final stage of a process that begins with denial and ends with acceptance.

The portrayal of women on the screen has changed through the years. In the classic woman's film, women did not so much have friends as confidantes who were either supportive sisters or wisecracking sidekicks. Genuine friendship between women was rare on the screen; women who seemed to be friends were actually rivals (*Old Acquaintance* [Vincent Sherman, 1943]). It was not until *Julia* in 1977 that American audiences saw a true friendship between women depicted on the screen. The title character and her friend Lily are not at odds with each other; they complement each other. Thus, the politically committed Julia inspires the apolitical Lily to take a stand against the spread of fascism that is soon to bring about a global war.

When Barbara Stanwyck played a young widow in *My Reputation* (Curtis Bernhardt, 1946) who refused to wear black as a sign of mourning, she scandalized her friends. In *Alice Doesn't Live Here Anymore* (Martin Scorsese, 1975), Ellen Burstyn plays a widow who would no more wear black than she would mourn in silence. Instead, she takes her son on the road in an attempt to resume her singing career. In the classic woman's film, a woman torn between two men was expected to choose one of them. That may have been true in the 1940s when Daisy Kenyon (Joan Crawford), in the 1947 Otto Preminger film of that name, had to make up her mind between a married lawyer and a World War II veteran. If the film were remade today, Daisy could decide she wasn't interested in either.

Perhaps the most significant difference between the way women were portrayed on the screen in the past and the way they are portrayed today is that women in contemporary films seem more like real people than icons or goddesses. Women's "liberation" and the increasing presence of women in jobs that had been restricted to men have resulted in a more realistic view of women which, in turn, has been reflected on the screen. One has only to compare the way Cora, the adulterous housewife, was portrayed in the 1946 and 1981 screen versions of *The Postman Always Rings Twice*. In the former, directed by Tay Garnett, Lana Turner played Cora, looking like the stereotypical "love goddess." In the latter, directed by Bob Rafelson, Jessica Lang played Cora, who looked and behaved like a person whose loneliness gave her a hunger for love.

THE HORROR FILM

The classic horror film involves a metamorphosis: an individual is tranformed into an animal (panther, ape), insect (fly), semi-human (werewolf), anti-human (somnambule, ghoul, zombie, vampire), anti-self (Dr. Jekyll), shrunken self (homunculus), or, as in the Frankenstein themes, a synthetic creation is turned into a living creature. The inanimate can also be an object of transformation: a house can change from a habitation for humans to a habitation for ghosts (*The Uninvited* [Lewis Allen, 1944]); it can even acquire an evil personality that affects those living there (*Burnt Offerings* [Dan Curtis, 1976], *The Amityville Horror* [Stuart Rosenberg, 1979]).

The ghost story is transformation in reverse, with the ghosts taking on human qualities. The ghosts may be benign or vengeful; both types are featured in *The Uninvited*. If they are not at rest, they may work through the living until they are vindicated (e.g., the mother's ghost in *Lady in White* that cannot be reunited with her daughter in the hereafter until her daughter's murderer is apprehended).

The prototypical horror film is *The Cabinet of Dr. Caligari* (Robert Wiene, 1919) whose visual style, pruned of its exaggerations, became standard for the genre. Visually, *Caligari* is expressionistic; its asymmetrical and bizarre settings suggest a world out of joint, a world not so much of our dreams as our nightmares. Chimneys look as if they

THE MONSTER AND THE GIRL
Caesare the somnambule and Jane in The Cabinet of Dr. Caligari *(Robert Wiene, 1919). (Courtesy MOMA/FSA)*

will topple over, windows are shaped like diamonds, walls seem on the verge of caving in. The American horror film uses a less extreme form of expressionism; the high-contrast photography of the German-made *Caligari*, in which there are no greys but only black and white, was not entirely discarded by American filmmakers but made less pronounced through low-key lighting that allowed for the interplay of light and shadow.

Caligari also features two plot devices that have become conventions of the horror film: the team of the mad doctor and his subhuman accomplice (whose most familiar successors were Dr. Frankenstein and his hunchback assistant in *Frankenstein* [James Whale, 1931]); and the creature's desire for a mate. In *Caligari*, the doctor's accomplice may be a somnambule, but he is not impervious to the heroine's charms; nor are the Wolf Man and Dracula of later films unaffected by the presence of the beautiful woman. Moreover, embalming does not stop the mummy from searching for his beloved Princess Ananka, even if she happens to be in Louisiana (*The Mummy's Curse* [Leslie Goodwins, 1946]). A synthetic creature like Frankenstein's monster needs a bride: when his bride rejects him (*Bride of Frankenstein* [James Whale, 1935]), he retaliates by destroying the laboratory where he was created. The monster's attraction to women is easily explained; the creature is the personification of the Id or the libido, which is virtually all that is left after the transformation. The creature's libido may even be more active because it is no longer under the control of reason.

The basic types of horror films—ghost, creature, dual personality, and mad scientist—had been established in the 1930s and 1940s along with the conventions of low-key lighting, shadowy surfaces, dissolve transformations, cellar laboratories with overflowing test tubes, fog-bound woods, and gothic mansions. While the musical and the western were photographed in either monochrome or color, the horror film was shot almost exclusively in black and white. In the 1950s, the use of color began with *House of Wax* (1953) and *Phantom of the Rue Morgue* (1954), but it was the British-made *Curse of Frankenstein* (Terence Fisher, 1957), the first of Hammer Films' horror series, that set the trend toward the color horror film.

While color and horror are not incompatible, as *Rosemary's Baby* (Roman Polanski, 1968) and *Carrie* prove, color cannot capture the shadowy world of the unconscious as well as black and white, which is also more conducive to horror by suggestion. Color is suited to gore, the hallmark of the latest kind of horror film, the slasher film. Like every addition to a genre, the slasher film is not without precedent: its parent is *Psycho*, which was a genuine horror film with a subtle transformation. The oedipal Norman Bates becomes so identi-

Larry Talbot (Lon Chaney, Jr.), whose transformation does not diminish his interest in the heroine in The Wolf Man *(George Waggner, 1941). (Copyright by Universal Pictures, a Division of Universal City Studios, Inc. Courtesy of MCA Publishing Rights, a Division of MCA Inc.)*

fied with his mother that he assumes her personality, even to the extent of dressing in her clothes and murdering in her name. Significantly, Norman does not die at the end of *Psycho;* and as the years passed and *Psycho* became a classic, the need for a sequel arose— *Psycho* II (Richard Franklin, 1983), then *Psycho* III (Anthony Perkins, 1986). As long as there is an audience for horror, there will be a *Psycho* of some sort.

The *Psycho* sequels illustrate a time-honored tradition in horror: the monster is destroyed only when the series or the cycle dies. Even though the monster clearly dies at the end of *Frankenstein* in the fire that destroys the mill, he is discovered in the mill's cellar at the beginning of *Bride of Frankenstein*. And even though the monster clearly perishes again in the inferno at the end of *Bride of Frankenstein,* he is resurrected for *Son of Frankenstein* (Rowland V. Lee, 1939) four years later and paired with the Wolf Man in *Frankenstein Meets the Wolf Man* (Roy William Neill, 1943) four years after he was revived by Frankenstein's son.

The same principle applies to the slasher film, the most popular being *Friday the 13th* (Sean S. Cunningham, 1980), although it is hardly the most inventive. That distinction belongs to *Halloween* (John Carpenter, 1978), which introduced a plot device that *Friday the 13th* and similar films (e.g., *Prom Night* [Paul Lynch, 1980], *Terror Train* [Roger Spottiswoode, 1979]) imitated: a prologue depicting a murder that has occurred prior to the main action and has definite bearing on the plot. *Halloween* led to three sequels (1981, 1983, 1988) but it was clear that the public was more taken with *Friday the 13th*, which, within eight years after its release, had spawned seven films.

The *Friday the 13th* cycle works from the same premise as other horror cycles and series: the premise of the undying monster. In *Friday the 13th*, two teenage camp counselors are killed because they were making love when they should have been rescuing the drowning Jason. The killer is Jason's mother, who herself is killed at the end. The sequels feature Jason himself, who emerges from the mud to continue his mother's work.

In addition to the obligatory prologue, the slasher film practices its own form of voyeurism: subjective camera. The camera is often stationed outside a window representing the point of view of someone looking in; it tilts up to a bedroom, as if someone were spying. The slasher film also uses off-center compositions and framing that excludes the killer, leaving only the victim in the frame.

While the slasher film is a lesser form of horror, its use of subjective camera is a feature worth noting.

SCIENCE FICTION

"There is no clearly recognized border between SF [science fiction] and such genres as fantasy and horror," notes a science fiction expert.[4] Such a statement is not surprising, since as we have seen, genres often overlap or share conventions. While the western and crime film portray both sides of the law, the designations are different: bandits in one, criminals in the other; sheriffs in one, police officers in the other. Moreover, what one critic would call horror, another might term science fiction. In *Science Fiction in the Cinema*, John Baxter considers *The Birds* science fiction even though it is neither futuristic nor a fantasy. *The Birds* does, however, deal with an invasion—not of Martians but of killer birds. The invasion motif justifies its inclusion under science fiction; the transformation motif (benign creatures turning malevolent) merits it a place in horror. On the other hand, utopian, fantasy, and doomsday films, as well as those about space travel and warring planets, are never mistaken for anything other than science fiction.

Nonhumans, often extraterrestrials, play a major role in science fiction; they are also a diverse lot and even differ in their attitude toward humans. While some extraterrestrials seek the destruction of the planet (*War of the Worlds* [Byron Haskin, 1953]), not all are treacherous. Some have come to warn humankind of the dangers of nuclear testing (*The Day the Earth Stood Still* [Robert Wise, 1951]); others, to enlighten humans about the nature of aliens in the hope of bridging the gap between Us and Them (*Close Encounters of the Third Kind* [Steven Spielberg, 1977]); still others to use Earth's resources for their own purposes (*This Island Earth* [Joseph N. Newman, 1955]). The aliens in *It Came from Outer Space* (Jack Arnold, 1953) mean no harm; they merely wish to repair their spaceship so they can continue exploring the universe.

The creatures themselves represent various life forms: plant life (*The Thing* [Christian Nyby, 1951]); aquatic life (the gill-man in *The Creature from the Black Lagoon* [1954] and *Revenge of the Creature* [1955], both directed by Jack Arnold); a protoplasmic mass (*The Blob* [Irving S. Yeaworth, Jr., 1958]); birds (*The Giant Claw* [Fred S. Sears, 1957]); spiders (*Tarantula* [Jack Arnold, 1955]); grasshoppers (*Beginning of the End* [Bert I. Gordon, 1957]); and ants (*Them!* [Gordon Davis, 1954]).

In *Seeing Is Believing*, Peter Biskind argues that just as the western is bipolar (wilderness vs. civilization, West vs. East, etc.) so is science fiction, with its political extremes of right and left.[5] Conservative science fiction portrays science, the federal government, and the military as forces for the good. In conservative science fiction (*It Came from beneath the Sea* [Robert Gordon, 1955], *The Thing*), science succeeds in destroying the alien. Liberal science fiction either depicts science, the federal government, and the military as ineffectual or criticizes their methods. In *I Married a Monster from Outer Space* (Gene Fowler, Jr., 1958), salvation comes not from the government but from a dog. In conservative science fiction, aliens have no redeeming features. In liberal science fiction, they are portrayed sympathetically. (In *The Seven Year Itch*, The Girl (Marilyn Monroe) remarks on how moved she was by *The Creature from the Black Lagoon*.)

Since creatures are often found in horror films as well as in science fiction, there should be some method of determining whether a film is more properly classified as science fiction than as horror. One must determine the role that science and technology play in the film, the sense of time reflected in it, and the effects of the experiments—individual, local, or global—conducted in it.

While neither horror nor science fiction mirrors the real world, science fiction tries to convince us that it does by dealing in specifics. Horror tends to be more general. We never know how Dr. Pretorious in *Bride of Frankenstein* shrinks humans to the size of miniatures. In *Dr. Cyclops* (Ernest Schoedsack, 1940), on the other hand, we know that the physicist creates his homunculi by subjecting humans to atomic radiation. Because science is the film's point of departure, *Dr. Cyclops* is considered science fiction.

The horror film, like the gothic novel, tends to be set in remote times. Even when a horror film is set in the present, it recalls cults (the cat cult in *Cat People*) and practices (devil worship in *Rosemary's Baby*) that go back centuries. Science fiction, on the other hand, can either reflect the present or evoke the future. The futuristic film is easily recognized. Less evident is the way science fiction can mirror the present.

In the 1950s, science fiction movies preyed on Americans' two deep fears: flying saucers and the atomic bomb. The possibility of extraterrestrial life resulted in one of the era's best science fiction movies, *Invasion of the Body Snatchers* (Don Siegel, 1956), in which aliens descend upon a California town and take possession of the inhabitants by an ingenious method of transformation: pods are placed under their beds, absorbing the inhabitants' personalities and leaving them as parodies of human beings. The implications of the film were far-reachng: aliens threatened the race with a unique form of extinction—the extinction of the human personality. The threat to civilization posed by the atomic bomb triggered a host of science fiction movies that imagined the results of atomic detonations: mu-

Science fiction as mythology in Return of the Jedi *(Richard Marquand, 1983): The confrontation of Good and Evil, Luke Skywalker (Mark Hamill) and Darth Vader (David Prowse). (Courtesy Lucasfilms Ltd.)*

tants in the form of giant ants, creatures dislodged from the ocean depths, humans turned into steel.

In the 1950s, a villain that was a computer would have made sense only to a few. By 1968, the name of Hal, the dispassionate computer of Stanley Kubrick's *2001: A Space Odyssey*, entered the movie vocabulary, joining such unforgettable names as Rick Blaine and Rhett Butler.

In the 1970s, the science fiction movie took an interesting turn. The threat of the atomic bomb had mushroomed into the fear of nuclear destruction. Since, as T. S. Eliot observed, "humankind cannot bear very much reality," George Lucas in *Star Wars* (1977) amalgamated science fiction, which was never a pure genre to begin with, not with horror but with adventure. The result was not mindless escapism but a return to myth in its earliest stage: fairy tale or dream narrative with stock characters rather than individuals—heroes, princesses, villains, half-humans, nonhumans, animal-like humans, and human-like animals—that we have met many times before in our dreams. In the *Star Wars* trilogy, the characters include the pure-hearted Luke Skywalker, the virginal Princess Lela, the evil Darth Vader, the 900-year-old Yoda, the patriarchal Ben (Obi-Wan) Kenobi, Chewbacca the Wookie, the treacherous Jabba the Hutt, the porcine Gammorean guards, the reptilian Admiral Ackbar, and a lovable pair of robots, C-3PO and R2-D2.

Equally important are the contributions of Steven Spielberg to the genre. While Lucas added adventure and an uncritical form of myth to science fiction, Spielberg humanized the genre. *Close Encounters of the Third Kind* portrays real people—a man, a woman, and a child—whose response to aliens reflects the film's philosophy. The child and the childlike characters in the film do not fear the aliens. What Spielberg is arguing for is the tearing down of the wall dividing one group from another, one race from another, and humans from extraterrestrials. The aliens bring love; thus, one can learn from them.

Those who return at the end of *Close Encounters* have clearly been changed—for the better. Likewise, in Spielberg's *E.T. The Extra-Terrestrial* (1982), a human—again a child—learns from an alien.

While there has been a tendency to dismiss science fiction as "lowbrow," the genre has produced enough classic work to merit serious consideration.

NOTES

[1] James Kitses, *Horizons West* (Bloomington: Indiana University Press, 1969), 8–27.

[2] Stanley J. Solomon, *Beyond Formula: American Film Genres* (New York: Harcourt Brace Jovanovich, 1976), 12–15.

[3] Jack Shadoian, *Dreams and Dead Ends: The American Gangster/Crime Film* (Cambrige, Mass.: MIT Press, 1977), 2.

[4] William Johnson, "Journey into Science Fiction," in *Focus on the Science Fiction Film*, ed. William Johnson (Englewood Cliffs, N.J.: Prentice-Hall, 1972), 1.

[5] Peter Biskind, *Seeing Is Believing: How Hollywood Taught Us to Stop Worrying and Love the Fifties* (New York: Pantheon Books, 1983), 102–59.

5
Film Subtext

How often have you read a story or seen a film that you felt was not entirely about what it seemed to be? Many college freshmen read "The Widow of Ephesus," a tale from Petronius' *Satyricon,* written in the first century A.D. In this frequently anthologized story, a woman is so shattered by her husband's death that she cannot practice the ancient rites of mourning (breast-beating and hair-tearing). Instead, accompanied by her maid, she retires to the underground tomb where the body lies. A soldier, patrolling a crucifixion site nearby to prevent the bodies from being taken down from the crosses, notices her presence, enters the tomb, quotes Virgil, and finally wins her attention. When a corpse disappears from one of the crosses, the soldier fears his negligence will cost him his job. But after three consecutive nights of love-making, the widow of Ephesus offers him her husband's body as fair exchange.

What was just summarized was the story's plot, which consisted of a situation (a widow in mourning), its complication (the soldier's appearance), and its resolution (the substitution of the husband's body for the criminal's). However, a classic tale like "The Widow of Ephesus" cannot be reduced to its story line. In every narrative worth studying, whether a work of fiction or a work of film, there is a subtext, a complex structure beneath the narrative consisting of the various associations the narrative evokes in us. In other words, there is a surface meaning and a deeper meaning. "The Widow of Ephesus" has a surface wit that cannot mask the underlying cynicism. The surface meaning is that love conquers all; the deeper or subtextual meaning is that love conquers lovers, generating such passion in them that they think nothing of sleeping three nights in a row next to a corpse.

Film also has a subtext. Whether or not we realize it, film has a dual nature. There is the film projected *on* the screen, and the film projected *from* the screen. The first is the text in the literal sense of the word; something woven together of various strands, the collaboration between a director, a screenwriter, a cast, and a crew. The second is the subtext, the harmonization of the text and the myriad associations it evokes in us. Such associations can be mythic, iconic, intellectual, musical, or some combination of these. An iconic association can be mythic in the sense of recalling a particular myth; however, it is primarily an association between the actor's screen persona and the character portrayed rather than between the character and a mythic type or mythological figure.

MYTHIC ASSOCIATIONS

The Nature of Myth

To understand how myth is part of a film's subtext we must examine our understanding of myth. Although myth is usually identified as falsehood in the popular mind, in film and literary criticism it has another meaning altogether. William York Tindall defined myth as "a dreamlike narrative in which the individual's central concerns are united with society, time, and the universe."[1] Erich Fromm called myth "a message from ourselves to ourselves."[2] Parker Tyler regarded myth as "a free, unharnessed fiction, a basic prototypic pattern capable of many variations and distortions, even though it remains imaginative truth."[3]

Myths are ultimate truths about life and death, fate and nature, God and humans. Thus, myths can never be false; they endure long after the civilizations that produce them vanish because they crystallize in narrative form unchanging patterns of human behavior. Although the Greek deities no longer command belief, they have taken other forms. Wherever there are the sworn virgin and the youth who weakens her resistance, there are Diana and Endymion; whenever a society is polarized between reason and emotion, it is reenacting the eternal conflict between Apollo, who embodies the powers of reason and order, and Dionysus, who represents the life forces of creativity and anarchy.

Film is receptive to myth for two reasons. First, film and myth can speak the same language—picture language. Long before the advent of writing, myths were transmitted orally through epics and visually through artwork on walls, vases, bowls, and wine vessels. Thus from the very outset myth was oral and visual; and so was film, for even during the silent period there was generally some form of sound, as we have seen. Another reason why film and myth are so compatible is that both are intimately associated with the dream. The dream was the first form in which the myths made their appearance, and as Parker Tyler has noted, film is a kind of "daylight dream."[4] We dream individually, but we also dream collectively. The stuff of our dreams is the stuff of fairy tales, legends, and romances: quests, evil enchanters, enchanted princes and princesses, talking animals, transformations of humans into beasts and ugly ducklings into beauties. This dream material belongs to the human race, and thus our dreams make us one with humankind. Psychologist Carl Jung compared the dream to a screen on which the history of the race is projected. World literature and world cinema abound in works about heroes and villains, maidens and sorceresses, scapegoats and questers. When these figures appear in literature or in film, they strike a responsive chord in us: they are familiar because we have encountered them before—in our dreams.

Film has a dream level to which we respond the way we respond to myths—instinctively, never questioning their origins or even their existence. Making a mythic association involves remembering a pattern of experience that is universal. Sometimes we can determine the specific myth that is operating in the film; but often these unchanging truths are difficult to isolate except as archetypal themes (death/rebirth, the return of the hero, the descent to the underworld, etc.).

Mythic Analysis of *Shane* (George Stevens, 1953)

Every critic who has written about *Shane* has sensed a mythic subtext in the film. In *Shane* there appear to be at least three mythic levels.

Shane as a Christ Figure

Shane begins with the credits, with Alan Ladd as Shane entering on horseback from the left to the "Shane theme," a melody suggesting cantering horses and deer drinking peacefully from a stream against a background of snow-decked mountains. Shane is descending into a valley; he is not moving horizontally across the frame like a gunfighter, although he will later change both speed and direction during his ride of vengeance. But for the moment he is moving *downward*—in symbolic terms, he might be said to be lowering himself—as he descends into the lives of the Starretts, a family of homesteaders.

Shane can be seen as Christ figure. Just as Christ descended from heaven and humbled himself by assuming a human nature, Shane descends into the valley, temporarily putting aside his divinity to serve humanity. The resemblance of Shane to Christ has been noted by critic Donald Richie:

> Shane . . . came from nowhere and he is going nowhere—like the vagrant Jett Rink in *Giant,* like the hitchhiking George Eastman [in Stevens's *A Place in the Sun*], like Jesus Christ. . . . His difference from the romantic hero is that he—like Christ himself—rather than merely feeling that he ought to do something to express his inner values and to affect the world, actually does something about it.[5]

Shane's past is as enigmatic as Christ's. Christ's life before he began his public ministry at thirty is a mystery. And so is Shane's; Shane simply appears one day looking like a god in white buckskins. As part of his ritual incarnation, he sheds his divine trappings and dresses in the clothes of mortals—blue denim and dark trousers. But he will not retain that outfit forever. Before he avenges the death of Torrey (Elisha Cook, Jr.), he changes back to his buckskins, becoming a god once more.

Jesus Christ preaches meekness: "If someone strike thee on the right cheek, turn to him the other also" (Matt. 5:40). Shane displays his meekness when Chris (Ben Johnson) challenges his manhood after Shane orders a bottle of soda pop for young Joey Starrett. Chris offers Shane a "man's drink" by spilling a jigger of whiskey on his shirt. At that moment Shane does not retaliate; but later when he returns to the saloon, he reciprocates by buying Chris a drink and disposing of its contents in the same way. In the ensuing brawl the abandon with which Shane swings his fists suggests a wrathful god not unlike the Christ who overturned the tables of the moneychangers as he drove them out of the Temple of Jerusalem. Meekness and righteous anger are not incompatible.

Shane's message is for the chosen. It is for the homesteaders, not for the cattle ranchers. Sometimes, as history has proved, the chosen must take up arms. Thus, Shane teaches young Joey how to shoot. When Marion Starrett (Jean Arthur) finds Shane teaching her son how to handle a gun, Shane's explanation is simple: "A gun is as good or bad as the man using it." Joey, who has a male child's notion of manhood (men do not flinch when turpentine is applied to an open wound, and they settle disagreements with their fists), is given a rare opportunity to see his theory put to the test when he watches Shane

Shane's farewell to Joey in Shane. *Shane leaves Joey (Brandon de Wilde) with the command to grow up "strong and straight" as he departs, presumably to aid another family of homesteaders. (Courtesy Paramount Pictures)*

kill Wilson (Jack Palance), the gunfighter. Shane leaves Joey with the command to grow up "strong and straight." Now Shane is no longer a man but a god delivering one of his commandments before he disappears from view.

Shane as Apollo-Hercules

One writer has called Shane "the frontier Christ, coming down from a Western Olympus."[6] This description characterizes Shane as part Christ, part Greek deity.

In Greek mythology, Zeus punished Apollo for killing one of his sons by forcing him to spend a year of servitude in the household of Admetus, the King of Thessaly. Admetus respected Apollo's godhead, and in gratitude Apollo allowed him the privilege of living beyond his allotted time, provided he could find someone to die for him. Unable to find a volunteer, Admetus turned to his wife Alcestis, who agreed. During the funeral, Hercules stopped off at the palace on one of his labors, learned what had happened, wrestled with Death, and restored (or so the legend goes, although Euripides' *Alcestis* is intentionally vague on this point) Alcestis to her husband.

Although Shane's golden hair is a good metaphor for Apollo's radiance, Shane is as much a Hercules as he is an Apollo. Shane's power of endurance is Herculean; in one scene a stubborn tree trunk is uprooted, a task that required Shane's perseverance as well as Starrett's brawn. Two themes are common to both *Shane* and the Greek myth: a god's bondage in a mortal's household in expiation for a crime, and a god's saving a mortal's life. As we have seen, Shane's life is a mystery, yet from the way he draws when little Joey Starrett clicks the trigger of his unloaded rifle, he seems to be an ex-gunslinger. That he humbles himself through voluntary servitude suggests that he is atoning for his past.

Just as Apollo served the family of Admetus, Shane serves the Starretts; just as Hercules restored Alcestis to her husband, Shane restores Starrett to his wife. Instead of allowing Starrett to kill Wilson (and lose his life in the bargain), Shane knocks him unconscious and goes in his place, thus increasing Starrett's lifespan and saving him for Marion and Joey.

Shane as Knight Errant

According to André Bazin, the subtext also encourages us to think of Shane as a "knight errant in search of his grail," pursuing the ideals of courtly love in the American West.[7] While it is Starrett whom Shane aids, it is Marion whom he serves. But in the courtly love tradition the knight not only served the lady, but tried to emulate her gentleness and thus acquire some for himself to offset his rough ways. Physically, there is a great resemblance between Shane and Marion. Both have golden hair, blue eyes, and a diminutiveness that suggests a gentle heart, not a natural failing. It is significant that Shane chooses to wear blue, one of the lady's favorite colors. However, the medieval knight was a living paradox; the lady he honored as the embodiment of natural perfection was frequently the unsatisfied married woman he took to his bed.

Here the analogies cease; the closest Shane comes to Marion is dancing the Varsouviana and shaking her hand in a farewell gesture. Yet *Shane* is a magnificently subtle film. When Marion is tucking Joey into bed, we hear his voice from behind the closed door: "Mother, I just love Shane." Goodnights are exchanged; Marion enters her bedroom, and Shane retires to the barn. "Goodnight, Shane," Joey calls, but there is no answer. A declaration of love has taken place, shared by mother and son, but in different ways. Marion's graceful entrance into the bedroom is neither slinking nor erotic but willowy and feminine. She may be retiring to her husband's bed, but she is clearly

Chuck Tatum (Kirk Douglas) of The Big Carnival (Ace in the Hole [Billy Wilder, 1951]), un-earthing his story. Tatum allows cave-in victim Leo Minosa (Richard Benedict) to remain entombed longer than necessary so he can win fame as a reporter. (Courtesy Paramount Pictures)

thinking of Shane. The mythic hero has many faces. Three of Shane's have been described here.

The Genesis Myth in *The Big Carnival* (Billy Wilder, 1951)

In *The Big Carnival* (or *Ace in the Hole*) an unscrupulous reporter deliberately allows the victim of a cave-in to remain entombed for a longer period of time so that he can cover the rescue operations. Chuck Tatum (Kirk Douglas) is en route to cover a rattlesnake hunt when the victim's wife (Jan Sterling) informs him of the cave-in. Sensing a story, he accompanies her to the site of the cave-in, where he strikes up a friendship with Leo, the entombed man, promising to immortalize him in print. Tatum never gets to the rattlesnake hunt, but in a perverse way the rattlesnakes come to him in the form of the pet rattler of the local sheriff, who carries it around in a cardboard box. Tatum convinces the sheriff that a dramatic rescue would ensure his reelection. As the pact is ratified across a table where a snake moves restlessly in his box, it suddenly becomes clear what Wilder is doing: he is using as the film's subtext one of the oldest myths known to man—the lost paradise, the Eden infiltrated by the evil serpent. We are back in an archetypal garden, here a New Mexico desert community, where an innocent Adam lies transfixed in a cave, his Eve bites into an apple as if she were glorying in the taste of forbidden fruit (an unforgettable shot), and a serpent's coils vibrate against cardboard.

The film then becomes an inversion of the book of *Genesis*, complete with a parody of the six days of creation. Had the rescue operations taken place as planned, Leo would have been freed in sixteen hours. But he cannot last the week. A priest administers the last rites; a host is placed on the end of a long-handled device, which resembles a serpent creeping toward the dying communicant. Leo succumbs on the sixth day, his death bringing the grotesque parody of the creation myth to a close as the shadow of a snake passes across his resigned face. The desert is still; presumably the seventh day will be one of rest.

ICONIC ASSOCIATIONS

In medieval art, an icon is a pictorial representation of a religious subject. Invested with a spiritual aura, the repesentation (icon) itself becomes worthy of veneration. An icon of the Virgin Mary, for example, depicts not just a woman with a halo but a woman who is the mother of Jesus Christ. By imparting a spiritual dimension to a material image, an icon calls attention to its inherent duality. Iconic associations are also based on duality. An iconic association arises from the perception of shared features or similarities between (1) the actor's screen image and the character the actor is portraying (Humphrey Bogart in any of his major roles, Katharine Hepburn in any of hers); (2) an actor's screen image and a historical figure or traditional type (e.g., an actor playing a Christ figure in a film where the actor's persona coincides with the traditional image of Christ; an actor playing a rebel in a manner consistent with the popular image of the rebel); (3) an actor's performance style and that of another actor who is not in the film but whose iconic presence is clearly felt. The third requires a specific example. In *Running on Empty* (Sidney Lumet, 1988), River Phoenix plays the older son of radical parents wanted by the government. Phoenix embodies the quiet intensity of Montgomery Clift and James Dean and acts in the naturalistic style they made famous. Since Phoenix's performance evokes theirs, it acquires an iconic quality even though River Phoenix is not—or is not yet—a screen icon.

The following are examples of iconic associations.

THE ACTUAL AND INTENDED
STARS OF *HIGH SIERRA*
(RAOUL WALSH, 1941).

Humphrey Bogart, who played Roy Earle in the film. (Courtesy Collector's Book Store)

George Raft, who was slated for the part of Roy Earle but refused to be in a movie where he had to die. (Courtesy Collector's Book Store)

Humphrey Bogart in *High Sierra* (Raoul Walsh, 1941)

Humphrey Bogart might never have appeared in *High Sierra*, the movie that made him a star, if George Raft, who was originally slated for the part of Roy Earle, had not refused to be in a film in which he had to die. Raft, however, could never have suggested that inward drive for freedom that propels Earle to the summit from which he falls. *High Sierra* is a movie about existential freedom, that freedom to which a human being is condemned, as Jean-Paul Sartre would say. Bogart's becoming an existential cult hero is not surprising because he projected the image of a figure living in the present, striving for freedom, and performing meaningful actions to achieve it—financing an operation for a girl with a club foot (*High Sierra*), helping a young husband win enough at roulette to buy visas for himself and his wife (*Casablanca*), even putting a spiritually lost intellectual out of his misery with a bullet (*The Petrified Forest* [Archie Mayo, 1936]). At the end of *High Sierra*, when Earle lies dead at the foot of the mountain, Marie (Ida Lupino) asks Healy (Jerome Cowan), "Mister, what does it mean when a man 'crashes out'?" "That's a funny question for you to ask, sister," Healy replies. "It means he's free." "Free," Marie says as she walks triumphantly into the frame, knowing that Earle has won his freedom—and his essence—through death.

The existential implications of "crashing out" would have eluded Raft; Bogart understood them and embodied them in his performance, thus giving the film its existential character. Even Bogart's face was extraordinary and fittingly existential. It was not a neighborhood face, nor was it especially handsome. It was a face that knew the mixed blessings of life; a face that did not slacken with age but grew tauter, the eyes retreating into their sockets until by the end of his career they had settled into omniscience.

Al Pacino as Frank Serpico (Serpico [Sidney Lumet, 1973]), one of the few visually acceptable Christ figures in film. (Courtesy Paramount Pictures)

Al Pacino in *Serpico* (Sidney Lumet, 1973)

When *Serpico* opened, several critics noted a resemblance between Al Pacino, who interpreted the title role magnificently, and the pop art pictures of Jesus Christ. Critic Vincent Canby of the *New York Times* also compared Pacino with St. Francis of Assisi. All sensed that there was more to Pacino's Serpico than just great acting; behind his Serpico they saw either a god-man doomed to suffer for his love of humanity or a saint who resisted the attempts of the religious establishment to interfere with his mission.

It was not merely Al Pacino's beard, his mesmeric eyes, or his uncontrollable rage at corruption that caused the critics to think of Jesus Christ. Certain details of Serpico's life also recalled similar details in Christ's; thus the text (Serpico) is coordinated with the subtext (Christ), and both come together in the person of the star (Pacino). This coincidence does not occur with every movie-hero police officer or every actor. The identification of Christ with Serpico (a cop who found his apostolate on the streets and underwent the traditional scapegoat cycle of harassment, betrayal, and desertion) was characterized in Pacino's performance in a way it was not in the performances of Stacy Keach in *The New Centurions* (Richard Fleischer, 1972) and Robert Duvall in *Colors* (Dennis Hopper, 1988), both of which are "hero cop" movies.

Simone Simon in *Cat People* (Jacques Tourner, 1942)

The horror films Val Lewton produced at RKO in the 1940s are singled out today for serious consideration because they represent an exotic, and for their time advanced, kind of subtext. In *Cat People* the casting of Simone Simon as the cat-obsessed Irena led to various interpretations of the film, each of which has some validity. The script tells of an Irena who is the ill-starred descendant of a Serbian cat cult. The visuals go much further; they tell of an Irena who cannot unleash the animal part of her nature; an Irena who wants a man as a friend, not as a lover, and who registers disgust whenever her husband tries to touch her.

Because of Simon's performance, some critics also saw Irena as a repressed lesbian whose animal nature was roused to anger by the male, to passion by the female. While such an interpretation may seem unwarranted, it can be suggested by the visuals, particularly the episodes in which Irena stalks her rival through Central Park and

Irena (Simone Simon) and her husband in name only (Kent Smith) in Cat People *(Jacques Tourneur, 1942). (Courtesy MOMA/FSA and RKO)*

follows her down the stairs to the swimming pool of a women's residence club.

Simone Simon had the appearance of a dream figure, and dream figures are never stable; they can be alternately sensuous and sexless. When she was cast in a film with ambiguous sexual overtones, she brought them to the surface, thereby activating the subtext, which in *Cat People* catalogued the various forms sexual repression could take (antipathy to men, tormenting of women, a self-administered penance in a scalding bath)—all rather daring for a movie of the 1940s.

Jack Nicholson and Louise Fletcher in *One Flew over the Cuckoo's Nest* (Miloš Forman, 1975)

The impression made by an actor's performance is based on many factors, including such seemingly irrelevant details as hairstyle and wardrobe. Yet it is through such details that filmmakers realize their intentions; it is also through such details that we see in characters what directors want us to see.

When Miloš Forman was about to direct *One Flew over the Cuckoo's Nest*, he was faced with the task of making a movie out of a cult book of the 1960s. During the last few years of that decade, Ken Kesey's novel seemed a tragically accurate mirror of America. The animosity between Randle P. McMurphy and Big Nurse paralleled similar confrontations between the pacifist and the draft board, the militant Students for a Democratic Society and the police, the student activists and the campus administration.

However, in 1975 Vietnam was a memory, the draft had been suspended, and campuses were quiet. To make the film meaningful, Forman had to deemphasize all the political overtones the novel had

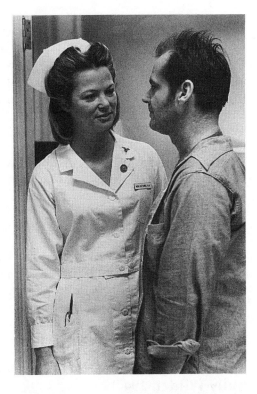

HAIR-STYLE AS A VISUAL
ASSOCIATION
*Nurse Ratched (Louise
Fletcher) and Randle
McMurphy (Jack Nicholson)
in* One Flew over the
Cuckoo's Nest *(Miloš For-
man, 1976). Louise
Fletcher's hairstyle is a
throwback to the 1940s.
(Courtesy Fantasy Films)*

*Sheila Ryan in an authentic
1940s hairdo. (Courtesy Twentieth Century-Fox)*

acquired in the 1960s. The film's text emphasized the humanism and comedy of Kesey's novel; the subtext transformed the conflict between McMurphy (Jack Nicholson) and Nurse Ratched (Louise Fletcher) into a battle between man and woman. Forman capitalized on Nicholson's exposed and often vulnerable masculinity, but he also saw more in it than locker room bravado. There is an impishness about Nicholson; at times he seems to be putting us on, challenging us to make the hackneyed connection between a man's height (Nicholson is not tall) and a man's ego. Little details about Nicholson's portrayal of McMurphy suggest the imp: the cap pulled down over the ears, the hornlike tuft of hair that gives the impression of a satyr, the eyes that dart from one direction to another as if they too were free spirits.

Although the time of the film is the 1960s, Louise Fletcher's hairstyle came out of another era. Forman had her wear her hair the way women did in "lady executive" movies of the 1940s, which were typified by such movies as *Take a Letter, Darling* (Mitchell Leisen, 1942) and *They All Kissed the Bride* (Alexander Hall, 1942). These films, however, were a harmless type of screwball comedy featuring women as executives and men as their subordinates. *Cuckoo's Nest* is hardly screwball comedy and Nurse Ratched, by her hairstyle and manner, is a savage parody of the female executive of the 1940s.

Barbara Stanwyck in *Double Indemnity* (Billy Wilder, 1944)

The name of the *femme fatale* in James Cain's novel, *Double Indemnity,* is Phyllis Nirdlinger. When Billy Wilder was working on the screenplay for the film version, which he also directed, he changed the character's last name to Dietrichson. He wanted audiences to think not of Marlene Dietrich herself but of Dietrich's persona, the embodiment of the extremes of desire and danger, passion and aloofness, femininity and masculinity. Wilder even had Barbara Stanwyck, whom he cast in the role, wear a blonde wig. Thus, throughout the film one senses something about Stanwyck that suggests Dietrich— behind Stanwyck's performance lurks Dietrich's persona.

INTELLECTUAL ASSOCIATIONS

When we make a mythic association, we are reminded of universal patterns true of all human beings at all times. When we make an iconic association, we perceive a likeness between an actor's persona and the character, or between the actor's performance and another's persona. When we make an intellectual association, we relate the film

BARBARA STANWYCK AS MARLENE DIETRICH
Fred MacMurray and Marlene Dietrich in The Lady Is Willing (Mitchell Leisen, 1942). (Courtesy Columbia Pictures)

Fred MacMurray and Barbara Stanwyck in Double Indemnity *(Billy Wilder, 1944). Wilder changed the name of Stanwyck's character to Dietrichson and had the actress wear a blonde wig to evoke the Dietrich persona. (Copyright ® by Paramount Pictures, Courtesy of MCA Publishing Rights, a Division of MCA Incorporated)*

as a whole—not just one aspect of it—to history, to another medium (literature, opera, etc.), to another film, or even to an earlier version of itself.

Historical Relations

John Schlesinger's film of Nathanael West's novel, *The Day of the Locust*, has a historical subtext. West intended his novel as an anti-

Hollywood tract, but it was also a subtle indictment of the political apathy that breeds moguls in the movie colony, dictators in the world at large. The 1975 film version followed a similar course. Nothing in the script's language implied there was a political dimension to the plot. Therefore, Schlesinger had to supply that dimension visually; he had to show a Hollywood where life is a soundstage and where reality becomes illusion and remains such even as the armies of Europe are preparing for World War II. Sometimes Schlesinger's cutting is so abrupt that it blurs the distinction between the real and the illusory. For example, he cuts from a father calling his daughter to passengers waving from a ship. At first this is puzzling until the ship is shown to be a soundstage prop whose passengers are movie extras.

The climax of the film is the brutal death of Homer Simpson (Donald Sutherland) on the night of a Hollywood premiere. Homer's death is a grim reminder of the price a nation pays when it turns inward upon its myths (where the dream is more glorious than the reality), and worships those who promise to make the dream come true. Schlesinger prepares us for the apocalypse earlier in the film with images of decay and perversity: a boy with platinum curls unsexed by his fame-hungry mother so he can look like Shirley Temple; a dead horse in a swimming pool; a death face peering into Homer's backyard; a bloody cockfight intercut with flashes of the gaudy dress Faye Greener (Karen Black) waves in front of Homer with a rhythm that matches, beat for beat, the quick jabs the roosters are giving each other.

The Hollywood depicted is an insular community that resents the intrusion of history and reality. Faye and her beaus leave the movie theater before the newsreel begins; having seen a film in which she had a bit part, Faye is uninterested in a newsreel about the rise of Hitler. On the night of the premiere a newspaper blows down Hollywood Boulevard, its headlines announcing the advent of World War II. The master of ceremonies for the event is a Hitler lookalike, and the fans are the kind that would turn out for a premiere or a Nazi rally. Again Schlesinger crosscuts, this time between the premiere and the death of Homer. He is not crosscutting between illusion and reality but rather between two forms of madness, as in the cockfight/swirling dress scene.

In the climax, all the associations merge: political detachment, fascism, and the mob's need for a scapegoat. Adore, the boy too old for his feminine curls, strikes Homer in the head with a stone. In a rage Homer pursues him into a parking lot and stomps him to death. His reaction is our reaction: we want this unnatural product of a twisted dream destroyed before it grows up into something worse.

But the mob is so crazed by the sight of the gods and goddesses at the premiere that it turns on Homer and tears him apart. As Tod the art designer watches in horror, he envisions the fans as zombies with death-mask faces, American grotesques mobilized to kill the destroyer of the dream.

By crosscutting between the premiere and Homer's ritual dismemberment, Schlesinger creates associations that are only implicit in the script. In the text the crowd destroys Homer because he kills Adore; in the subtext the crowd destroys Homer because he kills what Adore represents—the necessity of perverting one's nature to become a star. And if one must become dehumanized to be a star, one must do the same to worship the star; thus movie fans can be as grotesque as the objects of their worship, knocking down barricades to get a touch of mink or a piece of shirt. There is another motive for their behavior, a motive as old as the one that impelled the worshipers of Dionysus to kill the intruder who witnessed their sacred rites. Homer has wandered into a sacred ritual, the ritual of the Hollywood premiere; but Homer is also unclean from the blood of Adore. Thus, the fans turn on him because he has polluted their rites and shed the blood of one of their own.

Thus, a film can be set in a particular era and yet evoke that era indirectly. Such a film does not declare itself "historical" in the sense of dramatizing a historical event the way, for example, *Tora! Tora! Tora!* recreates the Japanese attack on Pearl Harbor. Yet to appreciate this kind of film one has to know history; unlike the historical film, the script does not provide the information.

A knowledge of the Great Depression enables one to look at *It Happened One Night* as something more than just a screwball comedy. And yet it is not coincidental that screwball comedy was born in the Great Depression; its breeziness and happy endings offered escape and enjoyment to the beleaguered audiences of that era. This kind of comedy, in which social barriers fell like the walls of Jericho, was ideal for Depression audiences who delighted in seeing a society woman put in her place by a man who didn't even wear an undershirt. *It Happened One Night* is pure fairy tale, a variation on "The Princess and the Commoner" set in the early 1930s. The associations we bring to the film—breadlines, soup kitchens, strikes—enable us to see it as a fable of the Great Depression.

Easy Living, another screwball comedy, is best remembered for the automat sequence in which Mary Smith, swathed in the sable that has literally dropped to her from the sky, is sitting by herself, eating a beef pie, completely oblivious to the fighting that goes on when the food suddenly becomes free. In the context of the film, the scene is uproarious; in the context of Depression America, the sight of people sliding on a food-covered floor is disquieting. When the camera roams around the automat, observing a fur-clad Mary eating in the foreground with the masses fighting in the background, it does more than record a comic free-for-all. By highlighting the extremes of affluence and poverty, it defines the Great Depression as a time of sable for the lucky and rags for the luckless.

Filmic Relations

Last Tango in Paris (Bernardo Bertolucci, 1972) is ostensibly about a woman caught between two men, one of whom debases her while the other idealizes her. Bertolucci used this narrative structure to work out a theory of film that he illustrates with references to movies of the past. Thus, when Pauline Kael reviewed *Last Tango*, and alluded to the film's constant "feedback," she meant that much in the film—the performances as well as the imagery—recalled other films.

"Movies are a past we share, and, whether we recognize them or not, the copious associations are at work in the film and we feel them," Kael observed.[8] As we have already seen, the way a movie is cast can create certain associations between the actor and his or her role. In *Last Tango* Marlon Brando plays Paul, an American in Paris, who meets Jeanne (Maria Schneider) when both of them show up to look at the same apartment; Jean-Pierre Léaud is Tom, the TV director and movie nut who is using Jeanne for a television film he is making. Brando and Léaud are not ordinary actors. Each epitomizes a style of acting and a type of film that revolutionized the cinema. Brando will always be synonymous with the Method, a system of acting requiring the performer to draw on past experiences, emotions, and memories for a particular role. Brando was the definitive Method actor of the 1950s—brooding, introspective, often inarticulate. Léaud was the discovery of François Truffaut, who cast him as Antoine Doinel, the problem child of *The 400 Blows*. Léaud and Truffaut then went on to make other films: the "Antoine and Colette" episode in *Love at Twenty* (1962), *Stolen Kisses, Bed and Board* (1970), and *Day for Night* (1973). Physically, Léaud had even begun to resemble the director. Truffaut typifies the New Wave, that extraordinary burst of creativity that started in France at the end of the 1950s when directors such as Truffaut and Jean-Luc Godard rejected literary scripts for shooting scripts and improvisation, filmed in the streets rather than in studios, demanded naturalistic acting instead of old-fashioned emoting, and quoted liberally from the movies of the past.

Just as Brando and Léaud represent two different eras of film

Cinderella in sable (Jean Arthur) is exposed to the grim realities of the Great Depression in the automat sequence of Easy Living *(Mitchell Leisen, 1937). (Copyright ® by Paramount Pictures, Courtesy of MCA Publishing Rights, a Division of MCA Incorporated)*

making, the characters they portray represent two different ways of life. Paul isolates himself in the apartment where he works out his sexual aggression on Jeanne; Tom roams the streets of Paris, scouting for locations for his movie. Jeanne is trapped not just between two men but between their worlds: Paul's closed world of the apartment and Tom's open world of the city. Yet filmmakers are in the same predicament: Do they remain within the closed world of the studio set as their predecessors did, or do they venture outside where an entire city can be their soundstage?

What Kael calls "feedback" is not limited to the eras Brando and Léaud evoke. Bertolucci used *Last Tango* as a vehicle for his ideas on film in the same way Paul and Tom were using Jeanne for their respective purposes. Thus, in the film Bertolucci invokes movies of the past that have some bearing on his own film. When Jeanne and Tom are on a barge, there is a life preserver with *L'Atalante* inscribed on it. *L'Atalante* is the title of Jean Vigo's classic film (1934), and the barge scene in *Last Tango* pays homage to Vigo's exquisite film in which a young bride leaves her barge captain-husband to experience the excitement of Paris, only to return to the secure world of the barge at the end. However, Bertolucci is also replying to Vigo's optimism: Vigo's bride can be reunited with her husband, but once Paul and Jeanne leave the apartment, no reunion is possible.

Last Tango is like a course in film history. The scene in which Paul looks out on the roofs of Paris before he dies recalls René Clair's *Sous les toits de Paris* (*Under the Roofs of Paris*, 1931), which the director made when he was thirty, the same age Bertolucci was when he made *Last Tango*. When Jeanne shoots Paul, the scene is a part not only of *Last Tango*, but of all those Hollywood movies in which a woman pulls a revolver and pumps her lover full of bullets. *Last Tango* purports to be about male-female relationships, but subtextually it is about the relationship between filmmakers and their art.

With its mix of animation and live action, *Who Framed Roger Rabbit* (Robert Zemeckis, 1988), set in 1947, seems to have a double subtext: the animated cartoons of the 1930s and 1940s and the private-eye films of the 1940s. While *Roger Rabbit* has been enjoyed by children who have never seen a private-eye movie and who know cartoons only from television, it speaks most directly to those with a knowledge of film history. The dancing hippos bring back memories of Walt Disney's *Fantasia* (1940); Roger's sexy wife, Jessica, with her red tresses and lowcut gown, recalls Rita Hayworth in *Gilda* (Charles Vidor, 1946); Eddie Valiant (Bob Hoskins), the private eye hired to trail Jessica, whose infidelity is causing Roger to forget his lines, is a seedier version of the 1940s' private detectives Sam Spade and Philip Marlowe.

However, the plot of *Roger Rabbit*—a detective's discovery of a scheme that would, if executed, change the face of Los Angeles—is not to be found in any cartoon or 1940s' detective movie, but in one

ASSOCIATIONS BETWEEN ACTOR AND ROLE

Jean-Pierre Léaud as Antoine Doinel in The 400 Blows *(François Truffaut, 1959), perhaps the most famous of the New Wave films. (Courtesy Janus Films)*

Léaud as Tom, the TV director in Last Tango in Paris *(Bernardo Bertolucci, 1973), with Maria Schneider. Even as Tom, Léaud typified the casual, naturalistic form of acting the New Wave directors encouraged. (Courtesy United Artists)*

The trio of These Three *(William Wyler, 1936), the first film version of Lillian Hellman's* The Children's Hour: *Miriam Hopkins as Martha, Joel McCrea as Dr. Joseph Cardin, and Merle Oberon as Karen. (Courtesy Samuel Goldwyn productions)*

particular film, *Chinatown* (Roman Polanski, 1974), the true subtext of *Roger Rabbit.* In *Chinatown,* private investigator J. J. Gittes (Jack Nicholson) uncovers a shady land deal involving Noah Cross (John Huston), who is buying up property in the San Fernando Valley where a projected reservoir will turn the area into choice real estate. In *Roger Rabbit,* Eddie Valiant discovers that Judge Doom (Christopher Lloyd) plans to transform Los Angeles from a city that relies on trolley cars for transportation into a city of freeways. To do so, he must destroy Toontown, the enclave in which the cartoon characters live. If he succeeds, he will be destroying a venerable film tradition: the animated cartoon and the characters like Bugs Bunny, Donald Duck, and Porky Pig who are part of it.

Judge Doom's plan is thwarted through the combined efforts of Eddie and the Toons. The actual history of Los Angeles and Hollywood, however, has proved otherwise. Thus, moviegoers who remember a time when theaters featured a cartoon, two movies, a newsreel, and a chapter of a serial find *Roger Rabbit* bittersweet: the film conjures up a Hollywood of another time and place—to many, perhaps a better time and place.

The Original and Its Relation to the Remake

William Wyler's *The Children's Hour* (1962) is three degrees removed from the original. First, there was Lillian Hellman's 1934 play

The trio of The Children's Hour *(William Wyler, 1962): Audrey Hepburn as Karen, James Garner as Dr. Joseph Cardin, and Shirley MacLaine as Martha. The 1962 version, despite its fidelity to the play, is inferior in many ways to* These Three. *(Courtesy United Artists)*

of the same name about a malicious child who accuses her teachers of lesbianism. Then there was Wyler's 1936 film version, *These Three.* Since the Production Code forbade "sex perversion or any inference of it,"[9] the charge had to be changed. Thus, the girl accuses the teachers of being in love not with each other but with the same man.

Familiarity with Hellman's play makes it possible to hear the original dialogue as it is being modified to fit the new situation. In the play when Martha confesses her love to Karen, she says, "I have loved you the way they said." In *These Three,* the line becomes, "I have loved *him* the way they said." John Benson did much the same thing when he changed the pronouns in Shakespeare's "Sonnets to the Fair Youth" to give the impression they were written to a woman. Yet Wyler preserved Hellman's meaning by having Miriam Hopkins play Martha as if she were in love with Karen, thereby recreating *The Children's Hour* within *These Three.*

In the early 1960s, Wyler was able to film *The Children's Hour* as Hellman had written it; but the times had changed, and the entire venture was a mistake. Oddly enough, *These Three* was closer in tone to the original—a 1930s movie of a 1930s play—than the 1962 version, which followed the play closely but never captured its liberal spirit. Yet moviegoers familiar with *These Three* watching *The Children's Hour* are having an unusual experience. It is almost as if they were seeing the two films concurrently; if they know the play, it is a triple experience.

When we watch a movie that is a remake of one we already know, the original becomes part of the remake's subtext. Louisa May Alcott's *Little Women* was made twice—in 1933 by George Cukor and in 1949 by Mervyn LeRoy. When Jo (June Allyson) of the 1949 version jumps over the fence, we see both June Allyson and Katharine Hepburn, who played Jo in the original, hovering over her successor like a spectral presence or a TV ghost. "I've seen this before," we often say of a particular movie; quite possibly we have. Twentieth Century-Fox was constantly remaking its musicals: To see *Wabash Avenue* (Henry Koster, 1950) is to see *Coney Island; How to Marry a Millionaire* (Jean Negulesco, 1953) was a remake of *Three Little Girls in Blue* (Bruce Humberstone, 1946), which in turn derived from *Moon over Miami* (Walter Lang, 1941). Often the time and place were changed and music was added, but the situation remained the same: Raoul Walsh's *Colorado Territory* is his *High Sierra* in a Western setting; *I Died a Thousand Times* (Stuart Heisler, 1955) is *High Sierra* with Jack Palance in the Humphrey Bogart role. *High Society* (Charles Walters, 1956) is *The Philadelphia Story* (George Cukor, 1940) with a Cole Porter score; *Against All Odds* (Taylor Hackford, 1984) is not only a remake of *Out of the Past* (Jacques Tourneur, 1947)—it also includes one of the original's stars, Jane Greer.

MUSICAL ASSOCIATIONS

Music has two main functions in a film: it either advances or enhances the narrative. When it advances the narrative, it is a plot device and not subtextual. In *Lady in the Dark* (Mitchell Leisen, 1944), a childhood song the heroine tries to remember is the key to her neurosis. Many a Twentieth Century-Fox musical included a tender ballad the heroine was belting out until the hero taught her how to sing it properly (*Coney Island, Wabash Avenue*). We have already seen how in many musicals working out the melody or the lyrics to a song was the significant moment in the film. There are also songs that drift in and out of the characters' lives, becoming *their* song and playing at appropriately dramatic moments; the classic example is "As Time Goes By" in *Casablanca*. Some movies have a classical score, usually a ballet or an opera, that catapults an unknown to stardom (*The Red Shoes* [Michael Powell, 1948]) or notoriety (the synthetic opera *Salammbô* in *Citizen Kane*). Sometimes a piece of music forms the film's climax, achieving an effect that words cannot: "Remember My Forgotten Man" in *Gold Diggers of 1933* (Mervyn LeRoy, 1933), George Gershwin's Concerto in F in *Rhapsody in Blue* (Irving Rapper, 1945), the title ballet in *An American in Paris* (Vincente Minnelli, 1951).

Music is even more functional as an element of the subtext when it does not so much advance the narrative as deepen it. Take, for example, a musical phrase that is repeatedly associated with a character, a mood, or a situation. Such a recurring musical phrase is a *leitmotif*. When a leitmotif identifies a character, it becomes the character's musical signature. Heard in conjunction with the appearance of a character, or representation of an idea, the leitmotif is inseparable from the individual with whom it is associated or the idea it under-scores. It also enjoys a kind of autonomy. A leitmotif can confirm a declaration of love, but it can also recur when the lovers are quarrel-ing or parting, mocking what it had previously celebrated. As part of the character, a leitmotif can remind the audience of what the char-acter is feeling at a particular moment. In *I Confess* (Alfred Hitchcock, 1952), when Ruth (Anne Baxter) tells her husband she does not love him, we hear the leitmotif associated with the man she really loves.

The leitmotif expresses aspects of the character that lie beyond the capacity of language. The nursery tune that opens the 1942 ver-sion of *Cat People* is the first indication that the movie is not an ordi-nary horror film. It is fitting that such a singsong motif should be Irena's signature, for she is emotionally a child.

The leitmotif also concretizes abstract themes. "Power" is an ab-straction, yet Bernard Herrmann, who composed the music for *Citizen Kane*, called one of the leitmotifs of the film "Power." As a musical phrase "power" is no longer abstract because we hear it. The Power motif is heard for the first time as the camera ascends the gate of Xanadu, taking us into the pleasure dome and then to Kane's death-bed. But it is a *synesthetic* experience: We see, feel, and hear Power. We watch its calculatingly slow rise, feel the isolation it brings, and hear the grim consequences it holds for those who seek it.

There are all kinds of motifs—love motifs, death motifs, and even love-death, or *Liebestod*, motifs. At the end of *Duel in the Sun* (King Vidor, 1947), which must have one of the lushest scores ever com-posed, Pearl Chavez (Jennifer Jones) crawls over sun-baked rocks to die in her lover's arms. As their blood mingles, the love motif heard when they first met seems to surge out of some chasm in the great Southwest to become their *Liebestod*.

For *The Private Life of Sherlock Holmes* (1970), Billy Wilder fash-ioned a love motif out of a few measures of Miklos Rosza's Concerto for Violin and Orchestra. It is a bittersweet but dignified theme ex-pressing a yearning never to be satisfied—in this case, Holmes's love for Ilse von Hofmannstahl. When Holmes receives the news of Ilse's death, the same theme is heard, no longer an expression of unfulfilled love but of love irretrievably lost.

Music is also capable of forging ethnic and national connections. In the pre–civil rights era, blacks were stereotyped both dramatically and musically. When they appeared on the screen, the original sound-track often ceased, and a spiritual was heard, presumably because it was more fitting. Even in such a brilliant film as *The Little Foxes*, blacks were given this kind of musical treatment, which not only equated them with their music but also perpetuated the misguided image of the Southern blacks as passive. Music, whether it wishes to or not, equates, and a moviegoer's earliest associations are equations: "Deep River" = blacks; *The International* = Soviet Union; a few gongs = the Mysterious East; "*Deutschland über Alles*" = Nazi Germany; a tarantella (or "O Sole Mio") = Italy, etc. Although only the slightest references were made to the title character's being Jewish in *Mr. Skeffington* (Vincent Sherman, 1944), a leitmotif that was vaguely based on traditional Jewish melodies left no doubt about it.

During World War II, movie music programmed its audiences to patriotism. People not only saw flag-wavers; they also heard Old Glory hymned on the soundtrack. Planes streamed across the sky to the accompaniment of "Wild Blue Yonder," which also doubled as death music for the marines who went off to be executed by the Japanese at the end of *The Purple Heart* (Lewis Milestone, 1944). To evoke American values, Frank Capra frequently incorporated typical American songs like "Red River Valley" and "Buffalo Gals" into his films.

Using classical music that was written centuries previous is a special case, since it is music not composed for a specific film. Yet the media have made extensive use of classical music. When radio was a mass medium in the 1930s and 1940s, listeners were exposed to classical music without many ever knowing it. Rossini's *William Tell* Overture ushered in *The Lone Ranger*; Sibelius's "Valse Triste" introduced *I Love a Mystery*; Prokofiev's March from *Love for Three Oranges* was the theme of *The FBI in Peace and War*; the second movement of César Franck's Symphony in D Minor heralded the opening of *Quiet, Please*. Thus, associations were created between the radio programs and their introductions, which were the equivalents of musical signatures.

Movies used classical music in the same way. Before many moviegoers even knew what Rachmaninoff's Second Piano Concerto was, they had heard it as background music in *Brief Encounter* (David Lean, 1946). In fact, for people who know the film, the concerto has such indelible associations that it never fails to evoke a dingy railroad station where two married people, on the verge of committing adultery, choose to say good-bye and never meet again.

Thus, the Rachmaninoff Second Piano Concerto took on associations of extramarital love, and was used for that purpose in *September Affair* (William Dieterle, 1950) where it forms the background for a story of adultery. Like any venerable device, the Rachmaninoff Second ended up being parodied; still, parody attests to its associations. In *The Seven Year Itch*, in which a husband whose wife is away for the summer imagines himself seducing the woman upstairs, Billy Wilder parodies the tradition. In a fantasy sequence, the husband fancies himself a great pianist, sitting down at the piano and breaking into the concerto to impress his potential conquest.

Since classical music is added to a film rather than being composed for it, it may already have produced certain associations within us; the film may either reinforce those associations or change them, so that thereafter we associate the music only with the movie. Certainly it is difficult to disassociate the Rachmaninoff Second from *Brief Encounter* and, in a totally different way, from *The Seven Year Itch*. This should not be surprising since few *Lone Ranger* fans can separate the *William Tell* Overture from the program.

Wagner's music occupies a peculiar place in the American film. There has always been a connection between Wagner and the Third Reich. Wagner was Hitler's favorite composer; in fact, Hitler identified with Wagner's Siegfried and maintained that to understand National Socialism (Nazism) one must first understand Wagner. To Hollywood of the 1940s then, Wagner was the composer of the Third Reich: It is difficult to recall a movie in which Nazism was not orchestrated with a Wagnerian motif. In *Brute Force* (Jules Dassin, 1947), Munsey (Hume Cronyn), a prison captain, tortures an inmate to the Venusberg music from Wagner's *Tannhäuser*. Munsey performs a kind of ritual before the torture, strutting around with his chest sucked in beneath a skintight undershirt. That the captain is a homoerotic sadist is evident in the film, but Wagner's music, with its historical and erotic associations, characterizes him even further. Music unites his lust for power and his need for sex, neither of which he can achieve except through the degradation of others.

Although *Apocalypse, Now* (Francis Ford Coppola, 1979) deals with America's tragic involvement in Vietnam, the film uses Wagner in much the same way as it is used in *Brute Force:* as a symbol of sexual energy channeled into miltarism. The "Ride of the Valkyries" from *Die Walküre* orchestrates the parade of the helicopters sequence. Had the same music been used in a World War II movie in which bombs rained down on German cities, American audiences would have applauded; in the light of the Vietnam debacle, "The Ride of the Valkyries" is accusatory rather than nationalistic. It is as if Coppola is accusing America of emulating Nazi Germany by invoking the spirit of Wagner to justify war.

The use of Wagner's music in *Apocalypse, Now* is ironic. However, irony is not the easiest of devices to manipulate. It can backfire, becoming blatant, as happens in *The Night Porter* (Liliana Cavani, 1974) when two inmates in a Nazi concentration camp perform an act of sodomy to the music of Mozart's *The Magic Flute.* What should have been a devastating moment becomes merely appalling. Far more intel-

Karin (Harriet Andersson) in Through a Glass Darkly *(Ingmar Bergman, 1961) as she discovers her father is using her schizophrenia for his novel. At that moment the haunting opening of Bach's Suite No. 2 in D Minor for violincello is heard. (Courtesy MOMA/FSA and Janus Films)*

ligent is Ingmar Bergman's use of Bach in *Through a Glass Darkly* (1961) when a schizophrenic daughter discovers her father is using her sickness as material for a novel. The nobility of the music points up the father's ignoble intentions.

In some films, classical music constitutes the entire subtext. It is not just a question of repeating motifs, but of using music—either one work or several works—from beginning to end. What happens to music in *A Clockwork Orange* (Stanley Kubrick, 1971) is what has happened to society. The social order gives way as thugs and disenchanted youths, leather boys and loafers become the citizens of the future. There is a corresponding degeneration of music; it becomes estranged from art, perverted, capable of producing effects its composers never intended.

One of the most innocent songs ever written is "Singin' in the Rain," which brings to mind Gene Kelly sloshing around without missing a tap in the classic 1952 musical of the same name. It is hardly the kind of song we would associate with violence, yet in *A Clockwork Orange* Alex does a soft shoe to it while brutalizing a writer and his wife.

Rimsky-Korsakov's *Scheherazade* is an exotic piece of music, lush and sensuous, the kind associated with a veiled courtesan on a chaise lounge upholstered in leopard skin. Yet this is the music heard when Alex imagines himself as a Roman centurion lashing Christ on his way to Calvary. *Scheherazade* is one of the most pleasurable compositions ever written, as Alex would be the first to admit. But the pleasure we receive from it is clearly not his.

Alex is also a lover of Beethoven's Ninth Symphony with its ringing affirmation of humanity in the last movement. Alex knows that such sublime music can only be the result of intense suffering. While Alex listens to it, on one occasion masturbating to it, Kubrick cuts to various shots of Christ, as Alex associates Christ with suffering and suffering with music. Therefore, the sublimity of the music inspires the hearer to make others suffer. "Preposterous!" we say; or, if this is so, how can the love of music be the mark of an cultivated person? It would be better to raze the concert halls and ban recordings. But in Alex's world, where good and evil have lost their meaning as moral terms, music has no value except the value put on it. In such a society it makes no difference whether one meditates to Beethoven's music or masturbates to it. Yet Alex is not alone in misusing the classics; his elders have discovered an equally perverted use for the Beethoven Ninth. During his rehabilitation, Alex is forced to watch Nazi films while the last movement of the Ninth is played electronically.

While *A Clockwork Orange* draws on the works of several composers for its musical associations, *Moonstruck* draws on one: Puccini's opera, *La Bohème*. In *La Bohème*, Mimi meets Rodolpho and within minutes they are pouring out their love in a soaring duet. In *Moonstruck*, Loretta (Cher) no sooner meets her fiance's brother than he whisks her off to bed to the music of *La Bohème*, his favorite opera. Later, he takes her to the Metropolitan Opera House to see it.

Moonstruck celebrates the passion that brings men and women together, using opera as a point of departure, where the characters experience such powerful emotions that they cannot express them except through song.

A film has an outer and an inner world, a text and a subtext or, if you prefer, a narrative and an "infra-narrative." Beneath the text woven by the filmmaker's creativity and technology is the subtext with its network of associations and implications that, when understood, broaden our knowledge of the film. Because what lies beneath the surface is usually more intriguing than what lies above it, one may be tempted to proceed to the subtext before the text is understood. However, as in literature, a work's symbolic level cannot be appreciated before its literal level is clear; so in film, the narrative must be grasped before it can be transcended. Only then are we free to seek out the associations—mythic, historical, iconic, musical—that provide access to the film's inner world.

NOTES

[1]W. Y. Tindall, *James Joyce* (New York: Grove Press, 1960), 102.

[2]As quoted in W. Y. Tindall, *A Reader's Guide to James Joyce* (New York: Noonday Press, 1959), 129.

[3]Parker Tyler, *Magic and Myth of the Movies* (New York: Simon & Schuster, 1970), xviii.

[4]Parker Tyler, *The Hollywood Hallucination* (New York: Simon & Schuster, 1970), 230.

[5] Donald Richie, *George Stevens: An American Romantic* (New York: Museum of Modern Art, 1970), 62.

[6]Michael T. Marsden, "Savior in the Saddle: The Sagebrush Testament," in *Focus on the Western*, ed. Jack Nachbar (Englewood Cliffs, N.J.: Prentice-Hall, 1974), p. 97.

[7]André Bazin, "The Evolution of the Western," in *What Is Cinema?*, Vol. 2, trans. Hugh Gray (Berkeley: University of California Press, 1971), 152.

[8]Pauline Kael, "Introduction," *Bernardo Bertolucci's* Last Tango in Paris: *The Screenplay* (New York: Dell, 1973), p. 17.

[9]For the various prohibitions with which the filmmaker had to contend, see Benjamin B. Hampton, *History of the American Film Industry* (New York: Dover, 1970), 300–02.

6
The Film Director

If film is a collaborative effort, no one person should get the credit for a particular movie. Yet it is standard practice to speak, for example, of "John Ford's *Stagecoach*," "Frank Capra's *It's a Wonderful Life*," and "Alfred Hitchcock's *Psycho*," The practice of prefacing the title with the director's name is an outgrowth of *auteurism*—a theory of filmmaking in which the director is considered the primary creative force behind a film—whose impact is still seen in the way the *New York Times* lists film revivals: the director's name precedes the film title much as an author's name precedes a book title. Certain film critics (e.g., Andrew Sarris, David Denby) still designate films this way, while most film texts and film histories place the director's name in a parenthesis along with the release date. In either case, the director is singled out for special consideration in a way that the screenwriter or the cinematographer is not.

Directors are also honored with retrospectives and are subjects of books and articles even though they may have made movies from scripts written by others. Why is it, then, that we speak of John Ford's *Stagecoach* and not Dudley Nichols's *Stagecoach* if *Stagecoach* could not have been made without Dudley Nichols's script? The answer to that question involves an understanding of *auteurism*.

AUTEURISM
The Beginnings of *Auteurism*

During the German occupation of France in World War II the French were denied American movies, but after the war was over, they began to rediscover the greatness of the American cinema. The movies Americans often took for granted, the French took seriously. André Bazin wrote appreciatively of William Wyler and Orson Welles; Jean-Luc Godard saw more in the B movies of Monogram studios than the American kids did who saw them as the second half of double bills at their neighborhood theaters.* The rediscovery of American films by the French led to a reconsideration of the director as artist. What impressed the French was the fact that Hollywood directors could be—and frequently were—handed a screenplay, a cast, and a crew (none of which they had personally selected) and still managed to leave the stamp of their personality on the films.

In 1951 André Bazin and Jacques Doniol-Valcroze began publication of *Cahiers du Cinéma*, a journal that evolved into a critical forum for young film enthusiasts (Jean-Luc Godard, François Truffaut, Eric Rohmer, Claude Chabrol, and others) who expressed themselves in its pages and later went on to become directors. *Cahiers du Cinéma* had the reputation of a maverick; it was often pretentious and erratic in its preference of one director over another. Still, whatever one may think of the journal and the eccentric taste of its writers (e.g., Luc Moullet, who found in films such as Edgar G. Ulmer's *Bluebeard* the theme of the loneliness of humanity without God), it moved directors from the background to the foreground, establishing them as creators instead of studio orderlies.

For the first three years of its existence, *Cahiers du Cinéma* had no real editorial policy; in 1954 Truffaut provided it with one in his famous essay, "Une certaine tendance du cinéma français," which attacked classic French cinema for preferring literary scripts to shooting scripts, adaptations to original screenplays, studio sets to actual locations, and a team of specialists to a single *auteur*. Truffaut argued for

---

*Monogram made low-budget movies and "series pictures" (The Bowery Boys, Charlie Chan, Bomba the Jungle Boy, the Cisco Kid). The Monogram product was undistinguished except for an occasional melodrama like *Suspense* (Frank Tuttle, 1946).

"a cinema of auteurs"; and so it was that *auteur,* the French word for "author," entered the critical vocabulary of film.

Cahiers du Cinéma now had a policy: *la politique des auteurs,* "the policy of authors," which has had various interpretations, the most common one being that the journal was partial to certain directors (e.g., Orson Welles, Alfred Hitchcock, Jean Renoir) but indifferent to others (e.g., John Huston, René Clair, René Clément). Another interpretation was that *Cahiers du Cinéma's* favored directors were infallible and incapable of making bad films. Bazin corrected this misconception in 1957 when he pointed out what should have been obvious: A great director can make a dud, and a mediocre director can occasionally make a classic. Essentially, Bazin endorsed the policy of ranking directors, although he was often disturbed by the indiscriminate taste of some of his writers. Bazin summed up his position in the equation: author + subject = work.

That equation was adopted as the critical principle of Andrew Sarris, through whom *auteurism* entered America. In his essay "Notes on the *Auteur* Theory in 1962,"[1] Sarris defended the ranking of directors as an extension of a policy that has always prevailed in the arts. We rank Shakespeare over Ben Jonson, Beethoven over Brahms, Mozart's *Don Giovanni* over Beethoven's *Fidelio.* It was inevitable that Sarris would establish a ranking order of his own. In *The American Cinema,* he divided American directors into eleven categories, including the "Pantheon" (Charles Chaplin, John Ford, D. W. Griffith, Howard Hawks, Alfred Hitchcock, Orson Welles, etc.); "The Far Side of Paradise" (Robert Aldrich, Frank Capra, Samuel Fuller, Vincente Minnelli, etc.); "Expressive Esoterica" (Tay Garnett, Arthur Penn, Edgar G. Ulmer, etc.); and "Less Than Meets the Eye" (John Huston, Elia Kazan, William Wyler). Despite the historical importance of *The American Cinema,* it is the kind of book that requires periodic revision. The current critical estimate of Huston and Wyler, for example, suggests there is more to each of them than met Sarris's eye.

Sarris reduced the *auteur* theory, which is how *la politique des auteurs* came to be known in America, to three principles. (1) An *auteur* is technically competent. (2) An *auteur* has a personality that manifests itself in recurring stylistic traits that become his or her signature. (3) An *auteur's* films exhibit a tension between the *auteur's* personality and his or her material—that is, there are aspects of an auteur's personality that will seep into the films, aspects that may not be readily discernible but may come out when a number of the *auteur's* films are studied and analyzed. Thus, Hitchcock's ambivalence toward women, especially blondes, is not immediately evident; yet after analyzing such films as *The Thirty-nine Steps, Saboteur, Psycho,* and *The Birds*, we see that while blondes held a certain fascination for him, he often subjected them to various forms of degradation—being handcuffed to a man, being slashed to death in a shower, having their faces pecked by attacking birds.

On the basis of Sarris's criteria, it is possible to consider certain directors—admittedly, few—as *auteurs* or surrogate authors of their films. However, film is not the only medium in which *auteurism* is practiced; forms of *auteurism* exist in all the performing arts. A ballet lover may refer to Nureyev's *Romeo and Juliet* as opposed to another dancer's, emphasizing not Prokofiev's score, but its interpreter. A theatergoer who remembers Richard Burton's Hamlet is remembering not the play but the interpretation of the play by a certain actor. Plays are also sometimes designated in terms of the acting companies that produced them. Thus, one theatergoer might ask another, "Did you see the Abbey's *Juno and the Paycock?*," meaning not Sean O'Casey's play but its production by Dublin's Abbey Theatre. A symphony orchestra provides a good analogy with film. If the brass section is mediocre, if the woodwinds fail to come in on time, if the horns sound flat, the conductor shoulders the blame. Critics constantly berate the conductor who "led a sluggish performace of Franck's Symphony in D Minor" or "who failed to elevate the orchestra to the heights the music demanded." When Leonard Bernstein conducts a Mahler symphony, it is no longer Mahler's symphony but Bernstein's. Bernstein takes Mahler's work and, ideally, realizes the composer's intentions and communicates them to the orchestra. If Bernstein succeeds, he is praised; if not, he is criticized. Similarly, if a director is successful at blending the elements that make up a film into an organic whole that realizes the script's intent, the director is commended; if not, the director is criticized for being unable to achieve the necessary integration.

However, just as not every conductor is a Leonard Bernstein, so not every director is an Alfred Hitchcock. Hitchcock then clearly fulfills the criteria of the *auteur*: when we designate *Psycho* as Hitchcock's *Psycho*, we mean that Hitchcock has been successful at integrating the efforts of the writer, the cast, and the crew into a reflection of his vision of the material.

The Debate over *Auteurism*

Even though some film scholars agree that there is such a thing as an Alfred Hitchcock film and thus, that there are Hitchcockian elements in the films of others, many would argue against *auteurism* as a general theory of film on the following grounds:

1. The genesis of a film is often too complex to be attributed to a single person. Some films, in fact, are the result of a producer's conception rather than a director's. Victor Fleming is credited as the director of *Gone with the Wind* (although George Cukor and Sam Wood also had a hand in the direction), yet the film was the brain child of the producer David O. Selznick; if anything, then, it might be called a David O. Selznick film. The disaster films, *The Poseidon Adventure* (1972) and *The Towering Inferno* (1975), are associated with the producer, Irwin Allen, not the directors, Ronald Neame and John Guillermin, respectively. Although Val Lewton never directed a single film, he left his mark on everything he produced at RKO (*Cat People, I Walked with a Zombie, The Curse of the Cat People*, etc.). Thus, we think of *Cat People* primarily as a Val Lewton film and only secondarily as Jacques Tourneur's.

If there is a similarity between *Poltergeist* (1982) and *E.T.*, it is because Steven Spielberg, who directed *E.T.*, coauthored and produced *Poltergeist* (although he did not direct it). Directed by Tobe Hooper, *Poltergeist* bears the Spielberg signature and is imbued with the same childlike innocence that characterizes *E.T.* If *Batteries Not Included* (1987), in which aliens come to the aid of tenants whom a greedy developer is pressuring into moving, sounds like Spielberg again, it is because it is a Spielberg production, even though it was directed by Matthew Robbins.

2. Certain films, especially those made when the studios were at their peak (1930–50), bear the stamp of their studios more than that of any individual and thus are thought of as "MGM movies" or "Warner Bros. movies." *Singin' in the Rain* is clearly an MGM musical, specifically a musical that came from Arthur Freed's production unit at MGM. If one compares *Singin' in the Rain* with other Arthur Freed productions (e.g, *Easter Parade* [Charles Walters, 1948], *On the Town, An American in Paris*), one recognizes a common feature: the integration of the musical numbers with the action. While *Singin' in the Rain* was directed by Stanley Donen and Gene Kelly, film historians consider it an MGM musical or an Arthur Freed production, not a Donen-Kelly film.

3. Films involving special effects illustrate the limitations of *auteurism*. When David Denby and Terrence Rafferty reviewed *Who Framed Roger Rabbit* in *New York Magazine* and the *New Yorker*, respectively, each referred to "Robert Zemeckis's *Who Framed Roger Rabbit*." Yet Zemeckis was not responsible for the animation; animation director Richard Williams and his staff were. Furthermore, the film was a cooperative venture between Disney's Touchstone Pictures and Steven Spielberg's Amblin Entertainment. Spielberg is not the kind of producer who remains aloof from a production; in fact, he had certain

ideas on how the cartoon figures should look. (For example, he wanted Roger's mouth to resemble Thumper's in *Bambi*.) The answer to the question, "Who framed Roger Rabbit?" is easy. The answer to the question "Who made *Who Framed Roger Rabbit*?" is not.

Therefore, not every director can be considered an *auteur;* comparatively few, in fact, can be. These are the directors whose films are studied in film courses and who are the subjects of books, articles, and retrospectives. Such directors need not write their own script: Woody Allen does, John Ford never did. There have also been directors who worked within the studio system and still made films that were their own. William Wyler made some of his best movies for Samuel Goldwyn—for example, *Dead End* (1937), *Wuthering Heights* (1939). Shortly before Pearl Harbor, he was hired by MGM to direct *Mrs. Miniver,* which dramatizes the impact of World War II on a typical British family. In one sense *Mrs. Miniver* is an MGM film; it was made by a specific studio because its head, Louis B. Mayer, believed in the "family film." However, Wyler was able to make it a William Wyler film. Wyler always tried to encompass as much as he could in a single shot, thus minimizing cutting. *Mrs. Miniver* is filled with such shots—Kay Miniver sitting on the bed while her husband is off in the dressing room; the Minivers seated at the dinner table while their son is seen talking on the telephone in the alcove; Kay standing on the bridge with the station master below her and water behind him.

Directors who are taught, written about, and honored with retrospectives and tributes have the following in common: their work illustrates the collaborative nature of the medium because they frequently work with the same personnel (writer, stars, cinematographer, editor) in a succession of films; they repeat the same themes but in different genres; they allude to their earlier films; and they borrow from the films of others.

COLLABORATION

From a director's standpoint, collaboration can take several forms, the most common of which are as follows:

1. Collaboration between a director and a screenwriter. Sometimes a director will have the same screenwriter for several movies; undoubtedly, those movies will have certain features in common. Joan Harrison worked on the scripts for Hitchcock's *Rebecca, Foreign Correspondent, Suspicion,* and *Saboteur,* in all of which the wrong person was under suspicion. Billy Wilder and Charles Brackett coauthored the scripts for three Mitchell Leisen films: *Midnight; Arise, My Love* (1940); and *Hold Back the Dawn* (1941). All three entail some form of deception.

2. Collaboration between a director and a cinematographer. Historically, the most famous was that between D. W. Griffith and Billy Bitzer. Other creative director-cinematographer collaborations have been between Eric von Stroheim and William Daniels (*Blind Husbands,* 1918; *Foolish Wives,* 1921; *Greed,* 1924; *The Merry Widow,* 1925); Josef von Sternberg and Lee Garmes (*Morocco,* 1930; *Dishonored,* 1931; *Shanghai Express,* 1932); Ingmar Bergman and Gunnar Fischer (*Smiles of a Summer Night,* 1955; *The Seventh Seal,* 1957; *Wild Strawberries*).

3. Collaboration between a director and a composer. Examples of this type include John Ford and Alfred Newman (*Arrowsmith,* 1931; *The Hurricane,* 1937; *The Grapes of Wrath; How Green Was My Valley*); Federico Fellini and Nino Rota (*La Strada,* 1954; *La Dolce Vita,* 1960; *8½,* 1963; *Juliet of the Spirits*); and Hitchcock and Bernard Herrmann (*The Wrong Man; Vertigo,* 1958; *Psycho; Marnie*).

4. Collaboration between a director and actor(s). Notable here are John Huston and Humphrey Bogart (*The Maltese Falcon,* 1941; *Across the Pacific,* 1942; *Treasure of the Sierra Madre,* 1948; *Key Largo,* 1948; *The African Queen,* 1951); von Sternberg and Marlene Dietrich (*The Blue Angel,* 1930; *Morocco; Dishonored; Shanghai Express; Blonde Venus,* 1932); Truffaut and Jean-Pierre Léaud (*The 400 Blows; Stolen Kisses; Bed and Board; Day for Night*); Bergman and Liv Ullmann (*Persona,* 1966; *Hour of the Wolf,* 1968; *The Shame,* 1968; *A Passion of Anna,* 1969; *Scenes from a Marriage,* 1973; *Face to Face,* 1976); Billy Wilder and Jack Lemmon (*Some Like It Hot,* 1959; *The Apartment,* 1960; *Irma la Douce,* 1963; *The Fortune Cookie,* 1966; *Avanti!,* 1972; *The Front Page,* 1974; *Buddy,Buddy,* 1981); John Ford's stock company (Ward Bond, Victor McLaglen, John Wayne, Maureen O'Hara, Ben Johnson); Woody Allen and Mia Farrow (*Broadway Danny Rose,* 1984; *The Purple Rose of Cairo; Hannah and Her Sisters; Radio Days; September,* 1988; *Another Woman,* 1988).

5. Collaboration between a director and an editor. Examples here include Arthur Penn and Dede Allen in *Bonnie and Clyde, Alice's Restaurant* (1969), *Little Big Man* (1970), *Night Moves* (1975), *The Missouri Breaks* (1976); Woody Allen and Ralph Rosenblum in *Take the Money and Run* (1969), *Bananas* (1971), *Sleeper* (1973), *Love and Death* (1975), *Annie Hall* (1977), *Interiors* (1978).

6. Collaboration between a director and a producer. The best examples of this are Wyler and Samuel Goldwyn (*Dead End; Wuthering Heights; The Westerner,* 1940; *The Little Foxes,* 1941); Jacques Tourneur, Robert Wise, and Mark Robson, who directed the films Val Lewton produced for RKO; and William Dieterle and Hal B. Wallis at Paramount (*The Searching Wind,* 1946; *The Accused,* 1948; *Rope of Sand,* 1949; *Paid in Full,* 1950; *Dark City,* 1950; *Red Mountain,* 1951).

7. Collaboration between a director and a studio. Frank Capra

Billy Wilder with Jack Lemmon, who appeared in six Wilder films. (Courtesy the Margaret Herrick Library of the Academy of Motion Picture Arts and Sciences)

and Columbia, Ernst Lubitsch and Paramount, Preston Sturges and Paramount, Raoul Walsh and Warner Bros., Vincente Minnelli and MGM all collaborated in film efforts. Paramount was synonymous with sophisticated comedy during the 1930s and 1940s, and it was directors such as Lubitsch, Sturges, and, to a lesser extent, Leisen who gave Paramount that reputation. Lubitsch could do more with the closing of a bedroom door than most directors could if they kept it open.

VARIETY

A great director need not have a wide repertoire of themes; there is a difference between a varied body of work and a varied number of themes. The same themes can recur within that body of work, repeated or modified to fit the particular type of film. Billy Wilder's films, for example, center about two major themes: deception and its various forms (disguise, fraud, masquerade), and the impact of one social or political order on another (capitalism/communism, rich/poor, youth/age). Even the scripts that he and Charles Brackett wrote before he started directing reflect these themes: the female commissar of *Ninotchka* (Ernst Lubitsch, 1939) who comes in contact with capitalism and falls under its spell; the chorus girl of *Midnight* who impersonates a countess; the female reporter of *Arise, My Love* who rescues a man from prison by pretending to be his wife; the gigolo of *Hold Back the Dawn* who feigns love to become an American citizen; the college professors of *Ball of Fire* (Howard Hawks, 1941) who find themselves learning slang from a stripper.

Then there are the films that Wilder directed himself:

The Major and the Minor (1942): A woman disguises herself as a twelve-year-old to purchase a train ticket at half fare.

A career woman (Ginger Rogers) disguised as a twelve-year-old to ride half-fare to her home in Iowa in The Major and the Minor *(Billy Wilder, 1942). (Courtesy Margaret Herrick Library of the Academy of Motion Picture Arts and Sciences)*

Five Graves to Cairo (1943): A British officer impersonates a lame servant in a desert hotel.

Double Indemnity: An insurance agent tricks a man into signing a policy with a double-indemnity clause; the agent and the client's wife conspire to kill her husband to collect on the policy; the agent briefly poses as her husband on board a train.

The Lost Weekend (1945): An alcoholic is continually devising ways of concealing his bottle.

The Emperor Waltz (1948): An Austrian countess meets an American phonograph salesman (a "two orders" film).

A Foreign Affair (1948): An army captain in postwar Berlin tries to conceal his relationship with a night club singer from a visiting congresswoman.

Sunset Boulevard: An aging silent star deludes herself into thinking she can make a comeback as Salome; her kept man conceals his status from his girlfriend.

The Big Carnival (*Ace in the Hole*): A reporter deceives the victim of a cave-in into believing he is the victim's friend.

Stalag 17 (1953): An informer infiltrates a POW camp.

Sabrina (1954): A rich young man courts a chauffeur's daughter (a "two orders" film).

The Seven Year Itch: A summer bachelor plays at being Don Juan.

The Spirit of St. Louis (1957): This is an atypical Wilder film, which depicts Lindbergh's flight across the Atlantic.

Love in the Afternoon (1957): A May-December romance develops between an older man and young woman whose father is a detective.

Witness for the Prosecution (1957): A woman tricks a noted barrister into thinking she is a cockney.

Some Like It Hot: Two musicians dress up as women; a millionaire (male) falls in love with one of the disguised men.

The Apartment: A woman with a checkered past masquerades as a virgin.

One, Two, Three: An American Coca-Cola executive and a radical East Berliner clash ideologically.

Irma la Douce: To keep a prostitute from sharing her favors with others, her lover resorts to disguise.

Kiss Me, Stupid (1964): A single female bartender impersonates a married woman; a wife allows her songwriter-husband to think his song succeeded on its own merits although it became a hit because she spent the night with a famous pop singer.

The Fortune Cookie: A TV cameraman is persuaded by his brother-in-law to sue for nonexistent injuries.

The Private Life of Sherlock Holmes: Deception is implicit in any treatment of Holmes.

Avanti!: A married man and the daughter of his late father's mistress arrange to have a yearly rendezvous in Italy, repeating the deception their parents (his father, her mother) had practiced until their death.

The Front Page: An editor will do anything to get his star reporter back, even resorting to a lie that also happens to be one of the most famous curtain lines in the American theater: "The son of a bitch stole my watch."

Fedora (1979): A facially disfigured international movie star passes her daughter off as herself.

Buddy, Buddy: to prevent himself from being unmasked, a hit man attempts to save a television censor from suicide.

Variety is achieved more through genre than theme. While deception/disguise is a recurring theme in Wilder's films, it is a theme that manifests itself in farce (*The Major and the Minor, Some Like It Hot, Irma la Douce*), romantic comedy (*Sabrina, Love in the Afternoon, Avanti!*), political comedy (*A Foreign Affair; One, Two, Three*), social comedy (*The Apartment, The Fortune Cookie*), social realism (*The Lost Weekend, The Big Carnival*), espionage and wartime melodrama (*Five Graves to Cairo,*

Stalag 17), courtroom melodrama (*Witness for the Prosecution*), gothic melodrama (*Sunset Boulevard*), period pieces (*The Emperor Waltz, The Private Life of Sherlock Holmes*), film noir (*Double Indemnity*).

The films themselves derive from several sources: novels (*The Lost Weekend, Love in the Afternoon*), plays that are either adaptations (*Stalag 17, Sabrina, The Seven Year Itch, Avanti!*) or almost total rewrites with little of the original left intact (*One, Two, Three; Irma la Douce; Kiss Me, Stupid*), original scripts (*The Emperor Waltz, Sunset Boulevard, The Big Carnival, The Apartment, The Fortune Cookie, The Private Life of Sherlock Holmes*); and other films (*Buddy, Buddy*).

REPETITION

Repetition need not be a detractor for a great director, who will repeat favorite themes not only in different kinds of movies but also as motifs within those movies. Thus, the deception/disguise theme recurs as various motifs in Wilder's movies:

1. adultery (*Double Indemnity, The Seven Year Itch, Love in the Afternoon, The Apartment, Kiss Me, Stupid, Avanti!*)
2. insurance fraud (*Double Indemnity, The Fortune Cookie*)
3. women physically altering their appearance (*The Major and the Minor, Witness for the Prosecution, Fedora*)
4. men physically altering their appearance (*Some Like It Hot, Irma la Douce*)
5. a woman deceiving the man she loves (*The Major and the Minor, The Apartment, Kiss Me, Stupid, The Private Life of Sherlock Holmes*)
6. a man deceiving the woman he loves (*The Seven Year Itch, Some Like It Hot, Irma la Douce*)
7. men deceiving each other (*Five Graves to Cairo, Double Indemnity, The Lost Weekend, The Big Carnival, The Fortune Cookie, Buddy, Buddy*)

Similarly in the "two orders" films the following motifs can be found:

1. distinctions of class (countess/commoner in *The Emperor Waltz;* common girl/privileged boy in *Sabrina*)
2. distinctions of age (young woman/older man in *Sabrina, Love in the Afternoon, The Apartment,* and *Avanti!;* young man/older woman in *A Foreign Affair* and *Sunset Boulevard*)
3. distinctions based on war (allies/enemy in *Five Graves to Cairo* and *Stalag 17;* victor/vanquished in *A Foreign Affair*)
4. distinctions of ideology (capitalism vs. communism in *One, Two, Three;* freedom vs. fascism in *A Foreign Affair*)

Marlene Dietrich as Erika, a cabaret singer in post-World War II Berlin, and John Lund as her lover Captain John Pringle in A Foreign Affair *(Billy Wilder, 1948). (Copyright ® by Paramount Pictures, Courtesy of MCA Publishing Rights, a Division of MCA Incorporated)*

Marlene Dietrich as Christine, who meets her future husband Leonard Vole (Tyrone Power) in a Hamburg nightclub at the end of World War II in Witness for the Prosecution *(Billy Wilder, 1957). Wilder added the nightclub scene, which does not appear in the Agatha Christie play, to show how the Voles met. He is clearly repeating a plot device from* A Foreign Affair—*the smoke-filled basement nightclub where Pringle came to hear Erika sing. (Courtesy MOMA/FSA and United Artists)*

QUOTATIONS

Directors repeat themes, character types, characters' names, or visual motifs. Sometimes repetition is unconscious, but generally it is because directors assume the audience will interpret the repetition as a sign of continuity—not a lack of imagination. Thus, in casting John Wayne to play a character called Lt. Col. Kirby Yorke in *Rio Grande,* John Ford might have hoped the audience remembered that two years earlier Wayne played Captain Kirby Yorke in *Fort Apache.*

The opening credits of Ford's *The Man Who Shot Liberty Valance* are on broken crosses intended to evoke the opening credits of *My Darling Clementine,* which appeared on sign posts. In the years between *Clementine* (1946) and *Liberty Valance* (1962), Ford's vision of the West had changed from romantic to realistic. The stars of *Liberty Valance,* John Wayne and James Stewart, play roles that would have been more suitable for them twenty years earlier; hence the broken crosses to suggest that time has left its mark on both director and stars. In *Empire of the Sun,* when a boy is reunited with his parents amid a vast throng of people, Steven Spielberg repeats a composition from a movie he made ten years earlier, *Close Encounters of the Third Kind,* in which a man and a woman pushed their way through a crowd to find each other.

Hitchcock often quotes himself, but his quotes are rarely verbatim. Rowley's fall from the cathedral tower in *Foreign Correspondent* prefigures similar falls, but in different contexts, in *Saboteur, Vertigo,* and *North by Northwest.* The airplane wing that becomes a life raft when a plane crashes in the Atlantic in *Foreign Correspondent* yields to the real thing in *Lifeboat* (1944), a totally different kind of film that uses a more conventional form of survival at sea.

In *Family Plot* (1976) when Blanche (Barbara Harris) and her boyfriend are driving along in a car whose brakes give way, she grabs hold of his necktie, almost strangling him with it. Her action recalls the necktie murders in *Frenzy* (1972). Similarly, when the pair are on a deserted stretch of highway, we almost expect the crops duster from *North by Northwest* to materialize and spray them with bullets. And to avoid detection when in a jewel thief's home, the boyfriend takes the same precautions Marnie took in Hitchcock's film of that name: he removes his shoes and tiptoes past the kitchen. In fact, we wait for him to drop a shoe, as Marnie did. These are old tricks, but they appear in a new setting.

In *Witness for the Prosecution,* Billy Wilder added a flashback to show how Leonard Vole (Tyrone Power) met his wife Christine (Marlene Dietrich) in a Hamburg nightclub at the end of World War II. Dietrich had the same profession in Wilder's *A Foreign Affair.* Wilder must have had the earlier film in mind when he decided to open up the Agatha Christie play a bit by putting in the flashback. Yet *Witness for the Prosecution* is not *A Foreign Affair* any more than *Family Plot* is *Frenzy* or *North by Northwest.*

BORROWINGS

Wilder regarded Ernst Lubitsch as the unrivaled master of sub-tlety. Whenever someone in a Lubitsch film closed a door, drew the curtains, or shut the blinds, one always wondered, "Did they or didn't they?" In *Double Indemnity,* the camera dollies back from Phyllis and Neff as they sit snugly on the sofa in his apartment. "We just sat there," Neff's voice is heard saying. We no more believe him than we believe the Lubitsch heroine who closes the door of her lover's bed-room and in the next shot awakens in her own.

As a rule, great directors are not troubled by the question of originality because they see themselves as part of a tradition. Al-though they respect the past, they neither worship it blindly nor lean on it for support; instead, they view it as a legacy on which they can draw. The Odessa Steps massacre in *Potemkin* left its mark on many filmmakers, including Busby Berkeley, who paid it a curious tribute in the "Lullaby of Broadway" sequence in *Gold Diggers of 1935.* Hitchcock did the same in *Foreign Correspondent,* in which an assassination was staged on the steps of an Amsterdam conference hall. Brian De Palma paid homage to the Odessa Steps sequence in *The Untouchables* (1987), which even includes the careening baby carriage. Most directors are flattered when viewers evidence an awareness of a borrowing or a quote; in fact, in some cases, viewers are expected to notice the bor-rowings so they can appreciate the director's integration of past and present.

AN INTERVIEW WITH BILLY WILDER

Billy Wilder is an ideal director for study. He directed his first film in 1942; his last in 1981. He is also a true *auteur,* inasmuch as he coauthored the scripts of all the films he directed. Since *The Big Carni-val,* with a few minor exceptions, he produced his own films. Wilder has been the subject of retrospectives, doctoral dissertations, books, articles, and television tributes by the American Film Institute and the Film Society of Lincoln Center. He is a six-time Academy Award win-ner: twice for direction (*The Lost Weekend, The Apartment*); three times for best screenplay (*The Lost Weekend, Sunset Boulevard,** *The Apart-ment*); once for best picture (*The Apartment*).

D. H. Lawrence said, "Trust the tale, not the teller." Yet the teller

---

*The *Sunset Boulevard* Oscar was technically for story and screenplay.

HOMAGE TO THE ODESSA STEPS SEQUENCE
The Odessa Steps massacre in Potemkin. *(Courtesy MOMA/FSA and Janus Films)*

can have much to tell, especially one who writes, directs, and produces one's own tales. Wilder told much during an interview on June 11, 1976:

DICK: The critics who like to minimize the director's role will say that all a director did during the Studio Years was carry out the studio's policy. They would not speak of "Billy Wilder's films" but of "Billy Wilder's Paramount period [1942–54]." When you were at Paramount, were you conscious of turning out a Paramount product?
WILDER: Never, not even in the early days when I did not have script approval and the right of final cut. If this were true, then Lubitsch's pictures, Sturges's pictures, Mitchell Leisen's pictures, my pictures—in fact, all the pictures made during those interesting days at Paramount—would have been the same. They were not. Once Paramount and I agreed on the subject of the movie, the cast, and the budget, and once they realized I would not have censorship problems (and in those days we had to smuggle things past the censors)—once all of this was settled—I was on my own. I wrote the film the way I wanted to, I cut it the way I wanted to. Of course, I may have to give a little when a picture is sold to television and make a cut here or a cut there. But even when I was beginning and did not have the ultimate control I have now, never for a moment did I think of myself as a foreman on the Paramount lot.

You see, the *auteur* theory, in emphasizing the director who takes

Hitchcock's homage to the Odessa Steps in Foreign Correspondent *(1940). (Courtesy MOMA/FSA and United Artists)*

over someone else's script, has little to say about a director like myself who writes, directs, and produces his own. Although I do not belong to the producers' guild (I do, of course, belong to the screenwriters' and directors'), I think I can evaluate the *auteur* theory better than most critics. Being the writer, director, and producer of a picture, naturally I am the *auteur*.

DICK: Then you do not accept the *auteur* theory?

WILDER: I accept it only up to a point. The *auteur* theory does not emphasize the script. I deeply believe in the script and in the director's getting the maximum out of it. A mediocre director with a great script will still come out on top, but a brilliant director with a poor script will inevitably fail.

DICK: Is it easier to become a director now than it was when you began in the industry?

WILDER: It is much easier now because television provides you with a training ground. In the past there was no training ground except shorts and a series like MGM's "Crime Does Not Pay" where Fred Zinnemann got his chance. Otherwise, unless you worked on Broadway or had important connections, or unless powerful stars requested

Billy Wilder on the set. (Courtesy Billy Wilder)

you, it was extraordinarily difficult to get a break. You might think that by becoming an assistant director you would stand a good chance of becoming a director. Yet the assistant director had the least chance of ever becoming a director. The dialogue coach, the cameraman, the actor, the actor's relatives stood a better chance of becoming directors.

Of course, all that has changed with television. With the enormous demands it makes on one's time, you can learn by being on the set long enough. And with highly trained crews at his disposal, a director can't make a total ass of himself.

Directing is not Chinese glass blowing or the art of making Inca gold statuettes. It can be learned and it can be learned quickly if you have a flair and a style for it. It is also an exhausting profession and one that has a finality about it. In the theater, you can rewrite a play during its tryout; in my profession you can't say, "let's reshoot the film" if you don't like it. The sets are down, the actors are in Yugoslavia, and plans have already been made for the picture's distribution.
DICK: Do you have an image in your mind of what the film will look like in its final form?
WILDER: Even though you lose yourself in the picture while you're making it, ultimately it is back to what it was when you did the script, which is proof that the script was good and that the choice of material

was good. If a film doesn't work—and often it doesn't—it was because I was telling the wrong story or an uninteresting story; I was telling a story that didn't have a chance no matter how brilliantly I might do it. Maybe I chose the right story at the time but it turned out to be the wrong time for the picture. If I write an article for a magazine, it will be published a few weeks later. The mood of the public has not changed, and there is still interest in the subject. But my picture will not see the light of day for two years when the mood of the public may be entirely different.

DICK: Are your scripts complete when you begin shooting?

WILDER: They are complete in the sense that I know how the film will end; but I want to see how the first two acts will play before I go on to the third. They are not complete in the sense that every line has been written down. I am always open to suggestions. If a scene does not play well in rehearsal, I will change it. If an actor has a good idea or even an electrician, I can add it. But you must first have something to add it to.

DICK: Is there any truth to the story that Shirley MacLaine and Jack Lemmon were handed their dialogue for the final scene of *The Apartment* on the last day of shooting?

WILDER: Could be. But we knew very well how it would end: the boy would get what he wanted, give it up, and get the girl. Maybe the actual words were typed the night before. But we did not improvise; I never depend upon improvisation.

DICK: Your films evidence an incredible range—romantic comedy, farce, social drama, *film noir*, melodrama, biography. Did you aim for such diversity?

WILDER: I know a man who always wears a dark blue suit when he goes out in the evening. It's rather boring, you know. Why not a striped suit once in a while? Sometimes I wonder if I did the wrong thing by experimenting so much. Hitchcock, whom I greatly admire, stayed with one kind of picture. When people go to a Hitchcock movie, they know what to expect. Certain directors develop a style, refine it, and never give it up; they never leave their own neighborhood. I ventured out and tested myself. But whatever kind of film I make, there is always one quality I aim for: a complete simplicity of style, a total lack of pretentiousness; there is not one phony setup in a Billy Wilder picture.

Also making films is a matter of mood. Now I am in the mood for something a bit serious, so I will do *Fedora*,* which may remind some of *Sunset Boulevard* at least in texture, but it will be quite different.

*Fedora, the first novella in Thomas Tryon's *Crowned Heads* (1976), is about a movie star who does not seem to age.

DICK: It's well known that you write your scripts with a collaborator, but do you ever look upon your editor as a collaborator? I ask because Doane Harrison edited several of your early films.

WILDER: Doane Harrison was an old-time cutter, going back to the time when George Stevens was a cameraman for Hal Roach. He was very close to me when I made *The Major and the Minor*; he taught me a great deal because until then I had spent my life behind the typewriter, not behind the camera.**

DICK: How did you get behind the camera?

WILDER: How I became a director is very interesting. When I was writing scripts with Charles Brackett, we were never allowed on the set when the film was being shot. First of all, directors didn't want writers on the set; and second, we were off writing another picture. I decided to assert myself because I wanted some control over my scripts. So I started to raise hell, and Paramount finally let me direct a picture. Actually it was no big deal because at that time Paramount was turning out fifty pictures a year. They said, "Let Wilder make a picture and then he'll go back to writing." Everyone expected me to make something "fancy-schmancy." Yet I made something commercial. I brought back the most salable hunk of celluloid I could—*The Major and the Minor*.

You see, unless you control your film, you are also at the mercy of actors. It's easy for an actor to argue with a director who is weak or who isn't convinced about the script. I remember Mr. Brackett and I were working on the script for *Hold Back the Dawn*, which Mitchell Leisen was directing. We had written a very fine scene for Charles Boyer, who was playing an immigrant waiting for his visa to come through. Unkempt and unshaven, Boyer waits in a cheap Mexican hotel. Well, to show the kind of hotel it was and to suggest something about the character Boyer was playing, we included a scene where Boyer makes some cynical remarks to a cockroach climbing up the wall. I assumed the scene would be shot as we had written it. A short time later, I ran into Boyer and asked him how he liked the scene with the cockroach. He said, "We cut that scene." I was shocked. "Why was it cut?" I asked. "How can I talk to a cockroach when the cockroach can't answer?" was Boyer's reply. I was so angry I told Brackett, "If that son of a bitch ain't talking to a cockroach, he ain't talking to anybody." We hadn't finished the script yet, so we pared Boyer's remaining scenes down to the bare minimum.

**Wilder began his career as a reporter in his native Vienna. It was in Berlin in the late 1920s that he turned to screenwriting.

DICK: Is it important for a director to be able to write?

WILDER: It is more important for a director to be able to read. Many directors do not understand the script and they don't have the nerve to say so. But they go ahead and shoot it, regardless.

DICK: There is a great deal of confusion today about the role of the editor. Did an editor ever change the form of any of your films?

WILDER: No, I learned to shoot with utmost economy so there is not much an editor can do. I cut the film in the camera. I do not protect myself by shooting the scene eighteen different ways: it exhausts the actors, and the words begin to lose their meaning. I will go over the rushes with the editor and we will discuss them. I may say to him, "I need an additional shot here," but that is the extent of it. The worst that can ever happen is that I must alter my film or add to it.

DICK: Yet some directors rely very heavily on their editors. Dede Allen has become a legend in her own lifetime. Some critics have even said that she bails out Arthur Penn time and time again with her editing.

WILDER: I would not say she "bailed" him out; it was more like the way Maxwell E. Perkins helped Thomas Wolfe reorganize his novels for publication. If an editor bails a director out, it is because he shot crap. Dede Allen fully deserves the billing she gets because she makes the picture better. It is the same with Verna Fields who cut *Jaws*. She has the knack of knowing which frames to cut and how fast to cut them.

DICK: You edited *The Front Page* in four days, yet Terrence Malick supposedly spent a year editing *Badlands*.

WILDER: That is because he shot a great deal of film; I don't. I also work with very expensive actors, so I do not have the time. In the case of *Badlands*, you have a crew of very talented beginners who do everything themselves, including moving the camera from place to place. They can go out and shoot where they like; and by the time the sheriff comes around to ask if they have permission, they've gone. I must apply for permission and wait until I get it. If I pick up a chair on the set, I have the unions to contend with. Our approaches are totally different; it's like commedia dell'arte as opposed to the legitimate theater.

DICK: Did you go into producing because you wanted more control over your pictures?

WILDER: Yes, and also because there were so few creative producers. Look at this ad in *The Hollywood Reporter*:

Silver Streak

A MARTIN RANSOHOFF-FRANK YABLANS PRODUCTION

AN ARTHUR HILLER FILM

A MILLER-MILKIS-COLIN HIGGINS PICTURE

This is insane. What happens is that somebody buys a property or two people buy it, so their names must appear. If the star becomes involved in the production, then his name appears. The director says it must read "A Bill Friedkin Film" or "Bill Friedkin's Film." Then the schleppers and the hangers-on get into the act. The vanity game is enormous. Even in the theater, it's "a such-and-such production in conjunction with so-and-so." Ultimately, when it's all over, it's Josh Logan's *South Pacific*.

The true producers like Thalberg, Selznick, and Goldwyn would add to a picture and enrich it; they were there when you needed them for important decisions. When the picture was finished, they got the maximum exposure for it and arranged for it to be shown in the best theaters.

DICK: Since *Ace in the Hole*, you produced all of your films except for *The Spirit of St. Louis* which Leland Hayward produced and *Witness for the Prosecution* which Arthur Hornblow, Jr., produced. Was there any reason for your not producing these yourself?

WILDER: Leland Hayward was my agent when I first came to Hollywood, so there was no real problem with his producing my film. Arthur Hornblow produced my very first film, *The Major and the Minor*. He was also a friend of Marlene Dietrich who wanted the part in *Witness for the Prosecution* and asked me to direct so she would be sure to get it.

DICK: How do you feel about directors like Peter Bogdanovich who pay homage to the work of other directors?

WILDER: You know what we call Bogdanovich? "The Frank Gorshin of directors." He is so steeped in film history that it is difficult for him to find a style of his own.

DICK: Have you ever paid homage to other directors?

WILDER: If I did, it was unconscious.

DICK: What about Lubitsch? There is a Lubitsch quality about *The Emperor Waltz* and *The Private Life of Sherlock Holmes*.

WILDER: I advise everyone to stay away from Lubitsch; he cannot be imitated. I did not set out to make a Lubitsch film in either case. And incidentally, you picked two of my failures. *Holmes* didn't make a ripple. I even had to cut two episodes out of it.

DICK: It is a film that is gaining in popularity. It was recently revived as part of a Sherlock Holmes Film Festival in New York and those who have never seen it before were quite taken with it.

WILDER: It was, I think, the lushest of the Holmesiana and truest to the period.

DICK: Most of your films employ some form of disguise or deception. Would you agree?

WILDER: Some, but not all. Not in *Double Indemnity*.

DICK: It does appear in the way Neff gets Dietrichson to sign the insurance policy.

WILDER: Yes, I see what you mean. Well, there is a lot of that in *Fedora*, I assure you.

DICK: You said before that you were not conscious of any Lubitsch influence. Were you aware of the fact that in both *Five Graves to Cairo* and *The Private Life of Sherlock Holmes* you used a parasol as part of the plot and as a symbol of femininity? In *Five Graves*, Bramble places it on Mouche's grave; in *Holmes*, Ilse uses her parasol to send messages as well as to say good-by to Holmes.

WILDER: No, I was not conscious of *Five Graves to Cairo* when I was making *Holmes*. In *Five Graves to Cairo* the parasol was a sentimental touch; there are no flowers in Tobruk so he brings her a parasol. In *Holmes* Ilse used it for Morse code. And a parasol is so photographable, you know. There is something exquisite about it, especially when it is opened out against the sun. I am very fond of the proper use of props and I like to make them part of the script. In *The Apartment* I used a broken compact mirror as the means of identifying Shirley MacLaine as the girl Fred MacMurray had been bringing to Jack Lemmon's apartment.

DICK: Were you influenced by the book of *Genesis* when you were writing *Ace in the Hole*? I am thinking of the continual emphasis on serpents, the desert as a kind of Eden that turns into a carnival, the rescue operations that take six days.

WILDER: That is a very interesting theory. You see, personally my mind doesn't go that way. And if it did, I couldn't admit it.

DICK: Several years ago you made this statement: "We're just like the guys in Detroit, putting out cars, no matter what anyone thinks we are." This is rather strange coming from a man who is the subject of retrospectives, books, articles, and Ph.D. dissertations. Do you still believe it?

WILDER: I did not mean what people think. How do you interpret it?

DICK: That directors are assembly-line workers.

WILDER: What I meant was that it takes tremendous artistry to put something into an assembly-line product so it will not have that mass-produced look. If someone is writing a poem or composing a symphony, he is doing it himself and on his own time. In our business we are playing for enormous chips supplied by other people. They give me the chips to gamble with, and I in turn am responsible to them. In this kind of situation it takes more artistry to produce something of value—sometimes to sneak in something of value—than it does when you are given as much money as you want, with no strings attached, and told to go to Salzburg and bring back a two-hour film. If I get behind schedule or exceed my budget, or if I indulge myself, after a couple of such pictures I would be flat on my ass. I would not get a chance to work again. I must do something that is hopefully superior, hopefully innovative, and at the same time it must be profitable. I personally believe that anything worthwhile ultimately finds some kind of audience. If somebody says, "This is the goddamnedest greatest picture ever made but no one went to see it," then it is not the goddamnedest greatest picture ever made.

I assure you, I have as many sleepless nights and as many ulcers as the truest of artists. But I have an added burden. If a painter buys a canvas for a couple of dollars and does not like what he has painted on it, he can throw it away. My canvas costs $4 million; if I don't like it, it can't be thrown in the fire. It's going to be shown, reviewed, maybe even play to empty houses. In the theater the producers can decide to close a show on the road and not bring it to Broadway. I can't. I've always said that the trouble with making pictures is that we can't try out in New Haven. If a picture is bad, it will come back to haunt you on the late late show. Its stench will endure forever.

AN INTERVIEW WITH ALAN ALDA

In the movie industry, when a writer becomes a director, he or she is said to have "gone hyphenate." To use movie jargon, Alan Alda has gone double hyphenate: while Billy Wilder is a writer-director, Alan Alda is an actor-writer-director. Alda's career began on Broadway with major roles in *Purlie Victorious* (1961), *The Owl and the Pussycat* (1964), and *The Apple Tree* (1966), which won him a Tony nomination. When Hollywood beckoned, he began the second phrase of his career, appearing in such films as *The Paper Lion* (1968), *The Extraordinary Seaman* (1969), and *The Mephisto Waltz* (1971). When the success of the movie *M*A*S*H* led to the television spinoff in 1972, Alda's already varied career took another direction. As Hawkeye Pierce, Alda became one of television's most popular stars, a favorite among college students, and one of America's most sought after commencement speakers.

What contributed to *M*A*S*H*'s longevity on television was an emphasis on human relationhips that was quite different from the absurdist and often cruel humor of the film. The series underwent a transition from sitcom to human comedy, and Alda played a significant role in the change, first by writing some scripts and then by directing them. By the mid-1970s, Alan Alda was a former Broadway star turned Hollywood actor who was then acting in, writing for, and

Alan Alda on the set of Sweet Liberty *(1986). (Copyright ® Universal Pictures, a Division of Universal City Studios, Inc. Courtesy MCA Publishing Rights, a division of MCA.)*

directing some of the episodes of one of the most popular programs in the history of American television.

By the end of the 1970s, Alda had experience writing for television but had not yet written for the movies. The next stage in an already thriving career was to write his first screenplay, the highly successful *Seduction of Joe Tynan* (1979). However, Alda did not direct *Joe Tynan*. Thus, there was one more height to scale: directing an original screenplay in which he would also appear. He achieved that goal with *The Four Seasons* (1981), which proved to be a critical and a commercial success. Two other films followed which he directed and in which he appeared: *Sweet Liberty* and *A New Life*.

Alda's views on filmmaking are as valuable as Wilder's because, as a actor-writer-director, he understands the needs of three of the key members of the industry.

The following interview took place in Alan Alda's office at Martin Bregman Productions in New York on June 13, 1988:

DICK: Some writers become writer-directors, or "go hyphenate" as *The Hollywood Reporter* would say, because they want greater control over their scripts. Was that true of yourself?

ALDA: No. I think I became a director because I thought I would love directing; it turned out I did. When I started to direct, I was on *M*A*S*H*. I was eager to direct anything, whether I had written it or not. It would be a chance for me to work under the best conditions, where there were people who could catch me if I fell. Yet I can understand what writers go through when someone else directs their work. Unless a writer and a director are in close touch and are lucky enough to see things the same way, the result may be quite different from what the writer intended. My first *M*A*S*H* script had a very good director, yet the scenes didn't have the point I though they should; in some cases, the actors didn't get the jokes, and I just had to sit by helplessly. It's a good idea, in general, for writers to direct their own material, and for directors to write their own material—but only if the directors can write. Unfortunately, there are a lot of directors who can't write but who keep doing it. I have great respect for the written word; that comes from having been an actor first. Since I come from the stage, I would never think of changing a word in a script. And I wouldn't do it as a director, either, unless I consulted with the writer.

DICK: You don't believe, then, that the director is the author of the film, as the *auteurists* do?

ALDA: I have a problem with the *auteur* theory; the author of the film is the author of the script. I could understand if, by the *auteur* theory, you mean that the director contributes something to the film. If the director tells the story successfully through the lens, he or she has contributed something the writer couldn't because the writer told the story on paper. John Wayne contributed something unique to his movies, but you don't call a John Wayne film "A Film by John Wayne." After Marshall Brickman finished directing *Simon*, he was asked if he would like it called "A Film by Marshall Brickman." He replied, "No. It's a film by Kodak."

DICK: An editor also contributes something to the film. How much latitude did you allow William Reynolds, who edited *A New Life*?

ALDA: Since we had to get the film out in a hurry, I gave Bill a lot of latitude. As I watched the rushes, I made detailed notes about preferred takes and angles, and how I saw the scenes fitting together. I didn't sit over his shoulder. Actually, I liked the idea of loosening my grip a little. I think I was able to do it on *A New Life* because I was more secure. I told Bill what my ideas were; if he had a better idea or if he felt one of mine wouldn't work, he would tell me and we would proceed from there. I find that editing is like script writing. You refine what you've written and get other ideas. All the cuts have some of my ideas and some of Bill's.

DICK: Did you allow Michael Economou the same latitude on *Sweet Liberty*?

ALDA: No, and I'm sorry I didn't. The fact that I allowed Bill Reynolds more on *A New Life* represents growth on my part. Whether you have tight reins or loose reins, it all boils down to communication. No matter to whom you are talking—the editor, the cinematographer, the actors—you have to be able to describe what you see. You just can't say to someone, "This is the script; you do it." That's not the job of the director or even the producer; that's what the studio does. The studio says, "I like that script; I like that cast. Here's the money. Go make the movie." From that point on, everybody must start communicating with each other. The producer has to say to the writer or the writer-director, "Do you really need that scene? Do you think these lines are clear?" The producer does not do this to achieve the producer's vision, but the writer-director's. And the writer-director tries to get everyone else to realize the vision he or she has.

DICK: Do you have an image in your mind of how the completed film will look?

ALDA: For *Sweet Liberty* I storyboarded. There was a picture of every scene in the movie. An artist I was working with came back with a storyboard that represented the way he thought everything should look. I said, "Thank you, but that's not the point. They hired me to tell the story as I see it." A storyboard conveys a great deal of information; it's supposed to be a visualization of the script as well as an aid to all the departments involved in shooting the script. What I did was draw stick figures and discuss them with the artist so that he could draw the figures properly. Eighty percent of the film looked like the storyboard.

DICK: What about your relationship with the cinematographer?

ALDA: We would discuss what kind of lens, dolly, or crane we would use. I also had a specific shot list. That part of the job was over before I even got to the set, so we didn't have to waste half the morning wondering whether we would shoot this way or that.

DICK: Did you storyboard *A New Life* also?

ALDA: Not as much, since I didn't have an artist. I just drew stick figures.

DICK: Is storyboarding difficult if you're verbally oriented?

ALDA: No. I think in images. I usually start writing when I have a visual image. Novelists do the same, you know. John Fowles had an image of a woman at the end of a jetty, so he wrote *The French Lieutenant's Woman* to find out who she was.

DICK: Did *The Four Seasons* begin with an image?

ALDA: That film came from several sources. First there was Vivaldi's *Four Seasons*. Wouldn't it be interesting, I thought, to make a movie showing the same people on vacation in each of the four seasons? The musical form would dictate the form of the film. Then I had another image: I envisioned three couples getting out of a car. I kept seeing them getting out the car and walking somewhere, and doing it over and over. It was like seeing a film in a loop. It haunted me. I had to find out more about those people.

DICK: In the film, the car is a very unobtrusive way of starting the film.

ALDA: Yes, in the credits sequence, one couple picks up the other couples, so that by the time the actual film begins, you know who everyone is.

DICK: Did you plan to have *The Four Seasons* begin in spring and end in winter?

ALDA: It wasn't until after I had written the film that I realized the whole spring-winter progression corresponds to the four stages of friendship. There's a springtime to a friendship when nobody can do any wrong. In the glare of the summer sun, you see your friends as they are. In autumn, illusions fall away like leaves. In winter, you're "frozen" with your friends; you have to accept them as they are or find new ones who won't be a burden to you because you don't know who they are yet. I think this is what happens in the movie, but didn't understand it until I had written it.

DICK: Do you have a complete script at the time of shooting?

ALDA: Absolutely. I have to because I haven't got time to rewrite on the set. That's why I go through about a dozen drafts and am overly particular about what I want to shoot.

DICK: When you were in the theatre, you did improvisations as a member of the Second City [a Chicago-based improvisational group]. As a film director, do you improvise?

ALDA: If you mean during filming, very little. I may do a bit in scenes where several people are talking at once. In *A New Life*, I improvised a scene in which the character I play is arguing with a lawyer at a party. We did one episode on M*A*S*H that was an improvisation. It was called "The Interview" and consisted of someone interviewing the M*A*S*H unit as if for a documentary. Yet it was a highly controlled situation. We rehearsed for weeks by improvising into a tape recorder; the tape was edited by the writer, Larry Gelbart, who added some of his own jokes, and that became the script. But there were also last-minute questions that we had never heard before; that part of the episode was spot improvisation. There's a great difference between a spot improvisation and a script that has been derived from improvisation. When you're improvising, and it works, it is very hard to repeat the improvisation and get the same effect. It may take fifteen or twenty attempts for it to come to life again. If you're working from a script that came out of an improvisation, it's the same as working from any other script. Filmmakers should know that. There is a difference between improvising during rehearsal and improvising whole scenes in front of the camera. But a lot of young directors who have had little experience working with actors think that improvising is a technique that gets the actors to be more truthful. There's a danger that the values of the script will get lost in the improvisation and that nothing will replace them. Also, if the actors improvise in rehearsal, and something exciting happens, the director assumes that if the actors repeat these lines, the excitement will recur. The director doesn't realize that it wasn't the lines that were exciting, but the creative impulse that inspired them. The first time the impulse passes through the actor is thrilling, yet nobody knows the source of that impulse, and to rediscover it takes several more improvisations. You may or may not get it again.

Directors who feel it's the actors' fault if they improvise brilliantly during rehearsal but can't repeat what they did in front of the camera don't realize it has nothing to do with the actors; it's the way the brain works. Something mysterious might happen during an improvisation that brings the scene to life. What happens is that connections are made and impulses arise that should be explored. The actual words that are said are not nearly so important. Improvisation is useful to find out who the characters are and what their pasts have been, and I've used improvisation during rehearsals for that purpose. Once the actors understand their characters—and improvisation is one way of accomplishing this—they may be able to play the scene with more life. Improvisation also gets the actors to feel comfortable with one another and with the director.

DICK: To make them comfortable, would you change dialogue with which they are uncomfortable?

ALDA: That's a traditional way of making actors comfortable. I do it with caution, but I do it. What is important is what the script is communicating and the truth of the relationships expressed in the script. If changing a word here or there doesn't vitiate that truth, then I'm happy to. But if it wrecks the story, makes it illogical, or denies something truthful about the character, I explain to the actor that I can't. It's the director's job to keep the whole picture in mind. Every department may have a wonderful idea, but it might not fit into the whole scheme of the film. However, an actor may be uncomfortable with a line of dialogue, and after a few days of rehearsal, when the context is clear, the actor is not only comfortable with it but would kill to keep it. Improvisation and changing dialogue are only two ways to make actors feel comfortable. The most important thing is for the actors and director to eat dinner together.

DICK: Is that why food is so important in your films?

ALDA: That happens to be the way I am, the way I run my life. A lot of it is devoted to eating.

DICK: Do you believe in eating with the cast because the meal has always been a symbol of unity?

ALDA: That reason never occurred to me. I think that food is an image that comes to me a lot because I like food.

DICK: Since you've written both teleplays and screenplays, is the basic difference between them that the half-hour teleplay is in two acts, while screenplays are not divided into acts?

ALDA: Actually, a screenplay is divided into acts even though the acts may not be indicated as such in the script. Most screenwriters talk in terms of act one, act two, act three. You introduce the situation, complicate it, and resolve it. George S. Kaufman used to say that in act one you get the hero up a tree; in act two you throw stones at him; and in act three you get him down. All stories are like that. You introduce the characters in the beginning along with their goals; then there are complications in their achieving those goals because everyone wants something different. Thus, it won't be so easy for the main character to get what he or she wants because of the obstacles thrown in the way by the other characters. It's what Aristotle in the *Poetics* called "dramatic action"—action in the sense of the characters' trying to achieve something. The resolution is the final working out of their either getting what they want or not, or getting not what they want but what they need. In that case, they experience growth, sometimes tragic growth. They may no longer be able to do what they did in the past, but they have achieved insight. This may not always be apparent in what I write because I stress relationships and internal struggles, but I'm always thinking in terms of action—dramatic action, not car chases. Someone's always trying to accomplish something, even if it's just to understand something.

It's almost impossible for the actor to act unless the character wants something. That doesn't mean the character has to want something external; it can be internal. It may be peace, tranquillity, or self-knowledge. And a director must know what that goal is. Otherwise, if it's a play, you'll just hear a lot of talking, or if it's a film, you'll see a lot of fancy shots.

The writer must give the character a goal, even if it's a limited goal, as it is in *Rocky*. Rocky only wants to go the distance; the fact that he doesn't win is unimportant. He achieved his goal: he went the distance. An actor shouldn't be allowed to go on stage or before the camera if he or she is playing a character without an objective or a goal. If the character doesn't want something, turn the lights out and save electricity. The scene will go dark anyway if the actors are only feeding each other lines so the author can get the exposition out. Shakespeare knew how to handle exposition: in the opening scene of *Othello*, we learn who Iago, Roderigo, Desdemona, and Othello are without one expository line being uttered. Everything comes out of the action. The actors have not been forced to say to themselves, "Well, we just have to say these lines so the audience will get what's going on."

DICK: You have been speaking of writing, acting, and directing as if they were part of the same process.

ALDA: They are. The actors need an objective that the writer provides and that the director achieves. It's painful for me to see writers and actors at odds with each other. The writers complain, "Those damn actors aren't saying my words right." The actors complain, "Who wrote this crap?" They both work the same way, yet they'll never know it unless they sit down and talk with each other. If actors don't speak the dialogue properly, it's probably because they don't understand it. Writers blame actors because they fail to realize an actor must go through a certain process to absorb in a few days what it may have taken the writer two years to create. Being an actor, a writer, and a director, I understand all three.

DICK: If you had to describe the role of a director to someone outside the industry, how would you do it?

ALDA: A director gives direction; it's inherent in the job title. However, it's not a good idea to direct actors down to the last little movement of their pinkie. It's not only a bad idea; it can also wreck the picture. You must find out how you can communicate your vision to each department so that everyone will give you what you want from their heart. What's the point of hiring an art director if you say, "This is what I want—nothing else." All the art director will do is draw the set you designed. You want to be able to get design ideas from the art director, but those ideas must serve *your* vision. All of this is done through communication. You must be able to describe what you see to everyone, and you should be able to compare what you see happening with what you see can happen. But you must understand the specific capabilities of each department, what each can and cannot do. Actors cannot work from results. The first mistake a director makes is to say to an actor, "Be mysterious." That's a result; mystery is what you experience when the actor is doing the scene right. The director has to find out, with the actor, what the actor is trying to accomplish in terms of the action that will make the actor appear mysterious. You have to find the cause that produces the result. Actors can play a state; they can depict a state of drunkenness, for example. But once an actor establishes that the character is drunk, the actor has to achieve something, even if it's trying not to appear drunk.

DICK: It is possible to learn directing?

ALDA: The only way to learn anything is with a mentor who will go through the steps with you, then let you do it and go over your mistakes. It's like the way my wife and I taught our children to wash their hands. We would put all of our hands under the faucet and rub them back and forth with the soap. Then the kids got the feeling. It's the way an artist guides the hand of a pupil or the way the tennis instructor puts his or her hand over yours on the racket. But you still have to make the shots; still, it's better if you've had hands-on experience with someone who is experienced.

NOTES

[1]The article appeared in *Film Culture* (Winter 1962–63); it is reprinted in Gerald Mast and Marshall Cohen, eds., *Film Theory and Criticism: Introductory Readings*, 3rd ed. (New York: Oxford University Press, 1985), 527–40.

7
Film and Literature

"Film has nothing to do with literature," claimed Ingmar Bergman.[1] Like so many dogmatic statements, this one is only partially true. Certainly a student can analyze a film as he or she analyzes a work of literature—in terms of form, rhythm, imagery, and symbolism. A student does not, however, analyze it in the same way as a novel or a poem. A film's rhythm is often determined by the length of the strips of celluloid, not by variations of stressed and unstressed syllables, as in poetry, or by the alternation of description and dialogue, as in fiction. A film's imagery is visual. Imagery in literature is verbal.

A film's form is an inheritance partly from literary narrative and partly from the visual arts. Literature by its very nature implies something written. A screenplay may be literature in the root meaning of the word, but it is rarely literature in the traditional sense (e.g., a literary classic). While many films are works of cinematic art, most screenplays do not qualify as works of literary art. Some film classics, in fact, were even shot without a script (e.g, *The Birth of a Nation*, *Intolerance*).

While there are some published screenplays that read like literature (Ingmar Bergman's and Woody Allen's, for example), they are not always an accurate representation of the films. In his screenplay of *Through a Glass Darkly*, Bergman has Martin cut his finger; then Martin's wife Karin sucks the blood. From the way the incident is described in the screenplay, the reader would assume Karin is behaving bizarrely. What happens on the screen is far less extreme: Martin cuts his finger, and Karin kisses it. When Bergman wrote the screenplay, he may have envisioned the scene differently. When he directed the scene, he apparently decided to make it less dramatic. Since a screenplay is prefilmic, it may contain material that never reached the screen. Likewise, the film on which it is based may include scenes that were not in the screenplay.

A screenplay can be compared to an opera libretto. While there are many great operas, there are few libretti that deserve to be studied as literature. Just as a libretto needs music, a screenplay needs visualization.

The screenplay is a *play,* although a play intended for the screen; thus, it will have some characteristics of drama. The screenplay is also a form of narrative; thus, it shares certain techniques with fiction. Like a play, a film can have a prologue and an epilogue. In film, however, the prologue can be either in the form of print (an opening title) or it can be dramatized in the form of a credits or precredits sequence. Opening title and credits/precredits sequence are, of course, terms peculiar to film; even so, they are prologues—in one case, a prologue involving the written word; in the other, a prologue involving visualized action.

Film also uses many techniques found in literature, the most famous of which is the flashback.

THE FLASHBACK

In ancient epic, the flashback was a way of incorporating material into the narrative that could not be added in any other way. For example, since the *Odyssey* begins ten years after the end of the Trojan War, the only way Homer could describe Odysseus' postwar adventures was by providing him with an occasion—a banquet—where he could recount them. In the *Aeneid,* Virgil, imitating Homer, likewise has Aeneas summarize at a banquet his seven years abroad.

The flashback has always been a favorite device of authors who start in the middle of an action (Milton's *Paradise Lost*) or whose narratives work from the present back to the past where the explanation for the present resides (Thomas Pynchon's *V*). In a film, a flashback can be introduced by a slow fade out/fade in, a dissolve, a wipe, or a quick cut, and serves three basic functions: (1) to furnish information that is otherwise unavailable; (2) to dramatize a past event even at the moment it is being narrated because the event cries out for visualization;

(3) to connect past and present when none of the characters is knowledgeable enough to do so.

The first function is self-explanatory, but the others require some
examples. In Tennessee Williams's one-act play *Suddenly, Last Summer*,
Catherine Holly, in one of the great monologues of the American
stage, describes the death of her cousin Sebastian, whose flesh was
devoured by the boys he had tried to debauch. The 1960 film version,
directed by Joseph L. Mankiewicz, includes the monologue, which is
also partly dramatized as it is being delivered. The monologue demands some visualization, and Mankiewicz provides it.

Although most flashbacks are memory flashbacks, not all are.
Sometimes we are not within the consciousness of a character but, so
to speak, of the camera. *Godfather II* is a flashback film, but not a
memory film; no one in the movie is remembering the past because no
one knows enough about it. The purpose of the sequel to *The Godfather* is to integrate the lives of Vito Corleone and his son Michael.
Since Vito is dead when the film opens, director Francis Ford Coppola
could not crosscut the lives of father and son. Instead, he told Vito's
story in flashback. *Godfather II* illustrates the impersonal flashback,
which is not the result of a reminiscence, an inquest, or an investigation, but rather the integration of the past with the present under the
supervision of a central omniscience that can be termed the *omniscient
camera* or the *omniscient filmmaker*. *Two for the Road* (Stanley Donen,
1967) also illustrates the impersonal flashback. The film crosscuts a
European trip a couple is making with incidents from previous trips.
Because of the subtle way past and present intertwine, we never ask if
it is the wife or the husband who is remembering. It is established at
the outset that it is the camera—the same camera that had apparently
accompanied them on their former jaunts.

While filmmakers have always been partial to the memory flashback, it is often poorly motivated. A character will say something
banal like "it seems only yesterday that . . ." and the present will fade
out and the past in. In the best memory flashbacks, an object pro-
vokes the reminiscence. In *Kitty Foyle* (Sam Wood, 1940), a glass paperweight with a girl on a sled inside it sets Kitty remembering; in *Penny
Serenade*, phonograph records trigger a woman's memories of her
marriage; in *Brute Force*, the picture of a woman on a calendar causes
four convicts to remember the women in their lives.

There is an unusual flashback in *The Searchers* involving a letter
that Martin has written to Laurie. At first it seems as if the letter is
being used to summarize what the audience will not be seeing. But
that is not the case. Some of what is in the letter has already been seen

(e.g., the incident of the Indian woman who attached herself to Martin), but most of its contents are dramatized as it is being read. Because the sequence is so long, John Ford obtains some variety by alternating between Martin's voice as he writes the letter and Laurie's as she reads it.

THE FLASHFORWARD

A device that enjoyed popularity with filmmakers beginning in the 1960s was the flashforward, in which some aspect of an event is shown before it occurs. The flashforward is a distant relative of the literary device called *dramatic foreshadowing*, wherein one incident presages another, or some indication is given that an event is going to happen before it actually does. But the true ancestor of the flashforward is a rhetorical device termed *prolepsis*, in which a speaker anticipates and answers an objection before an opponent has even put it forth.

Sometimes what seems to be a flashforward isn't one. During the course of *They Shoot Horses, Don't They?* (Sydney Pollack, 1969), the narrator (Michael Sarrazin) speaks directly to the camera—or is he speaking to someone we cannot see? We discover at the end that he is speaking to a judge, explaining why he shot Gloria (Jane Fonda) at her request. The reason why flashforwards succeed in *They Shoot Horses* is that from the audience's point of view they exist in the future, but from the narrator's they exist in the past. In retrospect, it becomes apparent that the entire film was a flashback told to a judge.

Because of their anticipatory force, proleptic devices can be dramatically effective. In *The Greatest Story Ever Told* (George Stevens, 1965), after Pilate delivers Jesus to be crucified, an off-camera voice is heard saying, "And he suffered under Pontius Pilate." It is a compelling moment in the film, for it elevates a historical event to an article of faith without waiting for the Apostles' Creed to be written.

The way in which the credits appear on the screen often has a foreshadowing character. In *Saboteur*, during the credits the shadow of the saboteur moves from the right of the frame into the center. Billy Wilder used the same technique in *Double Indemnity*; in that film the shadowy figure is on crutches, a prefiguration of the results of Dietrichson's accident, which will make murdering him a bit more complicated.

Sometimes a shot has the impact of a flashforward although it is really a comment on an earlier incident. Well after the midpoint of *The Story of Adele H.*, François Truffaut inserts a shot of Adele on the Isle of Guernsey, gloriously confident as she prepares to sail for Halifax to reclaim the affections of Lieutenant Pinson. Her voice is equally self-assured: "This incredible thing—that a young girl shall walk over the sea, from the Old into the New World, to join her lover—this, I shall accomplish." Obviously this is an Adele we have not seen before since the film begins with her arrival in Halifax. Truffaut inserts the shot where he does to mark the end of Adele's fruitless quest and the beginning of her descent into madness. If the shot had appeared at the opening, it would simply have been a prologue. Appearing where it does, it has the force of dramatic irony: Adele did make a journey from the Old World to the New, but it was also a journey from one form of neurotic behavior (obsession) to another (self-inflicted degradation). At the very end of the film, Truffaut repeats the shot, this time drained of its color and looking like a faded photograph. Adele's voyage is now just an item of memorabilia.

POINT OF VIEW

Like a work of literature, a film can be narrated in the first or the third person. A first-person film, one recounted by an "I" in the same way as Dickens's *Great Expectations* is recounted by Pip and Sartre's *Nausea* by Roquentin—that is, an "I" who begins speaking at the outset and continues right up to the end—is rare. (*Double Indemnity* comes close, with all but the very beginning and the very end narrated by Neff.) What generally happens in film is that a voice-over of the "I" is heard at the beginning and perhaps intermittently thereafter. The semidocumentary may seem to be an exception since it is first-person narration throughout; however, the narrator is not a character but a disembodied voice. When the voice intrudes periodically, it acts like a fade out, demarcating the film into narrative blocks.

Something similar happens in *Radio Days*, which is narrated by an adult who is only seen in the film as a child. If *Radio Days* has a distinctly literary quality and seems like a filmed short story, it is because continuous first-person narrative calls attention to itself as narrative. There is also a credibility problem if the "I" relates something to which it would not have had access. Despite the excellence of *Radio Days*, even Woody Allen has difficulty explaining how a grade school boy can know what he does.

A film need not use "I narration" to acheive other first-person effects that suggest the first person without the presence of the narrating "I": subjective camera and subjective sound. (We have already discussed these techniques in Chapter 3.) In subjective camera, the camera doubles as a character so that we are aware of both an "I" and an "eye," as in the slasher movies, when the camera looks in through the window from the outside. There the camera is both an "I" (the predator) and an "eye" (the predator's eye and, by extension, ours).

Thus, point of view in subjective camera is not that of an "it," but of an "I," a definite presence relating something to the viewer as an "I" would relate something to a "you." Subjective sound is similar: when a character hears something, the character is no longer a "he" or a "she" but an "I" telling "us" what he or she is thinking or hearing.

It is important to remember that voice-over narration does not necessarily mean a first-person film. Since the voice tends to come and go, one soon forgets there is a narrator. Far more important is to see how film emulates first-person narrative through subjective camera and subjective sound.

Omniscient Author

In fiction, the omniscient author tells the story in the third person, moving from place to place, time to time, and character to character, disclosing or concealing details at will.[2] The film equivalent, omniscient camera, is best seen in multiplot films or films that move back and forth in time. When the camera is omniscient, it behaves very much like an omniscient author. The camera in *Nashville* is omniscient. It can leave a freeway crack-up and move on to a hospital to look in on country singer Barbara Jean recovering from one of her breakdowns. It can abandon the Reese home for the local tavern, a nightclub for a smoker, a church for an automobile graveyard.

Omniscient authors can be intrusive if they pass judgment on what is seen, unintrusive if they suspend judgment. The camera can do likewise because omniscience does not mean impartiality. In *The Day of the Locust*, Homer Simpson (Donald Sutherland) is sitting in a wicker chair in the backyard of his Hollywood home. An orange drops from a bough with the sound of ripe fruit. In the yard above his, a woman looks down on this scene of otherworldly tranquillity. There is ripeness in her face, but it is the overripeness of rotting fruit. The camera has said nothing, but by moving from Homer to the woman, it makes its own comment on Hollywood as the earthly paradise for those who bask in the glow of an endless summer and those who decompose in it.

Instead of traveling back and forth among the characters, authors can select one of them as a "center of consciousness," to use Henry James's phrase or as a "reflector" through whose eyes readers will view the action. In film, the reflector method works well when the script involves a character trapped by his or her fantasies or victimized by some neurosis. In *The Lost Weekend*, Billy Wilder draws us into the consciousness of Don (Ray Milland), an alcoholic. Don becomes a genuine reflector; we share his experiences even when they are portrayed objectively, as they often are. Early in the film there is a scene in which Don is watching *La Traviata* and develops an uncontrollable urge to drink during the first-act "Drinking Song." Wilder cuts from Don to the stage where Violetta and Alfredo are toasting each other and back again to Don. Thus far the camera has been objective: what Don has been seeing on the stage is what everyone else in the audience has been seeing. But not everyone in the audience is an alcoholic; thus, Wilder allows the camera to turn subjective at this point as Don sees, superimposed against the stage, the checkroom where his raincoat is hanging, a bottle in one of the pockets. We clearly understand his craving and understand the effect the "Drinking Song" has had on him.

The Implied Author (Author's Second Self)

There is some fiction that is so impersonally written that it appears to be authorless. Hemingway's "The Killers" is often cited as the kind of story that seems to have been written by a vivisectionist rather than a novelist. In "The Killers" Hemingway obliterated his actual self and created a second self who mediates between Ernest Hemingway and the story that bears his name. Filmmakers can do likewise; they can suppress or mask their personal feelings so that they do not interfere with the film. This *implied author* method usually results in an impersonal movie because it does not encourage emotional involvement; thus, this kind of movie does not reach a high level of emotional intensity.

Barry Lyndon is such a film. First, it is Stanley Kubrick's *Barry Lyndon*, not William Makepeace Thackeray's; and it is Kubrick's film completely: He not only produced and directed it but he also wrote the screenplay. To say that Kubrick remains aloof from his characters is not the same as saying that he shuns them. The implied author approach is not emotional evasion; it is emotional noninvolvement. Kubrick was more interested in the characters as embodiments of their age than in the characters as human beings.

In adapting *Barry Lyndon* for the screen, Kubrick was dealing with a novel that was written in the nineteenth century but set in the eighteenth century. Thus, the tone had to be Victorian and the atmosphere neoclassical. Kubrick achieved an eighteenth-century air by framing scenes in the style of painters of that era—Watteau, Dayes, and Gainsborough—and by orchestrating them with selections from Bach, Handel, Vivaldi, and Mozart. He re-created a Victorian tone by using an off-camera narrator whose voice was fittingly snobbish.

The famous Barry Lyndon *candlelight. All the candlelight scenes were photographed with a special Zeiss lens and entirely with natural light. (Courtesy Warner Bros., Inc.)*

Seeing *Barry Lyndon* is like viewing a painting. A great painting draws a viewer toward it; but once face to face with it, the viewer instinctively walks backward to see it from a distance. Kubrick uses the same technique. He begins with a close-up; he then gracefully withdraws until he is satisfied with the distance he has put between the audience and the image. *Barry Lyndon* is like a tour of the world's great museums. The glow of candlelight is not the smoky haze it usually is in most films; specially created lenses give the candlelight in *Barry Lyndon* the look of melting gold. Light floods a window, not in neat spotlighting cones but in a burst of silver. To achieve such beauty, Kubrick had to sacrifice a certain amount of emotion.

FILM ADAPTATION

One common type of film is the adaptation of a novel, a story, or a play. The adaptation, however, occasions the greatest amount of criticism because the material has already appeared in another form which becomes the standard against which the film version is compared; hence, the often repeated charge, "Well, it wasn't the book (or the play)." There is only one answer to that charge: it wasn't intended to be. The adaptation is *a* version, not *the* version, since there can be several film versions of a particular novel or play. Which *Phantom of the Opera* is Gaston Leroux's novel *The Phantom of the Opera?* The 1925 version, the 1943 version, or the 1962 version?

Adaptation is not so simple as one might think. It is a given that the film version will differ from the original. Why else would a film-maker adapt a work for the screen, and why should audiences be expected to see the adaptation if they have read the book or seen the play? The adaptation must be different—but how different? The adaptation may preserve the essence of the original, even though it may alter plot details (perhaps even drastically), add or eliminate characters, and change the conclusion so that it is the opposite of what it was in the original.

Adaptations of Novels

The House of Seven Gables (Joe May, 1940)

The movie version of Nathaniel Hawthorne's *The House of the Seven Gables* (the movie's title drops the second *the*) is faithful to the spirit, but not the letter, of the novel. First, Hawthorne's narrative, which traces the fate of six generations of Pyncheons over two centuries, had to be considerably simplified. Second, relationships between the characters that might have been acceptable to nineteenth-century readers had to be changed for a 1940 movie audience. Third, any vagueness in the original had to be cleared up, especially in an era when movies were a mass medium and the fundamental rule was "show and tell."

That *The House of Seven Gables* (for which Lester Cole wrote the screenplay) is a version of Hawthorne's novel is evident from the way it begins: a book opens, presumably Hawthorne's novel, except that the words appearing on the screen are not Hawthorne's. Haw-thorne's novel begins, "Halfway down a bystreet of one of our New England towns stands a rusty wooden house . . ."—language too off-putting for a movie audience. The film's opening is more direct and accessible: "In the middle of the seventeenth century there lived Jaffrey Pyncheon." Such license was common: the film version of *Jane Eyre* also opens like a book about to be read, but the words that are seen are not Charlotte Bronte's. The opening sentence of the novel would be meaningless to anyone who had not read it: "There was no possibility of taking a walk that day." The movie's opening title goes right to the heart of the matter: "My name is Jane Eyre."

The screenwriter may take other liberties as well—including changing character relationships. In Hawthorne's novel, Clifford and Judge Pyncheon are cousins; Clifford and Hepzibah are brother and sister. A screenwriter, always taking the audience into consideration, must ask, "Is there any real drama in cousins' being rivals?" Certainly rivalry is more dramatic, and false allegations are more shocking, when brothers are involved. Thus, Cole made Clifford and Judge Pyncheon brothers. Therefore, Hepzibah and Clifford could no longer be brother and sister, so they became cousins—distant ones, so they could marry at the end. While this may seem a radical change, it is not entirely inappropriate. To a twentieth-century audience, the feelings Hawthorne's Hepzibah harbors for her brother seem midway between maternal and conjugal, but not especially sisterly. When Hepzibah and Clifford take their famous ride together in the novel, they seem like a couple in flight; when Clifford withdraws into himself, Hepzibah takes control, behaving like the proverbial all-suffering wife. (To a nineteenth-century audience, the nature of their relationship would have been more understandable because unmarried siblings often lived together throughout their adulthood).

The Pyncheons, except for Clifford, are corrupt. *Corruption*, however, is a general term, and a film must deal in specifics. The movie version specifies the type of corruption: slave trading. The slavery motif, once introduced, had to continue to the end; thus, the film's conclusion is different from the novel's, in which Judge Pyncheon dies like his ancestors—from a pulmonary hemorrhage. Hawthorne is vague about the circumstances, but the Judge's death seems to have been brought on by the sudden appearance of Clifford, looking more haunted than usual. A movie cannot afford to be vague. The Judge dies the Pyncheon death, but only after he is confronted by a mob of angry abolitionists whose funds he had appropriated to purchase the services of a slave runner. Once the Judge is dead, Clifford is free to marry Hepzibah, and the House of the Seven Gables is put up for sale.

In terms of Hollywood's approach to the classics, the film version of *The House of the Seven Gables* is a compromise between slavish fidelity to the original and total disregard for it. The film is the novel's essence distilled into a narrative form capable of being understood by a mass audience.

The Color Purple (Steven Spielberg, 1986)

Alice Walker's Pulitzer-Prize winning novel, *The Color Purple*, was not easy to adapt for the screen. On one level, it is a novel about written expression and the need to articulate feelings which, if they cannot be expressed orally, must be committed to paper, and, if they cannot be addressed to the right person, must be addressed to God. Clearly, it would be difficult to present this philosophy on the screen, yet the film repeats the exact words with which the novel opens: *"You better not never tell nobody but God. It'll kill your mammy."* These words are addressed to Celie, a fourteen-year-old black girl, by her "Pa."

*Whoopi Goldberg as Celie in
The Color Purple (Steven
Spielberg, 1986). (Courtesy
MOMA/FSA and Warner
Bros., Inc.)*

Actually, he is her stepfather, but at this point Celie does not know it. She only knows that Pa, whose real name is Alphonso (in the novel, several characters are not known by their real names), has raped her and that the two children she bore were taken from her shortly after birth.

Forbidden to speak of her suffering and shame to another person, Celie begins a series of letters to God. Thus, *The Color Purple* is an epistolary novel, consisting of Celie's letters to God, her sister Nettie's letters to her, and Celie's letters to Nettie. As we have seen in Chapter 2, the letter is a commonly used narrative device. However, a work that is both epistolary and a justification of the epistolary method must be considerably modified for the screen. While we can accept hearing some of the correspondence through voice-over narration or seeing some of it in title form on the screen, the bulk of the correspondence must be visualized.

Celie's correspondence, in particular, is filled with such drama that its contents can be visualized linearly, as moviegoers prefer. The story spans some thirty-four years, and although the novel specifies no particular time frame, the film does: 1909 to (approximately) 1943, with superimposed titles (Spring 1909, Fall 1930) to mark the passing of the years.

Menno Meyjes's screenplay repeats the novel's main episodes, although, like any adaptation, with alterations. Pa gives Celie in marriage to a man she calls Mr. in her letters, although his name is Albert. When Nettie spurns Mr.'s advances, he angrily ejects her from the house, separating the sisters for more than thirty years. Nettie, who eventually becomes an African missionary, writes to Celie, but Mr.

confiscates the letters. It is only through the blues singer Shug Avery that Celie learns about the letters and manages to obtain them. Shug also becomes Celie's lover, offering her the warmth and affection that she has been denied. Ultimately, Shug's effect on Celie is salutary; soon Celie is a successful pants manufacturer. Eventually, Celie learns the truth about Pa and is reunited with both Nettie and her children.

Just as a film has a subtext, so does a novel. But while the novel's narrative may transfer well to the screen, its subtext may not do so fully. Subtextually, the novel *The Color Purple* is about language as a vehicle of communication. Denied an education, Celie can only write in Southern Black dialect; Nettie, who has been educated, writes in standard English. Celie's letters provide the narrative; Nettie's provide a perspective and a commentary on the narrative.

As King-Kok Cheung has shown, the novel is an exploration of the nature of the written word.[4] When Celie learns that Pa is not her natural father, her perception of God changes from a "He" to an "it" that transcends gender. Once Celie stops regarding God as a substitute for a correspondent, her letters become more complex as she begins describing instead of merely recounting, and at times writing metaphorically instead of literally. Epistolary change, however, is outside the domain of the film. Menno Meyjes had to make certain choices, one of which was to give Nettie's letters a purely narrative function so they could fill in details that Celie would not have known. Since Nettie's letters are, for the most part, nondramatic, Spielberg generates some drama by having them visualized while Celie is reading them. As Celie is on her porch reading Nettie's description of life in Africa, an elephant appears in the background. When Celie is in church reading about the destruction of an African church, a bulldozer comes through the altar of the church where Celie is sitting. Concurrent visualization at least suggests the effect of language on the imagination, which is one of the novel's main points.

Not everything, however, can transfer from novel to film. In the novel, Celie leaves Albert after she discovers he has withheld Nettie's letters from her. She does the same in the film (although more dramatically as she unleashes all the anger and bitterness that had built up within her). In the novel, after Celie becomes a successful businessperson, Albert reenters her life. Celie bears him no animosity; indeed, she teaches him to sew, and soon he is making shirts to go with the pants that she sells. Albert even asks her to return to him— but Celie declines. Still, they become friends and remain such. The screenwriter, however, eliminated this reconciliation from the movie.

Although in the novel Celie's behavior is exemplary, most women, especially those who have undergone similar mistreatment, would find her reconciliation with Albert hard to take. While reading the novel, however, one can rethink, reread, and ponder; even though the reader may initially find it troubling that Celie would resume any kind of a relationship with Albert, this feeling may change to understanding once the reader realizes that Celie has grown in such a way that her inner peace and resolve allow her to forgive him.

The reader, however, did not *see* Celie's brutalization or witness Albert's attempt to rape Nettie; the reader was not present when Celie gave birth or when Albert unloosened each of Nettie's fingers as she clung to the doorpost, begging him not to send her away. The movie-goer, on the other hand, has seen all of this, and having seen it, could not accept a Celie who takes her husband back as a companion.

There is another reason for the omission of the Albert-Celie reconciliation in the film: it would eclipse the climactic reconciliation of Celie, Nettie, and Celie's children. The film builds up to this with two other reconciliations, each involving one of the other main female characters: Sofia with her family, and Shug with her father, the Preacher. The free-spirited Sofia leaves her husband and children but is reconciled with them after a lengthy prison sentence—the result of her public refusal to be the maid of the mayor's neurotic wife. In the novel, there is no mention of Shug's father; however, to soften the character of Shug, Meyjes introduces the Preacher, from whom Shug is estranged because of her lifestyle. Meyjes was influenced by an episode in the novel in which Shug states that she never found God in church. The reason might well have had to do with the way God was presented to her, perhaps by a minister; perhaps, even, by a minister who was her father. This is an example of the way an adapter's mind works: the novel affords clues about the character's background that are not developed in the written narrative. These clues can be embroidered to serve the adapter's purpose when the narrative is visualized. In one of the film's many moving scenes, Shug is entertaining servicemen at Harpo's waterfront bar while, across the water, she hears gospel singing from her father's church. Inspired by the music, she and the band make their way to the church where father and daughter are reconciled. "See, daddy; sinners have soul," Shug says as they embrace. The two preliminary reconciliations are arranged as emotional peaks, the second surpassing the first and both pointing to the grand reconciliation of the sisters at the end.

Interestingly, in the film Albert plays a role in the sisters' ultimate reunion. While he will not be reunited with Celie, he can change, as he did in the novel; his change must be made more acceptable to a movie audience than his learning to sew, which is symbolic rather than dramatic. Since *The Color Purple* is not a film in which the characters are virtuous or villainous, Albert is given a chance to perform one decent act. When a letter arrives from the immigration department apparently about Nettie's return to America, Albert does not hide it but seeks out the immigration officials and arranges for Nettie's trip. The film, then, comes full circle thematically: Albert, who separated the sisters, is, in a sense, partly responsible for their reunion—which he witnesses from a distance. The film also comes full circle visually. It begins in 1909 with the sisters clapping their hands together in a sunlit field, singing "Us never part / Us have one heart / Ain't no land / Ain't no sea / Can keep you away from me"; it ends in 1943 with the sisters, now middle-aged women, clapping their hands together in the dusk.

Visually, *The Color Purple* is a film of artful simplicity. While Spielberg has an arsenal of techniques that he has built up from his vast knowledge of film, he does not let technology overwhelm the human values of the story. Irises and wipes, two of his favorite devices, are absent since they are more appropriate to an Indiana Jones movie than to one about a black woman's struggle to achieve a sense of worth. However, Spielberg cannot resist a natural fade-out. When Celie asks Albert whether there is any mail, the camera replies by tracking into the dark interior of the mailbox, causing the screen to go dark.

Anyone directing *The Color Purple* would be confronted with a dilemma about how to film Celie. Although the story is essentially Celie's, she cannot be the visual focus of attention. Since she has been denied a significant role in life, Spielberg puts her in the extremity of the frame or in the background. She is often photographed over someone's shoulder or seen at the window as an onlooker rather than a participant. When she first sees Albert, for example, it is through a window. (Ironically, after she becomes a success, she glances through her store window and sees Albert in the street, the roles of outsider/insider now reversed.) Celie comes into her space for the first time, in close-up and medium close-up, in the love scene with Shug. As Shug expresses her feelings for Celie, each puts her hands on the other's shoulders, while the camera pans right to a tinkling glass mobile. This scene demonstrates another interesting aspect of the film: the human hand is used as a central image.

In earlier scenes, Celie and Nettie clap their hands together and embrace; in a particularly moving sequence, Nettie's fingers have to be dislodged individually from the doorpost. A hand can offer a gesture of affection or be a means of inflicting pain. If it holds a razor or a knife, it can shave, carve, or kill. Spielberg conjoins two separate incidents from the novel that involve hands and sharp instruments.

After Celie discovers Albert has concealed Nettie's letters from her, she is on the verge of cutting his throat while shaving him, until Shug intervenes. In one of her letters from Africa, Nettie describes a ritual initiation that leaves the face scarred. Spielberg crosscuts Celie's sharpening the razor with the preparations for the ritual, form cutting from razor to knives, from Celie's holding a razor under Albert's neck to hands holding knives against the faces of the children in Africa. By combining two separate incidents into one crosscut sequence, Spielberg creates a contrast between a crime of murder and a rite of passage. The former is interrupted; the latter completed.

Since every great film should have a subtext, what is *The Color Purple's*? As already suggested, the novel's subtext is the written word and its connection with those who use it. Film cannot deal with a subtext so specifically verbal, but it can suggest written texts. As a victim of oppression, Celie recalls other literary characters who also suffered indignities and abuse, the most famous being Oliver Twist. In the film, Charles Dickens's *Oliver Twist* plays an important role, although it is not even mentioned in the novel.

In the film, Nettie, on her way to school, is intercepted by Albert. Dropping her books, she runs away. One of the books—and a close-up makes certain we see the title—is *Oliver Twist*. This is the same book from which Celie learns to read, and the text that she repeats has special relevance to her own situation: "For the next eight or ten months Oliver was the victim of a systematic course of treachery and deception."

Despite its realistic plot, *Oliver Twist* relies heavily, as most of Dickens's novels do, on coincidence; to some extent, so does *The Color Purple*, although Walker's coincidences are not quite so contrived as Dickens's. For example, the two children that Celie bears and that are taken from her are raised by a local missionary couple and christened Adam and Olivia. After Albert expels Nettie from the farm, she is befriended by the same couple. Nettie accompanies them to Africa, along with Olivia and Adam. Thus, Celie's sister and her children are together; and when Nettie, Olivia, and Adam return to America, Celie is reunited both with the sister she has not seen since she was fourteen and the children she has not seen since their birth.

Menno Meyjes expects the viewer to recognize Oliver Twist and Celie as kin. Both are victims of "treachery and deception," yet through a combination of chance events and spiritual strength, both triumph over adversity, receive their rightful inheritance, and are reconciled with their families. Even if one has not read *Oliver Twist*, Celie evokes every victimized figure, from Joseph of the Old Testament to Cinderella, who ultimately came into his or her own.

On another level, Alice Walker's *The Color Purple* is about God, whose existence is so evident throughout the universe that it cannot be ignored. As Shug explains to Celie, "I think it pisses God off if you walk by the color purple in a field somewhere and don't notice it." God's love of humankind, as manifested in the bounty of creation, is as obvious as the color purple, which is too eye-catching to dismiss.

In the film, the color purple is also the color of nature, the color of natural innocence. The film opens with the sisters racing through a field of purple flowers. When Albert makes his advances toward Nettie, she drops her books on a dusty road strewn with purple petals that presage the end of innocence and the separation of the sisters. At the end of the film, the sisters stand in the same field of purple flowers, now muted in color by the setting sun.

While Shug speaks the same line to Celie in the film as she did in the novel, it is now associated with the opening/closing motif. Celie's worth should be as obvious as the color purple; that it is not is another indication of humankind's inability to see what is most clearly delineated.

As an adaptation, *The Color Purple* retains the integrity of Alice Walker's novel; yet by devising analogous subtexts, Spielberg and Meyjes have made a genuine film, not a filmed novel.

Dr. Jekyll and Mr. Hyde (Rouben Mamoulian, 1932)

Some films based on works of literature deviate so widely from the originals that they have to be treated independently of their sources. The 1932 film version of Robert Louis Stevenson's *Dr. Jekyll and Mr. Hyde* is such a film. Although the film deals with the phenomenon of the "double-self," Stevenson's classic novella is only its point of departure. Jekyll and Hyde are opposite sides of the same person, since Hyde is the reverse image of Jekyll. But they are not the only opposites in the novella. Two other characters, the lawyer Utterson and his friend Enfield, are opposites also. Utterson is cool and aloof while Enfield is the reverse—carefree and outgoing. Because Hollywood did not make all-male horror films, the male characters of Utterson and Enfield became Muriel and Ivy for the film. Muriel is the woman Jekyll courts, Ivy is the woman Hyde desires. Like Utterson and Enfield, they are mirror images: Muriel is an aristocrat, Ivy a prostitute.

The film makes it clear that Hyde is not only Jekyll's "dark side" but, more specifically, his sexual side. Since Jekyll is sexually repressed, he wants to marry Muriel as soon as possible. "I can't wait any longer," he insists. As Hyde, he does not have to wait; Hyde can go much further and do to women what Jekyll never could: brutalize them. The degradation to which Hyde subjects Ivy before killing her is still capable of shocking an audience.

The 1932 film is a study of the divided self inspired by Stevenson's novella as well as by Freudianism. The division within Henry Jekyll is not so much between good and evil as between sexual repression and sexual excess.

Adaptations of Plays

A play should be "opened up" for the screen. Material that had to be related because it could not be shown on stage can be visualized in film. Significant places mentioned in the dialogue can be shown.

William Inge's play *Picnic* takes place in a yard between two houses in a small Kansas town. But a vital scene, the Labor Day picnic that changes the lives of the main characters, cannot be shown on stage. Because audiences expected to see a picnic in the movie, the 1956 film version, directed by Joshua Logan, provided one that still remains a vivid piece of cinema Americana.

Gore Vidal, who adapted Tennessee Williams's *Suddenly, Last Summer*, opened up the play (which is set in Violet Venable's garden) by showing some of the places mentioned in the dialogue. In the play, Catherine Holly (Elizabeth Taylor) is committed to Lion's View State Asylum because she is considered insane. The film shows Catherine at Lion's View, and portrays the horrible conditions that exist in the mental institution. Since the plot hinges on whether or not Catherine will be lobotomized, the film opens with a lobotomy being performed in an operating theater. Most important, the details of the death of Sebastian Venable, Catherine's cousin, which she describes in her final monologue, are depicted on the screen.

When Blanche duBois arrives at her sister's New Orleans home in Tennessee Williams's play, *A Streetcar Named Desire*, she learns that her sister and brother-in-law are at the local bowling alley. The film shows Blanche's sister and her husband, Stella and Stanley Kowalski, at the bowling alley, so that we are introduced to Stella and Stanley at the same time we are introduced to Blanche. While theatergoers accept the existence of a streetcar named Desire, moviegoers expect to *see* the streetcar that Blanche takes to her sister's home in the French Quarter. The film version makes it clear that there indeed was a streetcar named Desire.

Single-set plays in which the action is almost inseparable from the setting are difficult to adapt. Since Lillian Hellman had confined all of the action of her play, *Watch on the Rhine*, to one setting, the hero must kill the villain in the living room. Although Dashiell Hammett did not open up the play very much when he wrote the script for the 1943 film, he at least moved the murder into the garage.

In Marsha Norman's Pulitzer-prize winning one-act play, 'Night Mother, a daughter tells her mother that she plans to commit suicide that night. The play observes the three unities of Greek tragedy: unity of action (one main plot), unity of place (one setting), and unity of time (the time covered in the play is identical with the time required to perform it). The plot of 'Night, Mother is so structured that a film version would also have to observe the unities. In the 1987 film version, the action was opened up a bit, but not enough to keep the moving images from becoming static pictures. Paul Newman's 1986 film version of Tennessee Williams's The Glass Menagerie had similar problems. Because of his great respect for the text, Newman scarcely opened up the action at all, and the result was like watching a photographed play.

Thus, strict fidelity to a work of literature does not necessarily result in a good film. Purists may be delighted that the text is intact, but moviegoers expect "moving pictures."

THE NATURE OF SCREENWRITING

If adaptation, which is merely one kind of screenwriting, is difficult, screenwriting in general can hardly be easy. Distinguished authors like William Faulkner and F. Scott Fitzgerald tried to write for the screen, but what they produced pales in comparison with their fiction. Fitzgerald genuinely wanted to write film scripts, but those that he wrote either contained dialogue the actors found impossible to speak, or were so cluttered with description that they had to be drastically pruned. Fitzgerald's talent lay in fiction, where he could narrate or describe without dramatizing, rather than in screenwriting, where he would have to suppress the urge to tell everything through words and delegate some authority to the camera.

The ideal screenplay advances the plot in two ways: verbally, through dialogue, and visually, through action. If a screenplay were total dialogue, there would be no difference between a screenplay and a stage play. Screenwriters must visualize the action as they write it. When the visual might be more effective than the verbal, the writer must suppress the desire to rely on dialogue and rather must indicate how the action can be visualized.

Julia has a literate—that is, well written and intelligently executed—script by Alvin Sargent, yet there are parts that contain no dialogue at all. Sargent knew when language was necessary to advance the plot, and when images were. For example, the scene in which Lillian is watching a performance of *Hamlet* in Moscow is crosscut with Julia's murder in Frankfurt. Sargent realized it would be more effective to have the murder take place without any dialogue at all so there would be a contrast with the performance of *Hamlet*, where dialogue is essential. Thus, a further contrast results: verbalized stage violence and nonverbal real violence.

All about Eve is another well-written screenplay, yet one of the most important moments in the film involves no dialogue whatsoever. To show that there will always be aspiring young performers, such as Eve Harrington, who ingratiate themselves with older stars, writer-director Joseph L. Mankiewicz concludes the film with Phoebe, the "new Eve," standing in front of a three-way mirror that magnifies her image to infinity. Not a word of dialogue is spoken; multiple image reminds us that the "Eves" of the world are too vast to be counted.

Although it is obvious that a screenplay is intended to be visualized, the consequences of visualization may not be so obvious. One such consequence is the kind of language with which the screenplay is written. Because audiences expect the photographed image to be realistic (as opposed to, say, a painting, which need not be), they also expect the characters to sound realistic. In real life, we point to an object, and call it a "this" or a "that." In film, a demonstrative can have a visual antecedent, so that a "this" or a "that" is something the audience sees. When Ellen (Claudette Colbert) sees the blanket partition that Peter (Clark Gable) has arranged between their beds in *It Happened One Night*, she says, "*That* makes it all right," glancing in the direction of the blanket. It is the glance that makes the grammar and the line all right, too. A screenwriter who is not thinking visually might have written: "The fact that you've put up a blanket between the beds makes it all right, I presume." Stage dialogue, which this resembles, tends to be more precise and grammatical than film dialogue; it can also turn off moviegoers.

Screen dialogue is often truncated—that is, sentences are frequently left unfinished, and speech is fragmentary. Thus, screen language is closer to actual conversation than any other kind of dialogue, even that of the most naturalistic kind of theatre. An example of stage dialogue is Nick's lines in Lillian Hellman's *The Autumn Garden*, "These are my oldest friends. I think as one grows older it is more and more necessary to reach out your hand for the sturdy old vines you knew when you were young and let them lead you back to the roots of things that matter." Even though these lines are supposed to sound pompous, they would sound doubly so in a film if they were delivered in close-up or even medium shot. The audience might even laugh. *The Autumn Garden* has never been filmed, even though it is considered Hellman's finest play. Yet if it were, and the screenwriter decided to retain the above lines, they would have to be changed to something like this: "These are my oldest friends. You might call them the vines that bring me back to my roots."

Movie dialogue is more like the exchange between Butch and Sundance in *Butch Cassidy and the Sundance Kid* (George Roy Hill, 1969):

> **BUTCH:** *How long you figure we been watching?*
> **SUNDANCE:** *Awhile.*
> **BUTCH:** *How much longer before you think they're not after us?*
> **SUNDANCE:** *A while longer.*
> **BUTCH:** *How come you're always so talkative?*
> **SUNDANCE:** *Born blabby.*

To appreciate the way a screenwriter economizes on language, you might compare the dialogue in a novel with the dialogue in a movie based on the novel. Often a screenwriter will incorporate dialogue from the novel into the screenplay if the dialogue is appropriate. However, spoken dialogue is not necessarily the same as written dialogue; screen dialogue has to be made compatible with the rhythms of human speech. In both Raymond Chandler's novel *The Big Sleep* and the 1946 film version directed by Howard Hawks, General Sternwood asks detective Philip Marlowe about himself. Here is what Marlowe says in the novel: "I'm thirty-three years old, went to college once and can still speak English if there's any demand for it. There isn't much in my trade. I worked for Mr. Wilde, the District Attorney, as an investigator once. His chief investigator, a man named Bernie Ohls, called me and told me you wanted to see me. I'm unmarried because I don't like policemen's wives."

Compare Marlowe's reply in the film: "I'm thirty-eight years old, went to college once. I can still speak English when there's any demand for it in my business. I worked for the District Attorney's office once. It was Bernie Ohls, his chief investigator, who sent me word you wanted to see me. I'm not married." Since Humphrey Bogart was playing Marlowe, the character's age had to be changed from thirty-three to thirty-eight. But the real difference is the succinctness of the screen version, which imparts the same information as the novel, but more concisely.

Economy of language, which is at the heart of screenwriting, is not the same as ellipsis, in which words are omitted for the sake of balance or parallelism. Ellipsis is rhetorical rather than dramatic, artificial rather than real. In a scene from the 1976 movie version of F. Scott Fitzgerald's unfinished novel *The Last Tycoon* (Elia Kazan), producer Monroe Stahr (Robert DeNiro) watches the rushes of a highly sophisticated 1930s movie in which the hero says to the heroine, "I love you," and she replies, "And I, you." Stahr is furious: " 'And I—you! ' Who talks like that?" Claudius in *Hamlet* does, for one: "And he to England shall along with you." But that is stage dialogue; in particular, Elizabethan stage dialogue. And nobody talked like that in Elizabethan England, either.

People talk in strands, in words and phrases strung together in a kind of beaded syntax, rather like Neff talks in *Double Indemnity*—in units of thought, where the ideas generate their own rhythm and their own grammar. Sometimes movie characters speak in epigrams, but these are movie, not stage epigrams. They are memorable because they compress a complex idea into an easily remembered line that is natural for the character to speak and not merely an occasion for the writer to wax clever. At the end of *Now, Voyager* (Irving Rapper, 1942), Charlotte (Bette Davis) says to Jerry (Paul Henreid), "Oh, Jerry, don't let's ask for the moon. **We have the stars.**" By using images (moon, stars) that everyone readily understands, she is summing up with marvellous precision humankind's perennial desire to overreach. Yet what Charlotte says is appropriate to the circumstances: Charlotte is happy just to take care of Jerry's daughter even though Jerry can no longer be her lover.

Movie epigrams are not stage epigrams which tell us more about the playwright's gift for language than about the character's motivation or psychology. Lady Bracknell's line, "Hesitation of any kind is a sign of mental decay in the young, of physical weakness in the old," in Oscar Wilde's *The Importance of Being Earnest* is a stage epigram because it functions not so much as dialogue but as an expression of Wilde's wit. While we may enjoy that wit, we sense we are hearing the author, not the character.

In *All about Eve*, when Margo Channing says, "Fasten your seat belts; it's going to be a bumpy night," she is parodying the airline cliché, "Fasten your seat belts; it's going to be a bumpy flight." Margo's line is not a turn of the phrase, but a variation on a phrase already turned. Unlike Oscar Wilde's epigrams, which can be quoted out of context and sound witty, Margo's "Fasten your seat belts" is the closing line of a specific sequence. Realizing that Eve is now her rival, Margo drinks too much at a party and becomes progressively ill-tempered. Downing one last Martini, she sweeps across the room, turns, delivers the line, and exits in the grand manner. The camera, which all the time has been tracking her, exits in a huff with her. As a curtain line, "Fasten your seat belts" might have fallen flat; as an exit line in a movie, it is ideal, particularly given Bette Davis's memorably corrosive delivery. [Nobody ever says, "Do you remember when Lady Bracknell said, 'Hesitation of any kind is a sign of mental decay in the young, or physical weakness in the old?' " They do say, "Do you remember when Bette Davis said, 'Fasten your seat belts; it's going to be a bumpy night' in *All about Eve?*"]

Just as the movie epigram differs from the stage epigram, the movie monologue—an extended speech in which a character reveals important information—differs from the stage monologue. In *All about Eve*, Eve delivers a monologue about her dreary childhood and tragic marriage, playing on the sympathies of her five listeners. Even if Joseph L. Mankiewicz had not directed his own screenplay, a director would have no other choice but to cut to the listeners on certain lines, as Eve either calls her listeners by name or alludes to something about them that causes them to respond. There are some seven cuts in Eve's monologue, yet the cuts are so unobtrusive that by the time Eve finishes speaking, the audience feels it has heard a monologue while it has really witnessed a scene. In the theater, the speech could never be a true monologue since Eve poses rhetorical questions to her listeners or makes references that necessitate a reaction from them, and these reactions demand close-ups. In the movie there is no question that one listener is moved, another close to tears, a third attentive, a fourth concerned, and a fifth mildly skeptical but ultimately convinced. It is important that we see, and see clearly, each listener's reaction since Eve is winning each of them over by her tale of woe—a tale, incidentally, that is fabricated.

By its nature, a screenplay is best appreciated after one has seen it brought to the screen. *Patton* (Franklin Schaffner, 1970) is best remembered for Patton's (George C. Scott's) opening monologue; yet taken simply as a monologue, it is not on a par with the great stage monologues like Hickey's in Eugene O'Neill's *The Iceman Cometh* or Blanche's in *A Streetcar Named Desire*. However, if while reading it, one tries to imagine Patton's growing progressively larger as he becomes more outrageous, which is what happens on screen, one can then appreciate how the words were translated into images. Patton progresses from a tiny figure against a gigantic American flag to a face filling the screen to a tiny figure again. It is like watching the ego puff itself up into bloatedness and then lose air.

One can write a novel by telling a story over several hundred pages without adhering to a strict code; the only division necessary is division by chapter or chapter equivalents. Writing a play requires division into acts and, if necessary, scenes within those acts. If the setting changes in a novel, it can be indicated by a phrase ("Meanwhile, in London . . ."); in a play, a change of location is marked by an act or scene change, as in Lillian Hellman's *The Searching Wind:* Act 1, scene 1, The drawing room of the Hazen house, Washington, D.C.; scene 2, a room in the Grand Hotel, Rome. In a screenplay, structuring the narrative and designating scene changes are even more complicated.

A screenplay follows a specific format. Every screenplay begins with the same two words in capitals: FADE IN. Fade in on what? Suppose you wanted to fade in on a cabin. That would be your first shot and must be numbered as all shots (or scenes if they entail more than just a shot) must be. So far we have FADE IN on shot one, a cabin in the woods. But that instruction is incomplete; shots must be described in terms of place (INTERIOR or EXTERIOR), and time (DAY or NIGHT). Thus, an incomplete opening might be:

FADE IN:
1. **INT—CABIN—NIGHT**

What is going on in the cabin? Suppose the first shot is to be of ELISE, the heroine, standing anxiously at the window, waiting for her husband to return. How is she to be shown? What will be the size of her image: CU, LS, MS? To convey anxiety, a CU is necessary. How will the audience know she is waiting for her husband? Voice-over narration (V.O.) will be used to reveal her thoughts. In screenwriting, characters' names or designations (ELISE, CROWD), camera movements (PAN TO), transitions (DISSOLVE TO), the word sound (SOUND of laughter), and sound effects (SF or SFX) are capitalized. Thus, the first shot as it would be filmed would be described:

FADE IN:
1. **INT—CABIN—NIGHT**
   CU of **ELISE** standing anxiously at window. A storm rages outside.

ELISE (V.O.)
John said he'd be back by nightfall, but it's close
to midnight. Dear God, not now . . . please, not
now.

To show John, the screenwriter would have to start a new shot.

2. **EXT—MAINE WOODS—NIGHT**
   ELS of **JOHN** trudging through snow. **SLOW ZOOM IN** to reveal face, weather-beaten but confident.

Note, for example, how Alan Alda observes the rules in this brief excerpt from the credits sequence in his *Four Seasons* screenplay:

7. **EXT: VILLAGE STREET—DAY**
    HIGH SHOT—station wagon makes its way down the street. Over this we HEAR:

                    DANNY'S VOICE
              Who ate the bread? What the
              hell is this? You started
              without me?

8. **EXT: 13TH STREET—DAY**
    The station wagon pulls up to the curb. **CLAUDIA ZELLER** is waiting for them holding a large unfinished painting and a box of supplies. She waves and smiles. Claudia is an Italian from the Bronx. Earthy, intelligent and strong. She gets in the car with the painting, passing it with difficulty over everybody's head as she gets into the back of the car.

                       DANNY
              You brought your work?

                      CLAUDIA
              It's almost finished. I'm hot.
              I'm cooking. I can't stop for
              a whole weekend.

                       DANNY
              I stopped *my* work for the
              weekend.

                      CLAUDIA
              Danny, please, you're a dentist.

                       DANNY
                     (to Anne)
              You hear this? I can sculpt a
              bicuspid that would fool God
              himself, but I'm just a dentist.

                      CLAUDIA
              I'll go out in the fields with
              the cows. I'll stay out of
              everybody's way.

She accidentally sticks the painting in Nick's face. Nick grabs at his eye and winces.

> CLAUDIA (contd)
> Oh, Nick, I'm sorry. Are you
> alright?

> NICK
> Fine.
> (to Danny)
> I'm glad you didn't bring your
> dentist's chair.

> JACK
> You hear about Janice and Hal?

> CLAUDIA
> I just got off the phone with
> her. It's a nightmare. Drive.
> Let's get as far away from the
> whole damn thing as we can.

The station wagon takes off.
CUT TO:

9. **EXT: MERRIT PARKWAY—DAY**
   The station wagon moves down the highway past the greens and
   reds and yellows of spring.

SPRING MONTAGE:
Crabapple trees spraying blossoms like fountains.

Lilac branches sagging with purple buds.

Dark rain clouds passing over the sun.

Forsythia shimmering in a spring rain, its buds dropping under the
weight of the fresh water.

Small wet birds in a nest shaking water drops from nearly feather-
less wings.

And finally, sunset in the woods. New leaves are everywhere. A
rabbit crawls slowly out of its hole and surveys the place.

10. **EXT: THE BARN—NIGHT**
    In the distance the station wagon pulls up to a barn that has been
    made into a house.

END OPENING TITLES.

Screenwriting is an art that film history, which emphasizes the
development of film as a medium, the studio system and the stars

that came out of it, and the role of the director in the filmmaking process, has tended to ignore, perhaps because the script is pre-filmic. Even though most narrative films start with a script, the script recedes into the background as it changes from a verbal to a visual text, so that by the time the film has been completed, the words have been translated into images. Thus, moviegoers associate dialogue not with the writer, but with the actors speaking the lines or the scenes in which they are spoken. Still, a serious student of film will always look for the screenwriter's name in the credits.

NOTES

[1] Ingmar Bergman, "Film Has Nothing to Do with Literature," in *Film: A Montage of Theories*, ed. Richard Dyer MacCann (New York: E. P. Dutton & Co., 1966), 144.

[2] The terms used throughout the rest of this chapter (*omniscient author, author's implied self, reliable narrator,* etc.) come from Wayne C. Booth, *The Rhetoric of Fiction* (Chicago: University of Chicago Press, 1961).

[3] Ibid., 158–59.

[4] King-Kok Cheung, " 'Don't Tell ': Imposed Silences in *The Color Purple* and *The Woman Warrior*," *PMLA* 103 (1988): 162–74.

8
Total Film

Film provides an experience that cannot be found elsewhere. It can crystallize an emotion or an idea into a visual image. When film uses language, the words can be integrated with the images so that they become inseparable. Once we see *Casablanca*, a line like "Here's looking at *you*, kid" is irrevocably linked both with its speaker (Humphrey Bogart) and the one to whom it is spoken (Ingrid Bergman). We may not be able to dredge up the exact frame from our memory, but we know that Bogart said it to Bergman, and we can remember the look in their eyes.

When we recall certain films that have left an impression, we visualize them as pictures—sometimes just pictures, at other times talking pictures or even musical pictures. Thus, if we were asked what film is all about, we would probably cite our favorite movie, favorite scene, or favorite shot.

The Third Man ends with what is arguably the most unforgettable snub in film. Anna (Alida Valli) walks down a Vienna road through a drift of leaves, her face immobile, her eyes fixed on a never-ending present. Holly Martins (Joseph Cotten) leans against a cart and lights a cigarette, waiting to be recognized. As the autumn leaves fall in a silent shower, Anna moves out of the frame—and out of Martins's life—without even a glance in his direction. Martins grows progressively smaller until he is nothing but a tiny figure by the side of a road, ready to disappear like the smoke from his cigarette. The ending achieves what only film can: eloquence without words. Not one line of dialogue is spoken: the zither alone speaks as it plays with restrained sadness the famous *"Third Man* Theme."

The ultimate snub: The ending of The Third Man *(Sir Carol Reed, 1949) in which Anna (Alida Valli) walks past Martins (Joseph Cotten) without even a nod in his direction. (Courtesy MOMA/FSA)*

Someone else might maintain that while the ending of *The Third Man* is impressive, it cannot compete with Isak Borg's final vision in *Wild Strawberries* in which Sara, his boyhood love, leads him through a meadow to a bay. Across the bay, Isak sees his mother knitting while his father fishes, apparently with some success, for the rod is beginning to curve over the water. They wave at their son, and he smiles back at them. Isak's vision of his parents has the texture of an impressionist painting. Not only is the shot perfectly composed but it also captures the essence of its subject; the shot objectifies eternity as a state into which we do not freeze like figures in a mural but rather melt imperceptibly, the way spring softens into summer or summer ripens into autumn.

It is natural to have a favorite scene; yet scenes are parts of a whole, a fact we tend to forget when we single them out for special consideration. Is there such a thing, we might ask, as *total film*—a work that, in its totality and not merely in its parts, epitomizes everything peculiar to the art of film? In other words, a work that could never have been possible in any other medium?

Let us examine four films, three of which were created especially for the screen, and one originally for the stage that never reached Broadway.

CASABLANCA (MICHAEL CURTIZ, 1942)

Before there was *Casablanca*, there was a play called *Everybody Comes to Rick's;* the play, however, was never produced. Even if it had been, it would never have meant to the stage what *Casablanca* means to the screen, despite the fact that the plots are not that dissimilar. In the play, Rick Blaine is the jaded owner of a café in Casablanca. One evening, a woman from his past, Lois Meredith, enters the cafe with Czech freedom fighter, Victor Laszlo. Although Rick and Lois resume

Humphrey Bogart and Ingrid Bergman as the legendary lovers in Casablanca *(Michael Curtiz, 1942). (Courtesy MOMA/FSA and Warner Bros., Inc.)*

their relationship, Rick begins to develop a political conscience; realizing that Laszlo must continue to fight fascism and that Lois must go with him, Rick makes it possible for the two of them to fly to Lisbon while he stays behind in Casablanca to meet an uncertain fate at the hands of the Nazis.

In the film, Lois Meredith becomes Ilsa Lund. Also, the Production Code precluded Ilsa's sleeping with Rick as Lois did in the play. The background of World War II determined the way the film ends: Laszlo and Ilsa board the plane while Rick goes off to join the Free French with his friend, Captain Renault, who was even more indifferent to human concerns than Rick, but is now willing to do his bit to stop the Nazis.

If the plot sounds farfetched, it is. Yet generations have responded, and continue to respond to *Casablanca*'s romanticism because there is a solid mythic foundation beneath a rickety plot, a foundation that constitutes the subtext. While there is no particular myth that describes the subtext, there is a universal one: the myth of regeneration. *Casablanca* argues that as long as there are the uncommitted like Rick, who are capable of change, there is hope for the world. And once the uncommitted have changed, they make it possible for the Victor Laszlos to do what most of us cannot: make the world a better place.

We identify with Rick because we too may be more concerned about ourselves than about the world; we also identify with Laszlo because we aspire to his idealism. We even empathize with the patrons of Rick's cafe, a true cross-section of humanity, who show the kind of courage we envy. As the Germans bellow their anthem, the patrons respond defiantly with "La Marseillaise" and drown them out. When Rick tells Ilsa that "the problems of three little people don't amount to a hill of beans in this crazy world," he is admitting that there are times when individual needs must be subordinated to the common good. Yet this is not any man speaking to any woman, but Humphrey Bogart speaking to Ingrid Bergman, one icon to another. Each is the perfect embodiment of the character: Bogart, the cynic in need of regeneration; Bergman, the woman with the power to regenerate him.

With two other actors, the effect might not have been the same. Bogart and Bergman have such powerful screen personas that when they play characters like Rick and Ilsa, a coinciding of persona and character results, so that when one thinks of *Casablanca*, one thinks of Humphrey Bogart and Ingrid Bergman and not merely of Rick Blaine and Ilsa Lund.

THE GODFATHER, PART II (FRANCIS FORD COPPOLA, 1974)

In the sequel to *The Godfather* (Francis Ford Coppola, 1972), the lives of Vito Corleone and his son Michael are interwoven in a way that is truly cinematic. Since Vito is dead when the film opens, Coppola could not crosscut the lives of father and son. Instead, he tells Vito's story in flashback.

The first time the film moves from the present to the past, from Michael (Al Pacino) to Vito (Robert de Niro), Michael is putting his son to bed. Michael's face is to the *left* of the frame. Slowly the scene dissolves to Vito, his face to the *right* of the frame, as he puts his son Fredo to bed. The transition from son to father, from present to past, is balanced by a movement from left to right. The transition also brings about a corresponding change of rhythm: As the action shifts from 1957 to the turn of the century, the frenetic pace of the present yields to Old World ease. The color also changes as Lake Tahoe dissolves into Little Italy. Michael's world is dark and forbidding; Vito's is bright and sympathetic.

The first flashback ends as it began—with a shot of Vito and his son—and suddenly we are in the late 1950s again with Michael en route to Miami. By ending with a cut instead of another dissolve, Coppola points up the difference between the feverish pace of Michael's life and the tranquillity Vito knew, at least in his early manhood.

The second flashback begins when Michael hears that his wife Kay has had a miscarriage, which is later revealed to be an abortion. The scene again dissolves to Little Italy, where Vito is hovering over his son who is ill with pneumonia. Again it is a child that effects the transition. Coppola ends the flashback by showing Vito with the young Michael on his lap; then he cuts to a car making its way along a wintry road and proceeding through the forbidding entrance to Michael's Lake Tahoe home. The cut propels us into a present that is so loveless that Kay does not even look up from her sewing to greet her husband.

Coppola could not use a child as a bridge three times in succession. Consequently, the third flashback in *Godfather II* does not spring from a particular image. Coppola merely dissolves a shot of Michael speaking with his mother into one of Vito buying fruit and ends the flashback with the formation of the Genco Importing Company. In the first two flashbacks it was a cut that restored the action to the present; in the third it is a dissolve. Just as Vito is about to enter the import business, Coppola dissolves to a congressional investigation at which Michael is being interrogated. By dissolving from the Genco Importing Company to the hearings, Coppola establishes a connection between them. The legitimacy of the Genco Importing Company, the foundation on which Vito built his empire, is now the subject of an investigation. Michael, who has inherited his father's empire along with its foundation, plays the honest businessman who refuses to take the Fifth Amendment, claiming that he has nothing to hide.

The final flashback begins after Kay tells Michael that her miscarriage was really an abortion. Coppola cuts to Vito's return to the Sicilian town of Corleone in order to avenge the murder of his parents, who were victims of Don Ciccio's vendetta. Here the link between present and past is something quite different from a child put to bed or the establishment of an import company: The link is death. An admission of abortion becomes the occasion for a flashback of a Mafioso's assassination. It is also death that returns the action to the present. As Vito leaves Sicily after killing Don Ciccio, Coppola dissolves to a casket containing the body of Michael's mother, Mama Corleone.

Godfather II interweaves past and present, contrasting them in a way peculiar to film: through variations of rhythm, balance, and color.

THE PASSENGER (MICHELANGELO ANTONIONI, 1975)

On the surface, *The Passenger* is an "assumed identity" film. What distinguishes it from other films of this type is Antonioni's approach, which makes a movie about a man's assuming another's identity a movie about the limitations of knowledge. The film opens somewhere in North Africa where British-born, American-educated journalist David Locke (Jack Nicholson) is attempting to make contact with some guerrilla leaders whom he hopes to interview for a television documentary. Unable to locate them, he returns to his hotel, where he discovers that Robertson, the businessman in the next room, has died of a heart attack. Noting a physical resemblance between them, he assumes Robertson's identity and itinerary, as yet unaware that his look-alike was a gunrunner for Third World revolutionaries. Locke flies to London, then to Munich, where he is paid handsomely by two men from the United Liberation Front; and finally to Barcelona, where he meets a nameless girl (Maria Schneider) who becomes his traveling companion. In the meantime Mrs. Locke receives her "dead" husband's belongings, including his passport with Robertson's picture (the resemblance is by no means perfect) and a tape of a conversation between himself and Robertson. Mrs. Locke turns sleuth, the police are contacted, and the hunt is on. Urged by The Girl to keep an appointment that Robertson had made in Osuna, Locke proceeds to the place of the rendezvous, the Hotel de la Gloria. However, it is an appointment with death.

The plot seems simple enough; however, it is what Antonioni does with it that makes *The Passenger* a candidate for total film.

The first time we see Locke he is asking directions; the world-famous reporter and interviewer is now a tourist, speaking haltingly as all tourists do. Locke is a passenger, or rather, he is Every-passenger. "Do you speak English?" he asks the boy riding with him in his Land Rover. He repeats the question, this time in French. The boy appears to understand neither language, but things are rarely what they seem in Antonioni. "Stop!" the boy cries, darting out of the vehicle. Locke drinks some water from his canteen and then notices an Arab approaching on a camel. Perhaps this is his contact. The Arab is also a traveler, but with a destination; like the Levite in the Parable of the Good Samaritan, he ignores Locke out of apathy or lethargy and continues on his way. Suddenly a contact materializes; he is about to bring Locke to the rebels' camp when the sight of some soldiers frightens him and he flees. Locke returns to his Land Rover and tries to start it, but the wheels sink into the sand and churn up a fine powdery spray. Locke lets out a primal scream, lowering his head in the sand. In frustration he strikes the vehicle with a shovel; the camera responds by panning the mute desert.

Locke walks back to his hotel. The heat has even affected the cockroaches, which have trouble climbing the wall. He checks on Robertson in the room next to his. When there is no answer, Locke enters the room. Robertson is lying on the bed, apparently the victim of a heart attack. There is no thundering chord from the sound track, no close-up of a shocked face. The dispassionate Locke turns the body over and sits down on the side of the bed. He pages through Robertson's appointments book, noticing that the dead man has a date coming up with someone called Daisy at the Hotel de la Gloria in Osuna, Spain. Although the other entries in the book look promising, it is the rendezvous at the Hotel de la Gloria to which Locke keeps returning.

Locke studies Robertson's face; then he examines Robertson's passport and airline ticket, the latter bearing the number of a locker in the Munich airport. Finally, he notices Robertson's revolver. Casually, he lights a cigarette and then looks up at the ceiling fan, its blades cutting the air in an unchanging pattern. The sight of an object doomed to follow the same predictable course is all the encouragement Locke needs to become Robertson. Suddenly he finds himself wearing Robertson's blue shirt, which he had just picked up. He dresses Robertson in his checkered shirt. All that remains for him to do is to switch passport photos.

David Locke becomes David Robertson, achieving what many middle-aged men secretly desire—the ultimate trade-in. Having adopted Robertson's itinerary, he flies to Munich to determine the contents of locker #58, and discovers it contains requisitions for guns and grenades. Two men, one white, the other black, approach him in the airport. When the black man thanks Locke for the arms, we realize that Robertson was a gunrunner. To Robertson, Third World revolutionaries were a source of income; to Locke they are material for a documentary.

Throughout the first half of *The Passenger,* Antonioni incorporates excerpts from the documentary that Mrs. Locke and the producer are watching. The documentary is very much like the old Locke; by its very nature it is an impersonal form, leaving its maker little room for creativity. Since the documentary was part of Locke's past, it appears with the force of a flashback, for it represents the career he is abandoning. Locke wants not only to change lives but also to change films; as David Locke he was the creator of documentaries; as David Robertson he can be the star of a road flick or a cloak-and-dagger movie.

We know nothing about David Locke's earlier life except that he was born in London, educated in America, is married, and has an adopted child. Yet it is unimportant for us to know anything more about him. Since he is abandoning his past, there is little reason for us to see it. There is an abrupt flashback that not only crystallizes the differences between Mr. and Mrs. Locke but also explains his decision to lead the rest of his life without her. In Munich, Locke enters a magnificently ornate church where a wedding is in progress. Antonioni cuts to the backyard of the Lockes' London home where Locke is burning leaves, behaving the way children do around a bonfire. His wife looks at him incredulously and asks if he's mad. He replies joyfully in the affirmative. Antonioni cuts back to the church where Locke is stepping on the petals that have fallen from the wedding bouquets. Locke has terminated his marriage to both Rachel and his former life, which are as dead as the petals that clutter the aisle. But his new life is already present in the church; the men from the United Liberation Front have followed him. They thank him for the ammunition, pay him handsomely, and remind him that their next meeting will be in Barcelona.

In Barcelona he encounters The Girl. She is a drifter like himself with no past, only a present. She readily becomes Locke's traveling companion. Meanwhile, Rachel Locke becomes suspicious after she receives her "dead" husband's belongings, which include the Robertson tape and Robertson's photo in his passport. She and Martin Knight, the television producer, take off for Barcelona to check on Robertson while Locke and The Girl head south.

"What are you running away from?" The Girl asks as they drive along a tree-lined road in a white convertible. "Turn your back to the front seat" is his reply. She obeys and with childlike elation watches the road recede into the distance. This stunning tracking shot is typical of the film's rich ambiguity. The shot is ambiguous because the past is ambiguous. Subjectively, the past is no more permanent than the roads a person travels. Objectively, the past, like the road, exists whether an individual is aware of it or not. One road may be abandoned for another or a person may opt for a fresh present over a dead past but neither can be willed out of existence. The road taken seems to lie in the distance; actually, it connects the passenger's past with his or her present, bringing him or her closer to the destination—and his or her destiny. Robertson's destiny is now Locke's because Robertson's present is Locke's present.

Locke's present, however, will be short lived. When he learns from The Girl that his wife is in Barcelona to warn "Robertson" that he may be in danger, he replies naively, "In danger of what?" The answer comes not from The Girl but in the form of a cut to a wayside cross. Death has replied to Locke's question.

Plagued by car trouble and pursued by the police, Locke and The Girl reach a town in southern Spain where the streets are sun-blanched and the chalk-white buildings look as if they would crumble in a powdery residue if anyone leaned against them. An adventure that began in the dry heat of Africa ends in the white heat of Spain. Antonioni, who has been using some of the oldest plot devices in movie history (look-alikes, snooping wives, dragnets), has Locke send The Girl off to Tangier with the promise that he will meet her there in three days if all goes well. But she knows that Robertson had an appointment in Osuna at the Hotel de la Gloria and begs Locke to keep it. He agrees and proceeds to the ironically named hotel, only to discover that she has checked in before him. One cannot help recalling all those Hollywood heroines who boarded a Greyhound after a spat with their lovers; as the bus pulled out, the boy would walk away in dejection and then turn around for one last look, only to see True Love standing on the platform with her suitcase.

Locke is not surprised to see her, nor does he even ask how she got there. She will not stay long, for she knows he must keep the appointment by himself. Their leave-taking is as unemotional as their first meeting. After she leaves, Locke opens a window and looks out through the grille at the white, dusty square. Then he lights a cigarette and lies down.

What happens at this point almost defies description. A small white car pulls up; there is a sign on its roof advertising something, but it is difficult to make out the words because the camera refuses to leave the room. The Girl moves into the square; an old man is there, a boy, and a dog. Suddenly we notice that the camera has moved closer to the window grille. Another car, a much larger one, pulls into the square. The two men from the United Liberation Front step out; one stays outside and approaches The Girl; the other, the black man, enters the hotel. He is obviously going to see Locke. A door opens; then there are some ambiguous sounds. The camera, which could show us what is happening in the room between Locke and the revolutionary, has made more progress in its attempt to reach the window. The grille still faces us, imprisoning us and the camera with its bars. But then they begin to disappear until only two bars remain, which separate like sliding panels, revealing the square.

The camera is free, and we are also. But free for what purpose? To

David Locke/Robertson (Jack Nicholson) and The Girl (Maria Schneider) looking through the window grille of the Hotel de la Gloria. (Courtesy Margaret Herrick Library of the Academy of Motion Picture Arts and Sciences)

speculate on what is happening (or has happened) in the hotel room? Ironically, the frustration of not being out in the square has changed to the frustration of being in the square when we would rather be back in the room. A police car arrives with two policemen, one of whom tells the driver of the white car to move out of the square; another police car arrives with Rachel Locke and Martin Knight, who enter the hotel. But the camera does not follow them inside. Once liberated, it will not enter the Hotel de la Gloria again, although it should, to answer the many questions the action has given rise to: Did the black man murder Locke for not being able to deliver the anti-aircraft guns? Did he discover that Locke was not Robertson? And who is Daisy, the girl referred to in Robertson's appointments book? Like an eavesdropper, the camera hovers at the window, peeking at Mrs. Locke, Knight, the manager, and The Girl as they stare at the figure on the bed. The manager asks Mrs. Locke if she recognizes the man lying there. "I never knew him," she replies; it is a fitting answer, for she only knew David Locke. The manager asks the same question of The Girl. She answers in the affirmative, for she knew David Locke/Robertson.

The sun sets in Osuna, and a guitar plays a soothing melody. The Hotel de la Gloria assumes the colors of evening; the man whom we saw in the square ambles up the dirt road, and the dog follows him. It is a soundstage tranquillity, and the setting, once gritty right down to the powdery dust, now resembles something from an MGM musical like *Yolanda and the Thief* (Vincente Minnelli, 1945): a quaint hotel caught in a pink and blue sunset. The music is so mellow that it defies us to leave the theater in anything but a state of serenity. The sky laughs too, daring us to see crimson in those shards of pink or darkness in that blue expanse. Thus, *The Passenger* ends.

What has been described so far is the film's narrative. Turning to the subtext, we can conclude that while superficially *The Passenger* is about mistaken identity, it is really a commentary on the nature of knowledge, and a statement about the art of film.

Antonioni intended *The Passenger* to be something more than another variation on an old theme. By making mistaken identity his point of departure, Antonioni was free to explore a related idea: the impossibility of absolute certitude. "Can one know anything for certain?" Antonioni asks in the subtext. The closer a person gets to truth, the more elusive and the more ambiguous it becomes. Life conceals its secrets even from the scrutiny of the camera. Just as the camera was about to clarify what was happening in the square, something began to happen in the hotel room. But the camera had gone too far to turn back; if it did, it would be returning to the past, thus undoing everything Antonioni had set out to accomplish.

In the last seven minutes, Antonioni articulates a theory of film through the movement of the camera alone. This sequence is his answer to the question that continually plagues the artist: Can one ever record what is seen or experienced with total accuracy? It would seem that although this may not be possible with words, which can be fuzzy and inexact, the camera may have the ability to record reality with clarity and precision. Yet Antonioni would deny this premise, for film is also limited. Reality even eludes the camera, whose vision is more reliable than our own. In our folly, we think that the closer we get to an object, the better we can discern its nature; but in fact the closer we get to the object, the more ambiguous it becomes. The closer one gets to the *Mona Lisa*, for example, the more puzzling her smile appears. Is she smiling benignly or smirking? Is it the smile of contentment or the smile of complacency? Or is there a smile at all?

The final sequence of *The Passenger* states with wonderful economy Antonioni's position on the human capacity to know. Earlier the camera caught sight of a little white car with an undecipherable sign on the roof. At the end of the film, the car returns, this time with the sign more legible: We can make out the word "Andalusia." That we are in the south of Spain should come as no surprise after all those whitewashed dwellings and sepulchral villages. Recall also that the last shot of the film is of a man walking up a road followed by a dog, an Andalusian dog.

Luis Buñuel's first film was *Un Chien Andalou* (*An Andalusian Dog*, 1928); it was totally plotless, consisting of a series of dreamlike images, the most unforgettable being the slicing of a woman's eye with a razor. Summarizing what happens in the seventeen minutes of *Un Chien Andalou* would be like summarizing the contents of a dream. We can try to describe in words what happened in pictures but we would be giving our dream a form it never had. Antonioni's incredibly subtle bow to Buñuel in the final sequence is his explosion of the myth of objectivity. Truth is like *An Andalusian Dog*, a film that neither takes place in Andalusia nor has anything to do with a dog.

The Passenger can truly be classified as a total film experience because it fulfills all of the qualifications of great art in that medium. It is first a film whose ideas could not be realized in any other medium. Film was the only medium for *The Passenger* because Antonioni's purpose was to make us *see* the limitations of both human and cinematic knowledge.

NASHVILLE (ROBERT ALTMAN, 1975)

Nashville, another original screenplay, interweaves the lives of twenty-four people over a five-day period. The film depicts two worlds, each with its own rhythm, and each rhythm with its own set of variations. The political world is represented by the unseen Hal Phillip Walker, a rabble-rousing presidential candidate who advocates abolishing the electoral college, taxing churches, and scrapping the national anthem. The apolitical world is represented by the Grand Ole Opry, made up of performers and producers who are satisfied with the status quo.

Nashville opens with Hal Phillip Walker's campaign truck leaving a garage, with its loudspeaker filling the silent streets with prerecorded platitudes about America. Altman then cuts to the studio where Opry star Haven Hamilton (Henry Gibson) is recording "200 Years," a song as platitudinous as one of Walker's speeches. Hamilton, isolated from spectators in a sound booth, notices a BBC reporter (Geraldine Chaplin) and demands that she leave. The Opry distrusts strangers. Altman cuts from Hamilton to a black gospel group with its one white member, Linnea Reese (Lily Tomlin), as they record "Yes, I Do"—their free, handclapping vitality in sharp contrast to the forced solemnity of "200 Years."

Without our being aware, we have experienced hypocrisy, xenophobia, and, by way of crosscutting, sincerity. A movie with twenty-

Haven Hamilton (Henry Gibson) and Barbara Jean (Ronee Blakely), whose white dress will soon be stained with blood, at the climactic concert in Nashville (Robert Altman, 1975). (Courtesy American Broadcasting Companies, Inc.)

four characters will necessitate being crosscut, with the action broken up so one segment begins before another is completed. *Nashville* is, in fact, a study in crosscutting.

A bartender, looking for some unknown who would be willing to strip at a political smoker, hears Sueleen Gay (Gwen Welles) during an amateur night and knows he is in luck. Sueleen not only has an abominable voice; she also has neither style nor sense of pitch. However, the bartender is not interested in her voice, only in her body. As the bartender calls Del Reese (Ned Beatty), one of Nashville's leading attorneys, Altman interrupts Sueleen's song, but not her singing. We hear it the way it would sound over the telephone, the way Del Reese is hearing it. But by this time we are in the Reese home with Del's wife Linnea and their two children, who are both deaf. Linnea encourages her son to talk about his day in school. When her son does, there is applause—not for him but for Sueleen at the end of her wretched song. The scene then shifts back to the bar, to allow Altman to introduce another character: Tom (Keith Carradine), the egocentric rock star, who is calling Linnea for a date.

The sequence serves several functions. First, it introduces the manipulation theme. The political machine will make Sueleen serve its ends by exploiting her desire to become an Opry star like her idol Barbara Jean (Ronee Blakely). Second, it prepares the audience for one of the most poignant scenes in the film, the scene at the smoker where Sueleen does her pathetic strip. Third, it portrays a relationship of expediency, one of many such relationships that exist in the film. Tom sleeps with Linnea because he is a stud and she is available. Linnea sleeps with Tom because her husband is so indifferent to their deaf children that he does not even bother to learn sign language; hence his apathy when he overhears Tom's phone call to his wife.

The manipulation theme carries over into another sequence:

Sueleen's performance at the smoker, which is crosscut with Tom's performance in a nightclub. As Tom sings "I'm Easy," other women in the audience think he is singing to them. Altman cuts to their knowing faces but all the time the camera is moving toward the corner table where Linnea is sitting, the person to whom the song should have been dedicated if Tom could limit himself to one woman. The rhythm of manipulation, slow and serpentine, comes through in the editing: the very moment a rock star is playing on the women's emotions, some unsavory politicians are playing on the desire of an untalented waitress to become a star. Even before Tom finishes his number, there is lusty handclapping—not for him but for Sueleen. But the sequence does not end with her strip. After she finishes, we hear "I'm Easy" again, this time from a tape deck in Tom's hotel; he is in bed with Linnea, who apparently is no substitute for the sound of his own voice.

One of the themes in *Nashville* is religion and its various forms, which range from Lady Pearl's (Barbara Baxley) militant Catholicism that inspired her to campaign for the Kennedys, to Barbara Jean's ecstatic devotion to a Redeemer who is an extension of her own neurosis. Altman begins the religion theme with a shot of Tom lying on his bed, his long hair and messianic eyes giving him the appearance of a Christ. Altman then cuts from Tom to a stained-glass window of Christ as the Good Shepherd, contrasting the shepherd who exploits his flock with the shepherd who tends it.

However, the religion theme does not end with contrasting shots of two shepherd figures. What started as a simple shot of a rock star in bed grows into a four-part sequence portraying four different Sunday services as well as four different forms of worship. The camera tilts down the stained-glass window to the congregation. It is a Catholic service, with Lady Pearl, Sueleen, and Wade, the black man who looks after her, in attendance. Next the scene shifts to a white Baptist service, with Hamilton singing self-righteously in the choir, and then to a black Baptist church, where Linnea and her gospel group are singing with unfeigned enthusiasm. The mixed liturgy ends in a hospital chapel, where Barbara Jean, seated in a wheelchair, is pouring her heart out with pentecostal fervor. No sooner does she finish than Altman cuts to another part of Nashville, to the automobile graveyard through which Opal, the BBC reporter, wanders as she tries to find a suitable metaphor for the city.

The crosscutting in *Nashville* links the destinies of twenty-four people over a five-day period; it connects related themes through image and sound; it creates ironic associations by juxtaposing images (rock star/Good Shepherd, neurotic Opry singer/wrecked automobiles); it produces the film's manifold rhythm. The rhythm of *Nashville* is the rhythm of manipulation, which can be soft or blatant, genteel or crass; it can be as deliberately slow as Sueleen's rendition of a suggestive song or as shockingly quick as the bullet that strikes Barbara Jean.

Nashville accomplishes what film does best: it links the destinies of a number of people through a combination of musical associations, juxtaposed images, and variegated rhythm. Its subtext is not Nashville but America of the 1960s, of which Nashville is a microcosm. At the end of the film, the Opry is to perform at a Hal B. Walker rally where Barbara Jean will be the main attraction. In the crowd is a young man, who has been seen intermittently during the film. He seems innocuous enough, except that he now has a gun aimed at Barbara Jean. Just before he fires, he sees the American flag. The cut from the young man's eyes to the flag creates an association that is possible only in film. Clearly the young man is not firing at the flag, but at Barbara Jean. But to him—and this point is being made subtextually—Barbara Jean is as emblematic of America as the flag. Although her fans venerate her, she is as unstable psychologically as the United States was politically in the late 1960s when the country was polarized between the hawks who favored American intervention in Vietnam and the doves who opposed it. When he attempts to kill Barbara Jean, the young man is attempting to destroy an America that is falling apart like Barbara Jean. When the bullet rings out unexpectedly, it recalls similar bullets that also rang out unexpectedly during the 1960s, killing John Kennedy, Robert Kennedy, and Martin Luther King. Without mentioning Vietnam or political assassinations in America of the 1960s, Robert Altman has made a movie that is, subtextually, about both.

If you have a particular candidate for total film, first ask the following questions: Could it have been anything other than a film—a novel, a short story, or a play? If it is an adaptation of a work of literature, is it so different from its source that, for all practical purposes, it is an original work? How much of the film is told through images or camera movement without recourse to dialogue? If everything is conveyed through dialogue, the same effect might have been achieved if the film had been a novel or a play. Or do the camera and script collaborate, with each doing what it does best so that word and image are allies rather than enemies? What is the subtext? Without one, the film would have exhausted itself in one viewing. The subtext enriches the film, causing the viewer to return to it.

On the other hand, if a film has only a surface meaning with nothing beneath, a narrative that can be grasped in one viewing, and a visual style that matches the low level of the script, you know it is not total film.

CRITICISM AS THEORY

Most criticism from Aristotle to John Dryden is really theory of literature. Students reading Aristotle's *Poetics* for the first time may be disappointed if they expect a detailed analysis of a Greek tragedy. In the *Poetics*, Aristotle was practicing legislative criticism. He was setting forth certain principles (art as imitation, plot as soul, the tragic hero as midway between perfect goodness and utter depravity) and establishing various categories and distinctions (the simple versus the complex plot, the kinds of recognition). But he was not explicating a text or exploring its levels of meaning.

In *On the Sublime*, Longinus analyzed one of Sappho's poems, but most of the work is also legislative: how to achieve the sublime, how not to achieve it, what elements of the sublime can be learned, what elements are innate. Horace's *Ars Poetica* also ignores practical criticism, as does Sir Philip Sidney's *An Apology for Poetry*, which by its very title is a defense of an art rather than an interpretation of it.

Descriptive criticism, which is based on the analysis of a literary work, is relatively new; it began in 1688 with Dryden's *An Essay of Dramatic Poesy,* and not very successfully at that. Dryden was superb when he championed the cause of English drama, but deficient when he tried to analyze a particular English play, Ben Jonson's *The Silent Woman.* The kind of criticism to which most of us are accustomed— where a text is examined line by line, image by image—started with the New Critics (John Crowe Ransom, Cleanth Brooks, Robert Penn Warren, and others), who focused almost exclusively on the work, ignoring the historical milieu out of which it came as well as the author's biography.

Early film criticism was also theoretical and reflected the basic premises of literary criticism, namely, that criticizing a medium requires a knowledge of what the medium can and cannot do, and that this knowledge is obtained through theory.

THE HISTORY OF FILM CRITICISM

The Russians

Film criticism really began in Russia with the Revolution of 1917. It is true that before that time newspapers had reviewers, that in 1915 Vachel Lindsay published *The Art of the Moving Picture,* and that in 1916 Hugo Munsterberg's *The Photoplay: A Psychological Study* appeared. But no filmmaker attempted to explain the nature of his craft until Lev Kuleshov started writing in 1917. In the famous Kuleshov Workshop at the State Film School in Moscow, which included such famous pupils as V. I. Pudovkin and briefly Sergei Eisenstein, Kuleshov performed various experiments in montage, which he defined alternately as "the joining of shots into a predetermined order," "the alternation of shots," and "the organization of cinematic material." To show how editing can alter the face of objective reality, Kuleshov intercut a close-up of an actor's neutral face with three different shots: (1) a bowl of soup, (2) a woman in a coffin, and (3) a little girl with a toy bear. Audiences marveled at the actor's "versatility" in expressing (1) hunger, (2) sorrow at his mother's death, and (3) joy at the sight of his daughter.

Pudovkin continued in his teacher's footsteps. He idolized Kuleshov, and made the extravagant claim that while others made films, Kuleshov made cinematography. Kuleshov was not infallible; although much of his theory still has value, some of it is misleading. His belief that the shot is the equivalent of the word has led to a misunderstanding of what the shot can say and what it cannot; his comparison between a sentence and a sequence limits the sequence to imparting only the information of which a sentence is capable; his view that the way a film is put together is more important than what it means is equivalent to the fallacy that form is more significant than content.

To his credit, Kuleshov was critical of the way Russian directors shot scenes. A great admirer of American films, he contrasted American "fast montage" with Russian "slow montage." He envisioned a suicide scene where a despondent man would sit down at his desk, remove a pistol from the drawer, press it to his forehead, and pull the trigger. The American director would fragment the scene by breaking it up into its components: a close-up of the man's agonized face, a shot of his hand reaching into the drawer, an extreme close-up of the man's eyes, and finally the firing of the pistol. The Russian director would simply film the scene as if it were taking place on the stage.

What Kuleshov meant by montage in this example was nothing other than the editing technique that D. W. Griffith had perfected. Thus, when Kuleshov said montage developed in America, he was speaking the truth. Pudovkin continued to explore the implications of montage, which at this stage still meant editing. He argued that the foundation of film art is editing and that a film is not "shot" but "built" from individual strips of celluloid. Pudovkin was intrigued by what happens when two different shots are combined within the same narrative context. For example, in *Tol'able David* (Henry King, 1921), a tramp enters a house, sees a kitten, and immediately wants to drop a stone on it. Pudovkin read the scene in this way: Tramp + Kitten = Sadist.

To Eisenstein, Pudovkin was incorrect: The equation was not A + B = C, but A × B = Y. Shots are meant to collide, not join together. With Eisenstein montage was no longer a matter of combining shots or of alternating them, but of making them collide with each other: A × B = Y; fox × businessman = cunning. In *Tol'able David*, when King cuts from the tramp to the kitten, both the tramp and the kitten are part of the same scene; in *Strike* (1924), when Eisenstein juxtaposes the face of a man and the picture of a fox, the fox is not an integral part of the scene as the kitten is in *Tol'able David*. To King the kitten is a character; to Eisenstein the fox is a metaphor.

The Grammarians

As new terms (montage, dissolve, wipe, and so on) entered the vocabulary of film, definitions became necessary to explain their functions. In 1935 Raymond Spottiswoode published *A Grammar of the Film*, whose purpose was "to make as precise as possible the language and grammar of film."[1] Spottiswoode was critical of some of the ways in which film expressed itself. He had little use for the wipe because, unlike the cut, which is imperceptible, the wipe calls attention to itself. He believed that while dissolves could be justified, they generally interfered with the film's rhythm because they slurred over the bridge between shots and altered the tone of a scene. Although *A Grammar of the Film* was a serious attempt to analyze film techniques, much of it is passé by today's standards. One no longer speaks of "credit titles," and what were once known as "strip titles" are now "subtitles."

The Apologists

Spottiswoode combined a study of film terminology with a defense of the medium, arguing that movies can only become an art if they first become part of a nation's cultural life and that critics must help film develop a national character. He was forced to defend film, as Sidney was forced to defend poetry 350 years earlier, against its detractors, who called moviegoers "celluloid nitwits." However, few defenses of the filmmaker are as eloquent as Rudolf Arnheim's in *Film as Art:*

> [The filmmaker] shows the world not only as it appears objectively but also subjectively. He creates new realities, in which things can be multiplied, turns their movements and actions backward, distorts them, retards or accelerates them. . . . He breathes life into stone and bids it move. Of chaotic and illimitable space he creates pictures . . . as subjective and complex as painting.[2]

To Arnheim, the fact that photography is limited is precisely what makes film an art. Because photography is incapable of perfect reproduction, film ceases to be a mere replica of reality and becomes reality's ally or enemy but never its equivalent. Film is the art of partial illusion, the same illusion that exists on the stage, where we accept a room with only three walls. In a silent film we accept characters who speak but cannot be heard; in a black and white film we ignore the absence of color.

Because film is capable of distortion, it is not a purely realistic medium. To the doubters who think the camera reproduces the object as it is, Arnheim explains how the camera's ability to approach an object from different and unusual angles creates effects that are ordinarily found in great painting. "Art begins where mechanical reproduction leaves off,"[3] and Arnheim had no doubts that film was art.

The Realists

Since the first film critics based their theories on the silents, they were more sympathetic to montage than the critics who came of age with the talkies. Sound brought spoken dialogue, and once the pictures learned to talk, they were not so docile as they were when they were silent. Russian montage was not well suited to the narrative sound film, in which the combination of happy face and flowing brook could break the dramatic continuity or destroy verisimilitude.

"There are cases in which montage far from being the essence of cinema is indeed its negation," wrote André Bazin,[4] whose early death in 1958 was an irreparable loss to film criticism. What bothered Bazin about montage was its inability to offer more than a limited and frequently distorted view of reality. Bazin discerned two main traditions in film: montage and *mise-en-scène,* or the cut as opposed to the long take. It was *mise-en-scène* that he championed, and it was the *mise-en-scène* directors (Jean Renoir, William Wyler, Orson Welles, etc.) whom he favored.

Mise-en-scène, a term derived from the theater, is difficult to translate because it signifies a variety of things. It means staging a film with the same feeling for style and detail that a theater director (*metteur-en-scène*) brings to a play; it means that the director stages the action, positions the actors within the frame, dresses them in costumes suitable to the era and mood of the film, provides them with décor that is similarly evocative—in short, blends all the elements of filmmaking, from acting and make-up to the composition of the shots, into a whole to give as close an approximation of reality as he or she can.

Directors who work within the *mise-en-scène* tradition achieve a high degree of realism by shooting certain scenes in long take. In fact, some of the finest camera work in film is a result of the long take. The opening of *Touch of Evil* derives its power from being an uninterrupted tracking shot. The long take was particularly evident in *The Best Years of Our Lives* (William Wyler, 1946), a 172–minute movie with under 200 shots; the average film has between 300 to 400 per hour. Wyler filmed several scenes without making a single cut, creating action and reaction within the same shot. Bazin justly admired the famous ending: the wedding of Wilma (Cathy O'Donnell) and Homer (Harold Russell). All of the principals are present: Al and Milly Stephenson (Fredric March and Myrna Loy); their daughter Peggy (Teresa Wright); and Fred Derry (Dana Andrews), Homer's best man. Fred and Peggy are in love, but his inability to find a job has prevented their marriage. As Homer and Wilma exchange vows, Fred turns in the direction of

In the celebrated long take from The Best Years of Our Lives *(1946) William Wyler brings all the principals into the frame for the wedding of Homer (Harold Russell) and Wilma (Cathy O'Donnell). (Courtesy Samuel Goldwyn Productions)*

Peggy, who is standing with her parents. At that moment Wyler brings everyone into the frame. The vows seem equally applicable to Fred and Peggy; the result is the illusion of a double wedding. A cut at any point during the scene would have shattered that illusion.

Another scene Bazin praised was the one in which Fred phones Peggy to terminate their relationship. Fred, Al Stephenson, and Homer are in a bar, where Homer is playing the piano. In one unbroken movement the camera goes from the piano to the phone booth, pausing only for a quick look at Al. Another director might have used several cuts or allowed us to overhear the conversation between Fred and Peggy. The fact that Wyler did neither reinforces Bazin's thesis that Wyler did not have imitators, only disciples.

Bazin wanted film to encompass as much reality as possible, but *mise-en-scène* cannot produce realism by itself; it needs *deep focus*, a technique in which background and foreground are in focus at the same time. Thus, *mise-en-scène* and deep focus are allies. Deep focus has three other advantages for Bazin. (1) It brings spectators into closer contact with the image; (2) it is intellectually more challenging than montage, which manipulates spectators and annihilates their freedom of choice by making them see only what the filmmaker wants them to see (deep focus, by contrast, presents spectators with the whole image, from which they may choose to see only a part, such as the foreground); (3) it allows for ambiguity, which is absolutely essential to works of art, whereas montage reduces a scene to one meaning (smiling face + babbling brook admits of only one interpretation).

Bazin never expressed his theory of film in a full-scale critical work, but only in the form of essays and articles, not all of which have been translated into English. Yet it is clear that he was moving toward an aesthetics of realism. Bazin was especially impressed by the neorealistic Italian films that appeared after World War II—for example, *Open City* (Roberto Rossellini, 1945) and *Paisan* (1946), and *The Bicycle Thief* (Vittorio De Sica, 1949). He saw these films as showing the same respect for reality that deep focus does. Neorealism and deep focus have the same purpose: to keep reality intact. In a neorealistic film, Eisensteinian montage is impossible; nothing can be added to the existing reality. The cutting must follow the script, which cannot tolerate juxtapositions.

Initially, it was film's realism that caused its adversaries to regard it as a copy of nature. To Siegfried Kracauer, film's ability to capture reality, far from being a handicap, is its greatest asset. Just as in the *Poetics* Aristotle determined the nature of art before he discussed the nature of tragedy, Kracauer began his epochal *Theory of Film* not with film itself, but with its parent—photography.

Kracauer is unwilling to call photography an art for the same reason he is unwilling to call film an art: the photographer lacks the artist's freedom to create his or her own inner vision. Both the photographer and the filmmaker are more dependent on the material world than either the painter or the poet. In art the raw material of nature disappears; in film it remains.

Kracauer's reluctance to elevate film to an art form follows inevitably from his belief that film is better equipped to record physical reality than any other medium. Consequently, film should stay on the surface of reality, for when it tries to penetrate the surface, it becomes uncinematic. Parker Tyler challenged Kracauer's thesis by showing that film has successfully explored such themes as split personality (*Persona*) and the impossibility of certitude (*Blow-Up*) by moving from the surface into the realms of human consciousness, where the camera once feared to tread. Kracauer would probably agree with Tyler but then add: "*Persona* and *Blow-Up* are uncinematic," meaning not that they are inferior films (quite the contrary), but that they deal with a form of reality that is better suited to the novel. Kracauer's position is thoroughly classical. Each form reaches its highest stage of development when it accomplishes what no other form can.

To Kracauer, films are either cinematic or uncinematic. The more they reflect the material world, the more cinematic they are; as soon as they forsake physical reality for spiritual reality, they become less cinematic. Thus, he would call the following genres uncinematic by nature: (1) the historical film because it is an artificial reproduction of a bygone age; (2) the fantasy film because of its otherworldliness; (3) the literary adaptation because in a novel or a drama the physical world is not the only one that matters—there is the inner world of the characters, which the camera has difficulty entering.

Because film evolved from photography, it shares with it four characteristics: (1) an affinity for unstaged reality, (2) a penchant for the fortuitous and the random, (3) a sense of endlessness, and (4) a preference for the indeterminate. A fifth characteristic is peculiar to film alone: an ability to capture the open-ended flow of life as it appears in the stream of situations and occurrences that constitute human existence. Kracauer is not saying that film must never attempt to stage reality or that it must always deal with such themes as chance encounters and unpredictable events. He means only that film favors nature in the raw and resists the artificial; thus, film balks at being made to resemble a play. As we have seen, shooting a film from the point of view of a spectator in an orchestra seat is entirely different from shooting it from the point of view of the camera eye, which can look up, down, around, over, under, and beyond what it sees. Naturally, photography favors the fortuitous; some of the most memorable pictures ever taken were the result of the photographer's being in the right place at the right time.

When Kracauer says that film has a liking for the fortuitous, he does not mean that the camera will record whatever passes in front of its lens; he does mean that a good many movies involve chance occurrences on streets, in the badlands of the West, on ships, in airports, railroad stations, hotel lobbies, and so forth. Film tends toward the endless because physical reality is seemingly without end; thus, in a movie a change of scene may be a change of continent. The filmmaker had to learn how to bridge vast distances by creating transitions such as the fade and the dissolve.

Film is indeterminate because physical reality is indeterminate. The juxtaposition of laughing face and flowing brook evokes the same response the world over. But what of the meal of wild strawberries and milk that Mia offers the Knight in *The Seventh Seal?* Bergman has not falsified reality by making the strawberries and milk other than what they are. The context of the scene changes the strawberries and milk from picnic food to food for a eucharistic meal; it also changes those eating the food into communicants. Reality's indeterminacy is one of the glories of film, where an object can be both itself and a symbol at the same time. The strawberries and milk never cease to be what they are: a means of sustenance. The scene determines the *kind* of sustenance: spiritual as well as physical.

Toward the end of *Theory of Film* Kracauer distills the essence of his thesis into a myth. It is not an original myth but the old one of Perseus and Medusa's head. Because the sight of Medusa's head turned men to stone, Athena warned Perseus not to look directly at it but only at the reflection on his shield:

> Now of all the existing media the cinema alone holds up a mirror to nature. Hence our dependence on it for the reflection of happenings which would petrify us were we to encounter them in real life. The film screen is Athena's polished shield.[5]

Hence, the complete title of Kracauer's book: *Theory of Film: The Redemption of Physical Reality.* Kracauer does not believe that film deals only with nature in the raw as opposed to nature transfigured. Nature in the raw, of course, is film's starting point, as it must be; for nature in the raw—physical reality—is to film what language in the raw—words—is to literature: the means by which the work comes into being. Yet how does film redeem physical reality? The very fact that Kracauer speaks of holding a mirror up to nature, a polished mirror at that, provides the answer. A polished mirror will not catch a reflection of the physical universe as it is, but as something better than it is; it catches a higher form of reality, one that is no less real than what we see around us, but superior to it. How can art imitate nature and improve it? Aristotle never tells us. How can film mirror reality and redeem it? Kracauer never tells us. For the answer, we must examine the works of artists who knew the secret of working within the material universe without becoming mired in it.

The *Auteurists*

It was in the late 1950s that the cult of the director arose, resulting in a spate of books on the great and the not so great *auteurs*. Presently, there is a book, a section of a book, an encyclopedia entry, or a monograph on every director who made some contribution to the art of film, even if it was only directing a Republic western with verve and style, as Joe Kane did. That contribution could be revolutionary, as in the case of D. W. Griffith, or minor, as in the case of Edgar G. Ulmer. Yet if there can be critical studies of minor authors, there can be critical studies of minor directors. Minor does not mean mediocre; one's influence on a particular art form may not be pervasive but can nonetheless be noteworthy.

As we have seen in Chapter 6, *auteurism* is merely *one* way of looking at film. It enables those who need a "handle," so to speak, on film to have one. Certainly it is much simpler to deal with a work of known rather than unknown authorship; among other things, it affords a sense of control and security. Even though it is common knowledge that Shakespeare wrote *Hamlet* and Dickens *Great Expectations*, we still speak of "Shakespeare's *Hamlet*" and "Dickens's *Great Expectations*." To be able to say "Hitchcock's *Psycho*" means we can approach *Psycho* in the same way as we might approach *Hamlet;* just as a literary scholar can discuss *Hamlet* within the broader context of Shakespeare's plays, we can approach *Psycho* within the context of Hitchcock's work instead of viewing it merely as a horror film or as the prototype of the modern slasher film.

There are, of course, drawbacks to *auteurism*. The *auteurist* approach cannot be applied unilaterally. It would be something of a joke to write, "Edward Bernds's *Bowery Boys Meet the Monster* (1954)," although confirmed *auteurists* would think nothing of it. Whatever one may think of Edward Bernds (a competent director) or the film, such a designation is bound to strike non-*auteurists* as laughable.

Auteurists can teach us something about the way directors repeat compositions, framings, and certain types of shots. Frank Capra's love of bells, which ranges from the tolling bells in *Lost Horizon* (1937) to the bell on the Christmas tree in *It's a Wonderful Life* (1946), led to his using the bell as the logo of his short-lived production company, Liberty Films. No doubt Capra associated bells with the spirit of freedom and a feeling of joy. Hitchcock's high shots or "God's eye shots" may be a vestige of his Roman Catholicism or merely an attempt to suggest an unseen, omnipotent presence peering down at the world. At any rate, the high shot is a favorite Hitchcockian device, as is irising in D. W. Griffith, double framing in John Ford, long takes in Orson Welles and William Wyler, and a claustrophobic atmosphere in Edgar G. Ulmer. If writers in the *auteurist* tradition can deepen our understanding of a director's style, they have served film well. However, *auteurism* can only be considered a way of approaching film, specifically of approaching the films of selected directors.

The Mythographers

Parker Tyler was the first film critic to understand how mythic the movies are. In *The Hollywood Hallucination*, Tyler explained the extraordinary appeal of stars like Greta Garbo and Marlene Dietrich: They were mystery women, phantom ladies, moon goddesses like Diana. Their inaccessibility made them more desirable than they really were. If they ever loved a man, they could love him only in myth, where they would never have to yield. Even when a man would break down their resistance, we could never believe these goddesses could offer him anything more than fairy tale love.

To Tyler, even Mickey Mouse cartoons had mythic underpinnings. Intelligent moviegoers watch an animated mouse without feeling their intelligence has been insulted because they instinctively recognize some myth, some universal pattern of experience behind the cartoon. Tyler identified it as the Frankenstein myth, which is based on an even older myth of the artist who creates a human being out of inert matter (e.g., Prometheus who molded man from earth; Pygmalion who carved Galatea out of marble). We understand intuitively that Mickey Mouse is someone's creation. Tyler cited other similarities between Mickey Mouse and the Frankenstein monster: Both are mechanized beings; both are factory products (Mickey, the product of the Disney factory; the monster, of Frankenstein's laboratory); both obey their masters. There is also a difference between them: In *Frankenstein* the monster turns on his maker, but Mickey always remains an amiable mouse.

We identify with the underdogs in animated cartoons because they have the same problems we do. We forget they are ducks, mice, or pigs and think of them as humans running the same obstacle course as ourselves and encountering the same frustrations. Yet, Tyler asks, is it not the same situation in gangster films? Don't we empathize with the Little Caesars, the Dillingers, the Bonnies and the Clydes? Many moviegoers find gangsters sympathetic for various reasons: They are nonconformists who flaunt morality; their lives are colorful; they are upwardly mobile, often beginning at the bottom with petty crime and moving up the ladder of notoriety to bank heists and bloodbaths. Hollywood tends to humanize its gangsters, and to Tyler humanization equals glorification. Interestingly, Tyler made no distinction between Superman and the gangster. Who gave Superman the right to take the law into his hands? He is only a newspaper reporter, not a police officer. Yet we look the other way when Clark Kent ducks into a phone booth and emerges as Superman; or rather, our unconscious looks the other way as a reporter becomes a disrupter of the normal order.

In *Magic and Myth of the Movies* Tyler continued to explore the ways in which the unconscious sees films and to show how we accept certain actions in a movie that we would not tolerate in real life. Physical pain is never humorous, yet we laugh when comics slip on banana peels or get pies thrown in their faces. We do not laugh because we are sadistic; the comics give us the right to laugh by becoming scapegoats for our sake and suffering indignities on our behalf. It is the same with comics who distort their faces and mock themselves: they laugh at themselves first so that we can laugh with them. Yet if we read their actions correctly, the rubber-faced clowns are really asking for our approval, our love. They humiliate themselves to win our applause.

Tyler saw the stars of the 1930s and 1940s as gods and goddesses. Because the screen made them immortal, they could not die; they only underwent a ritual death, like the vegetation deities who die in winter and are resurrected in spring. A star can never really die because divinity makes death impossible. The almost universal interest in films of the past supports Tyler's thesis. Humphrey Bogart will live as long as his films are shown, and there is little likelihood that the world will call a moratorium on movies. To see Bogart in *Casablanca* is to see a man in his prime, not a man who died of cancer in 1957. In *The Happy Ending* (Richard Brooks, 1969), the heroine's husband accuses her of mooning over *Casablanca* whenever it is on television. When he reminds her that practically the entire cast is dead, she replies that Humphrey Bogart, Peter Lorre, Sidney Greenstreet, and Claude Rains are more alive than either of them.

The Semioticians

Semiotics emphasizes the way a film transmits its meaning through signs and codes.[6] Its approach is similar to that of the myth critics, who search out universal patterns and archetypal themes. Semiotics is also the theoretical side of structuralism, which is not so much a new discipline as a new approach to older disciplines such as linguistics, anthropology, psychoanalysis, and rhetoric, disciplines that are more concerned with signs than with objects. Thus, structuralists are invariably attracted to myth because myths are the first structures, the first messages of a culture.

But myths are coded; they are invisible patterns, "offstage voices," as Roland Barthes might call them. The structuralist tries to bring the voice from the wings to center stage. Myths remain coded until they become transparent; then society discards them as clichés. The reason myths were such unifying forces in ancient societies is that they resisted decoding. Frequently they appeared in binary form, reflecting the dualism inherent in nature (spirit/matter, male/female, life/death) and in culture (urban/rural, endogamy/exogamy, freedom/imprisonment). The great myths are inexhaustibly bipolar;

they resist any attempt to reduce them to a single meaning. Oppositeness is at the heart of Greek mythology—which is one reason why it is constantly being reinterpreted. The Oedipus myth, for example, embodies the polarities knowledge/ignorance, wife/mother, old order/new order, rationalism/mysticism, sight/blindness. Myths such as this are deathless because they are founded on natural, not artificial, opposites.

It is understandable that semiotics would be in such vogue today. Semiotics is studied in the university and in adult education centers, where "Semiotics for the Layperson" teaches students to translate the signs they encounter in daily life: the TV commercials that promise a world where young and old, white and black will stand together if they drink Pepsi or chew Juicy Fruit gum; the clothing ads that build sexual potency into their product; the body language that is spoken at parties but not always understood.

In *Mythologies*, Roland Barthes sees signs everywhere. A person's hairstyle can designate the class and era to which he or she belongs. In *Julius Caesar* (Joseph L. Mankiewicz, 1953), the fringed hair of the characters was a sign of their "Roman-ness." Wrestling abounds in signs. The wrestler with the fleshy, sagging body telegraphs certain messages to the spectator: repulsiveness, cruelty, cowardice. The wrestler's body determines the way he acts in the ring. The conventions of wrestling (the armlock, the twisting of the leg) are all parodies of tragedy. Just as the mask of tragedy is an exaggeration of the human face, so too is wrestling an exaggeration of human suffering. The opponent who lies flat on his back with his arms outstretched has been crucified. In wrestling defeat reaches the nadir of humiliation—crucifixion.

Even our detergents speak to us, according to Barthes. Chlorinated detergents proclaim they are absolute; as liquid fire, they blaze a path through the dirt and annihilate it. Powdered detergents are more selective; they liberate the dirt. Foam detergents, on the other hand, are useless. They are luxury items, airy and immaterial, as impractical as bubble bath.

If detergents talk, so does food. Fish 'n chips speak of nostalgia, of the British bearing up under the Blitz; steak speaks of virility, and if it is served rare and swimming in blood, of ambrosia that produces godlike strength. (In *Experiment Perilous* [Jacques Tourneur, 1944], a woman on a train orders steak for a male passenger because she assumes steak is a man's dish.)

On the surface, semiotics seems rather easy to understand. There is a signifier (say, a gold band) and the signified (marriage); there is denotation, by which a word keeps its literal meaning ("He lit the *fire*"), and connotation, by which it takes on other meanings ("She was consumed by the *fire* of passion"); there is *langue*, language system that can be verbal (English, German, and so on) or nonverbal (the "language" of poker, falconry, and so on), and there is *parole* (speech), the actual practice of a language system.

The problems begin when one attempts to apply this terminology to film. In film what are the signifiers? Can a movie denote and connote, or in film does denotation become connotation? There is also the haunting question: Is film a language system? To Christian Metz, the best known of the film semioticians, film is not *langue*.[7] In language, a word can acquire a different meaning merely by the addition of a single letter—for example, *d* or *r* added to *love*. But film has no words. Metz rightly rejects the shot-as-word theory and compares the shot to the sentence. Like a gifted child, film skipped the parts of speech and moved to a higher grade. But if film has no parts of speech, then it has no grammar. We know "He see the man" is ungrammatical in standard, edited English; but what is ungrammatical in a movie? Using a dissolve instead of a cut?

Another difference is that in words there is a distance between the signifier and the signified. *Sadness* can be broken up into its signifier (the sound săd'něs) and its signified (the concept of unhappiness). But in film the signified cannot be disengaged from the signifier. In a movie the sound of sadness is not săd'něs, but a child weeping, a man wailing, an American secretary sitting alone in an outdoor café in Venice while couples stroll past her. In a movie sadness is not a concept but an actual situation (a sad family) or an attribute of a specific person (a sad man). For the same reason denotation and connotation are not distinct in film. A movie denotes and connotes at the same time. When Isak Borg raises a glass of wine in Bergman's *Wild Strawberries*, he is Isak Borg who at that moment is having lunch with his daughter-in-law and some young hitchhikers; he is also Isak Borg the priest-figure officiating at a communion service and elevating not a wine glass but a chalice.

Metz claims that film is "like" language because it communicates. But how does it communicate? In two ways: syntagmatically and paradigmatically. A *syntagm* is a unit of actual relationship; thus, *syntagmatic relationships* result when the units of a statement or the units in a filmic chain follow each other in order. If we analyze the way the subplots of *Nashville* interconnect or trace the rise of a character such as Mildred Pierce from housewife to restaurant owner, we are approaching the film syntagmatically.

A *paradigm* is a unit of potential relationship; thus *paradigmatic relationships* are associative, not sequential. They are not concerned with the order of the links in the chain but with the meanings we associate with them. If we associate Frank Serpico with Jesus Christ or the madness that erupted at the Hollywood premiere in *The Day of the Locust* with the outbreak of World War II, we are approaching the film paradigmatically. Because paradigmatic relationships are independent of the order in which the events occur, they can also exist between scenes taking place at different times within the film. Shane's ride of vengeance at the end of George Stevens's film of the same name should, by its horizontal movement, recall the first appearance of Wilson the gunfighter, who also rode horizontally across the frame; yet it also contrasts with the way Shane rode down into the valley at the beginning of the film. If we associate descent with something positive (the desire to reform) and horizontal movement with something negative (the desire to murder), then we have made a paradigmatic connection.

It is not enough for the semiotician simply to isolate syntagmas and paradigms; the movie relays its messages through codes that the filmmaker used and that the semiotician must now reconstruct. There are all kinds of codes: codes of dress, color, lighting, and so forth. In certain simplistic westerns we may discover that white and black attire mean hero and villain respectively; in other westerns the dress code will yield to a landscape code, in which the signifier (Monument Valley) becomes the signified (America in microcosm).

Transportation codes are particularly meaningful in discovering a filmmaker's intentions. Karel Reisz saw the car as a vehicle charged with associations of death in *Isadora* (1969); in *Two for the Road*, the particular car in which the couple is traveling is related to a particular stage in their marriage. In *The Wild One* (Laslo Benedek, 1954), the motorcycle is the embodiment of raw virility, fascism, and arrested sexuality; but in *Easy Rider* (Dennis Hopper, 1969), the motorcycle epitomizes young, disenchanted America in the late 1960s. The Yuppies of the 1980s, however, do not travel by motorcycle; they go cross-country in a motor home in *Lost in America* (Albert Brooks, 1985), in which *Easy Rider* is mentioned so reverentially that the idealistic sixties becomes the yardstick by which to measure the materialistic eighties.

Sometimes codes are not quite so easy to decipher. Whenever Marlene Dietrich wore a tuxedo in a movie, as she did in *Morocco* and *Blonde Venus*, both directed by Josef von Sternberg, 1930s audiences were taken aback at the sight of such a sensuous woman in men's clothes. A dress code was operating, but what did it mean? In *Morocco*, it meant that a strange form of defeminization had taken place by which Dietrich had become the essence of Hollywood Woman (seductive, smoldering) decked out with the trappings of Hollywood

Marlene Dietrich looking androgynous in Blonde Venus *(Josef von Sternberg, 1932).* (Copyright ® Paramount Pictures, Courtesy of MCA Publishing Rights, a Division of MCA Incorporated)

Man (debonair, aggressive). Thus, the Dietrich figure in a tuxedo became androgynous.

Critics influenced by semiotics use a specialized vocabulary. For example, they do not think of film narrative solely in terms of plot. They distinguish between *plot, diegesis,* and *discourse.* The plot, or what Aristotle in the *Poetics* called the *mythos,* is the ordered arrangement of the incidents in terms of a beginning, middle and end. The diegesis is the story that is recounted, embodying everything pertaining to the story regardless of how much of it actually appears on the screen. The party in *Notorious* is an all-evening affair, but on the screen it only lasts thirteen minutes. Thus, there is a difference between diegetic time (all evening) and film time (thirteen minutes). The discourse is the manner in which the story reaches the audience. That story includes what is dramatized as well as what is implied; it is based on a script that is brought to the screen by a team who have broken down the action into various codes (color codes, dress codes, lighting codes, codes of manners); it is the result of the interaction between an "I" and a "You," between the one telling the story (the filmmaker) and the one perceiving it (the filmgoer); it is the result of decisions made before, during, and after production. Thus, the main title and the end credits would be very much a part of the film's discourse; a credits sequence, which is visualized action, is part of the plot (the film's structure) and diegesis (the film's world).

While semioticians have shown how complex film narrative is, one should remember that it is perfectly possible to write good film criticism without resorting to critical jargon. If understood properly, Aristotle's concept of plot is as applicable to film narrative as it is to literary narrative. "Plot is the structure of events," Aristotle wrote. Note that he does not call the plot the story line, as many would, but the *shape* of the story line and the *form* it takes. To Aristotle, the plot is the soul of the work—the source of its life. Remove the plot from a work of fiction and it ceases to be a work of fiction; remove it from a narrative film and it ceases to be a narrative film. Soul is structure; it is the harmony that exists when all the parts work together. Once plot is understood as the nucleus around which the incidents, the characters, the theme, and the setting gather, and the source from which they draw their life, it can then be perceived as the soul of the work and something quite distinct from the story line, which is a bodily part.

Semiotics is to film what linguistics is to literature. A knowledge of linguistics can be helpful in reading dialect literature or in interpreting poetry, since poets coin new words and use old ones in startlingly new ways. However, literature can be analyzed quite successfully without the terminology of linguistics. Similarly, semiotics can enhance our perception of a film by disclosing the way signs and codes operate in it, yet film can be discussed intelligently without resorting to the vocabulary of semiotics.

Feminist Criticism

Feminist film criticism, whose practitioners include Laura Mulvey, Julia LeSage, Annette Kuhn, and E. Ann Kaplan, is indebted to the work of French psychologist Jacques Lacan, especially for his theory of the mirror stage of development. Briefly stated, the image a child sees reflected in a mirror produces ambivalent feelings. The child is attracted to the image because it is an ideal image, but repelled by it because the real can never be the ideal; the ideal is *other than* real. The Hollywood studio system, a male-created and male-dominated industry, never seems to have gone beyond the mirror stage. In the classic Hollywood film, the separation of real and ideal made woman the other, an object rather than a subject. Specifically, the woman was an object of the male gaze; she was an exhibit or a spectacle rendered in terms of anatomy (bosom, legs, mouth, posterior) and fractured representation (close-ups, extreme close-ups). The idealization of woman (soft focus, front lighting, lenses smeared with vaseline or covered with gauze to give the face a glow) originates in the fear of castration. It was as if the male had unconsciously struck a bargain with the female: If she would not deprive the male of his potency, he would glorify her image. In this way, the universe would remain phallocentric, dominated by the symbol of male potency, the phallus, which, according to Lacan, is a signifier. The phallus represents male power as well as male presence, as opposed to female helplessness and female absence. Since the female lacks the organ on which the signifier depends, she denotes absence—the absence of power, authority, and speech. Speech is phallocentric, the prerogative of the male; speechlessness is the state of the female. Thus, even when women speak, they are passive; it might be more accurate to use the passive voice.

Although the woman's film of the 1930s and 1940s placed the woman at the center of the action, feminists would still argue that, despite woman's pivotal role, it is the male who sets the plot in motion. *Dark Victory*, a key woman's film, is ostensibly the story of Judith Traherne's acceptance of death from brain cancer. After Dr. Steele, a neurosurgeon, has diagnosed Judith's condition, she reluctantly submits to surgery. Later she falls in love with Steele, who cannot bear to tell her the operation was unsuccessful and her condition is terminal. Judith learns the truth by accidentally coming upon her medical record. Embittered, she turns on Steele, indulges in self-pity and drink, but finally returns to him, begging his forgiveness. Forgiveness for what, one might ask? She is the one who is going to die, not he. Judith even goes to his apartment and admits she has been a "fool." That visit, however, results in her marriage to Steele, without which the plot cannot be resolved. Judith knows that blindness will precede death. When her eyesight suddenly fails, she does not tell Steele, who must depart for an important medical meeting, but manages to help him pack while all the time acting normally. The ending of *Dark Victory* would have been impossible without the character of Steele, for it is Judith's marriage to him that gives her the courage to face not just death but death alone.

Like all theories, phallocentrism and the mirror stage cannot be proved scientifically. Thus, they may strike one as either probable or improbable. One can also argue that women were depicted as goddesses endowed with an aura denied to men because Hollywood believed that attractive women were "good box office." Women liked seeing themselves on the screen, and men liked seeing women on the screen. When both sexes were happy, the studio system thrived.

One cannot ignore Hollywood's ambivalence toward women. As Laura Mulvey states in an influential article, "woman . . . stands in patriarchal culture as signifier of the male other."[8] When woman is the object of the male gaze, she is given the full treatment; she is exquisitely gowned and impeccably coiffured. Her face is bathed in light that cleanses it of imperfections. A close-up transforms her image into a portrait. Woman as movie star is Other as Ideal, and the ideal should be idealized. However, other is also not-I, and in a phallocentric world, what is not-I is not Male. As not-male, woman is often relegated to a subordinate position in the frame. In westerns, she is frequently behind the hero, serving him or standing in the background looking terrified as he takes on the villain. When the hero rides off at the end, she becomes part of the landscape in the extreme long shot that concludes the film.

Although women are still objects of the male gaze in slasher, macho, and exploitation films in which they are portrayed as chattel or prey, a new generation of actors (Glenn Close, Meryl Streep, Kathleen Turner, Jessica Lange) has emerged that has been able to challenge the woman-as-object tradition. While the industry may still be male-dominated, there are a number of talented female directors (Penny Marshall, Joan Micklin Silver, Susan Seidelman) who do not use woman exploitatively. However, it is too early to say whether female directors will wrest control of "the gaze" from the male and give it to the female, reject the gaze with its domination-submission pattern, or resolve the polarities (active/passive, speech/speechlessness, voyeur/fetish) that the gaze creates.

The Reviewers

A film reviewer is not necessarily a film critic; few reviewers can be considered critics if, by critic, we mean a representative of the most insightful approach possible. If Alexander Pope's standards are applied to contemporary reviewers, only a handful would qualify as critics. Pope expected the critic to know everything about the work under evaluation:

> You then whose judgment the right course would steer,
> Know well each ancient's proper character;
> His fable, subject, scope in every page;
> Religion, country, genius of his age:
> Without all these at once before your eyes,
> Cavil you may, but never criticise.
> —*An Essay on Criticism* (I, 118–23)

Film reviewers write for newspapers and magazines or deliver their reviews on television and radio. Film reviewing, then, is a branch of print and broadcast journalism. Movies are a form of news; thus, they should be covered. The question is, by whom? Ideally, by someone knowledgeable about film. However, it often happens that the film reviewer of a local newspaper is a reporter assigned to the movie beat because there happened to be an opening in that department. A major newspaper, on the other hand, is likely to have several reviewers who know film and have a wholeness of vision reflected in their reviews. They can relate the film being reviewed to other films of its kind, to the director's or the stars' previous work, to the writer's former scripts. Their reviews are not valentines studded with superlatives; rather, they offer a reasoned and balanced judgment of a film so that if they use words like "greatest" or "best," we know they are not being hyperbolic.

Television critics are a special breed: limited sometimes to a mere minute of air time, they are almost forced to be glib to keep the viewer from switching channels. Thus, to base one's knowledge of film criticism on television reviewing is to limit criticism to one-liners.

Americans need and want film reviews. This was true even at the turn of the century, when the public was so hungry for some kind of film review that they even accepted plot summaries and naive accounts of the wonders of celluloid. By 1904, the *Philadelphia Inquirer* was reviewing movies: its review of *The Great Train Robbery* (1903) was superficial ("There is a great amount of shooting"), but at least it was a beginning. By 1906, the first film journals had been started. In 1909, the *New York Times* ran its first movie review, an archly written piece on D. W. Griffith's *Pippa Passes;* from that time on, film reviewing became a regular department in the *Times.* Since there were no special qualifications for reviewing films, anyone could write about them, and often did. Frank Woods, an advertising salesperson for the *New York Dramatic Mirror,* wrote a movie column in the *Mirror* under the pseudonym "The Spectator" from 1908 to 1912; later he went on to become a leading screenwriter.

Before he became a major playwright, Robert E. Sherwood served as film critic for *Life* magazine from 1920 to 1928. Men of letters such as Edmund Wilson, Joseph Wood Krutch, and Mark Van Doren also wrote occasional film criticism. However, Wilson, Krutch, and Van Doren made their reputations in literary criticism, not movie reviewing. The first writer to achieve a national reputation for movie reviewing was James Agee, who between 1941 and 1948 reviewed for both *Time* magazine and the *Nation.* In addition to being a critic, Agee was also a novelist, a poet, and a screenwriter; thus, his reviews had a literacy not generally found in movie columns. Agee could be vicious, but generally he was honest and regarded himself as an amateur conversing with his readers.

Agee's early death at forty-five prevented his leaving behind a fully developed theory of film; yet he demonstrated in outline, if not in detail, what a critic should be. It is clear from his review of *Mission to Moscow* (Michael Curtiz, 1943), made when Russia was an American ally, that he sensed the film's importance, not as art but as pro-Soviet propaganda. Although *Mission to Moscow* justified Stalin's purge trials, Agee was unmoved by the film's rationalizations. Instead he wrote:

> About the trials I am not qualified to speak. On surface falsifications of fact and atmosphere I might, but on the one crucial question, whether Trotsky and Trotskyists were or were not involved with Germany and Japan in a plot to overthrow the government and to partition the country, I am capable of no sensible opinion. I neither believe it nor disbelieve it.[9]

One imagines Agee would have been the kind of critic who could take a film on its own terms, however political those terms may be. His charge that *Mission to Moscow* indulges its audience is more damning than five paragraphs of invective. Agee was not the kind of critic who catered to prejudices and yearned to make his audience a reflection of himself, but the kind who believed that readers have the right instincts within them and only need the proper guidance to bring them forth.

Whether Agee would have become an *auteurist* is problematical. He was certainly conscious of the role of the director, as is evident from his review of *Hail the Conquering Hero* (Preston Sturges, 1944). Sturges's mother was a bohemian who gave her son a charmed life: private schools and early exposure to opera, theater, and ballet. Sturges's foster father was a down-to-earth Chicago millionaire. Agee saw Sturges as a man torn between his mother's love of the arts and his foster father's success in business. Thus in his films, Sturges was always floundering between art and popular entertainment, tending more to the latter than to the former. Agee realized he was doing something quite unusual when he invoked a director's life as background for his films. Here is one of those tantalizing glimpses into the kind of critic Agee might have become. He seemed to be on the right track with Sturges. In *Sullivan's Travels* John L. Sullivan (Joel McCrea), a liberal director who may well be Sturges's persona, abandons social consciousness films for comedies because "there's a lot to be said for making people laugh." In *The Palm Beach Story*, Sturges was completely ambivalent toward money, satirizing the gold diggers and the frivolous rich alike but resolving their problems before the fade-out.

Agee was not afraid to express admiration for B films. He must have known Val Lewton's movies would someday be classics, for he hailed *The Curse of the Cat People* and *Youth Runs Wild*, also a Lewton production, as the best "fiction films" of 1944. Agee also wrote favorably of *Phantom Lady* (Robert Siodmak, 1944), now regarded as a model of *film noir*.

Another important reviewer was Bosley Crowther.[10] Of all the newspaper reviewers of his era, he carried the greatest weight because from 1940 through 1967 he wrote for the *New York Times*. Since Crowther reviewed for the most prestigious paper in America, he did not waste his time on what he deemed "junk." Whereas Agee saw more in Val Lewton films than calculated fright, Crowther saw nothing in them. *Cat People*, he felt, was "labored and obvious"; and although he found *The Curse of the Cat People* sensitive, it did not make his Ten Best list.

Crowther wrote for that anomaly known as the *New York Times* reader: someone who was educated but not pedantic, conservative but not a book burner, liberal without endorsing every cause as right, a believer in human values without being a teary sentimentalist. Crowther had these qualities himself. When the National Legion of Decency condemned *The Miracle* (Roberto Rossellini, 1948) as an affront to the Virgin Birth, Crowther praised it as a work of art. But in the 1960s, his influence began to wane. The movies were changing and so were audiences. One of the last reviews Crowther wrote before his retirement was of *Bonnie and Clyde*. The review gave no indication of the sane judgments of which he was capable. Unable to see the film as a commentary on the Great Depression, he branded it as cheap, pointless, and marred by violence.

Dwight Macdonald, who devoted more than forty years of his life to movie reviewing, defined the concept of *film critic*: A critic will judge the film's quality, prove its quality, and compare the film with other films, giving it its proper place within the history of motion pictures.[11] Note how Richard Corliss of *Time* meets these criteria in his review of *The Last Temptation of Christ* (*Time*, August 15, 1988). He backs up his assertions, reveals his knowledge of Scorsese's other films, and places the film within the context of film history.

Sunday school may have taught them the words of the Gospels, but for millions of children, Hollywood provided the pictures. They were pretty pictures: stained glass in motion, from the First Church of DeMille.

Handsome men—their beards neatly curled and trimmed, their robes immaculate—trod on tiptoe through a Judaea as verdant and manicured as Forest Lawn. They may have represented Israelites of two millenniums past, but they often looked Nordic; God must have had blue eyes. And they spoke the King's English: King James', with an assist from any screenwriter willing to gussy up his fustian. In these prim tones, the heart's revolution that Jesus preached became an Oxford don's lecture, and his ghastly, redemptive death a tableau painted on velvet.

Martin Scorsese's first achievement in *The Last Temptation of Christ* is to strip the biblical epic of its encrusted sanctimony and show biz. He has re-created—in Morocco, and on a pinchpenny budget of $6.5 million—a Palestine of sere deserts and balding meadows. It takes hard men to work this holy land, men who labor under the twin burdens of poverty and occupying oppression. Their clothes are dirt-dry and sweat-drenched. Their faces, most of them, boast Semitic heritage; their voices hold the raspy, urgent cadences of Brooklyn, Appalachia and other frontier outposts of working-class America. (Only Satan and the Romans speak with British accents.) By jolting the viewer to reconsider Hollywood's calcified stereotypes of the New Testament, Scorsese wants to restore the immediacy of that time, the stern wonder of that land, the thrilling threat of meeting the Messiah on the mean streets of Jerusalem.

Scorsese is America's most gifted, most daring moviemaker. His style is impatient, intimate, conspiratorial, the camera scurrying ever closer to the heart of the matter—X rays of souls in stress. His films are also, thematically, the same film. In *Mean Streets* and *Raging Bull, The King of Comedy* and *The Color of Money,* he has made his own kind of buddy movie. Two men are bound by love or hate; one must betray the other and thereby help certify his mission. In the Nikos Kazantzakis novel and Paul Schrader's script, Scorsese has found a story vibrant with melodrama and metaphor. This Jesus (Willem Dafoe) is not God born as man. He is a man who discovers—or invents—his own divinity. And he is both tormented and excited by the revelation. This Judas (Harvey Keitel) is a strong, loving activist. He wants to overthrow the Roman occupiers, while Jesus wants freedom for the soul. To fulfill his covenant, Judas must betray not Jesus but his own ideal of revolution. He must hand the man he most loves over to the Romans.

Any Jesus film with sex and violence is bound to roil the faithful. For Scorsese, though, these elements are bold colors on the canvas, images of the life Jesus must renounce and redeem. The sex scene (in which Barbara Hershey's Mary Magdalene entertains some customers) exposes a strong woman's degradation more than it does her flesh. And the film's carnage is emetic, not exploitative. The crowning with thorns, the scourging at the pillar, the agonized trudge up Calvary show what Jesus suffered and why. Dafoe's spiky, ferocious, nearly heroic performance is a perfect servant to the role. He finds sense in Jesus' agonies; he finds passion in the parables.

This is not a movie for all believers—or for all moviegoers. But it is, nonetheless, a believer's movie. Scorsese believes in the power of Jesus' message. He believes in the power of cinema to rethink traditions, to make Jesus live in a skeptical age. And those willing to accompany Scorsese on his dangerous ride through the Gospels may believe he has created his masterpiece.

Naturally, not all reviewers can fulfill Macdonald's criteria as well as Corliss does. Several, however, can: Andrew Sarris (*Village Voice*), David Denby (*New York*), Stanley Kauffman (*New Republic*), and perhaps the most famous of all, Pauline Kael (*New Yorker*).

Much of Pauline Kael's criticism has been collected; *I Lost It at the Movies* (1965), *Kiss Kiss, Bang Bang* (1968), *Going Steady* (1970), *Deeper into Movies* (1973), *Reeling* (1976), and *Hooked* (1989). Because she identifies with the moviegoer, she is sometimes forced to assume an egalitarian, even an anti-intellectual pose. She constantly laments the teaching of film in the university, claiming that an overly scholarly approach will kill "movies" (her favorite term for the medium because in America we never say, "I'm going to the films," but "I'm going to the movies"). She scorns pretentiousness, believing that films like *Last Year at Marienbad* (Alain Resnais, 1961) will drive moviegoers out of the theaters. She champions American movies, yet she is not chauvinistic; she merely feels that they come closer to what movies ought to be than most European films. Although she scorns *auteurism*, she will come to the aid of beleaguered directors like Robert Altman and Sam Peckinpah. She may write for *The New Yorker*, but there is no wordliness in her style; there is wit, however, which may explain her association with that magazine.

If Pauline Kael sounds like a mass of contradictions, it is because on the one hand, she writes about an art form that, in its inception, was not taken seriously; movies were "flickers," and nothing more. On the other hand, she is writing about an art form that is now not only taken seriously but is the subject of undergraduate and graduate study. Thus, she maintains a "one of the people" stand by addressing the reader as a "you," a form of address that David Denby has also adopted. "What you keep reacting to is the film's exuberant doodles," she wrote of *Bull Durham* (Ron Shelton, 1988). Yet, as a critic whose knowledge of the other arts is on a par with her knowledge of film, she is more than just one of the people; she is the people at their most perceptive; she is the ideal moviegoer.

This does not mean she cannot make mistakes. No critic is infallible; one should remember that Tolstoy refused to consider Shakespeare a classic, and T. S. Eliot made the extravagant claim that Virgil's *Aeneid* is the only true classic of Western literature. Kael can also be hyperbolic when she feels strongly about a movie: she once compared the evening *Last Tango in Paris* closed the 1972 New York Film Festival with the evening Igor Stravinsky's *The Rite of Spring* premiered, calling each date a cultural landmark. Because she disapproves of *auteurism* (although she has favorite *auteurs*), she set out to discredit Orson Welles as the *auteur* of *Citizen Kane* in her essay, "Raising Kane" (1971), which first appeared in *The New Yorker* and then as the introduction to *The Citizen Kane Book*. Subsequent criticism, notably by Robert Carringer, has shown that Kael was not entirely correct in attributing the script wholly to Herman J. Mankiewicz. Kael certainly has her blind spots; she either failed, or refused, to see how Welles impressed his personality on *Citizen Kane* by drawing on his stage and radio experience (especially overlapping dialogue and musical bridges) to combine the best of both media in the film.

To her credit, Kael at least has a philosophy of film: It is a people's art form. Moviegoers loathe sham; they prefer "movies" to "cinema"; they want theorizing kept to a minimum; they cannot bear to see their values mocked. Thus, Kael reacted negatively to *A Clockwork Orange* because it argued that humankind's capacity for evil is never exhausted. Kael, who believes in people (or at least moviegoers), could not accept that. Consequently, she accused Stanley Kubrick of "sucking up to the thugs in the audience."[12]

Since Pauline Kael enjoys considerably more space than most reviewers, she can write about films at greater length, producing what are really essay-reviews. Her method is to reconstruct the film, incorporating into an essay-review her own impressions, comparisons with other films, and frequently comparisons with other art forms. Those who dislike Kael claim that in reconstructing the film, she creates an antifilm that bears little resemblance to the original. If Kael does this, and it is not often, the readers are at least afforded an X ray of her thoughts so that they can experience what was going on in her mind when she saw the film and later when she was writing about it. We may not always be able to see every movie we read about. What reviewers as critics can do is suggest how we might have reacted during the film and when reflecting on it. Pauline Kael can provide this vicarious experience better than most of her colleagues.

PRACTICAL CRITICISM

If fiction is a house with many windows, as Henry James alleged, then criticism is a house with many doors, each with its own key. No school of literary criticism has a monopoly on interpretation; each offers its own peculiar access to the work. The New Criticism stresses the text; historical criticism places the text within its time; biographical criticism, within the context of the author's life; Marxist criticism, within the framework of the class struggle; psychoanalytic criticism, within the workings of the unconscious; myth criticism, within the universal dreams of humankind.

That criticism is an applied art is evident from the ways a film historian, an *auteurist,* a myth critic, and a social philosopher might interpret *Citizen Kane.*

The Film Historian

The history of *Citizen Kane* is filled with so many untruths and half-truths that uncovering the real truth about the film is as complex as Thompson's attempt to solve the enigma of "Rosebud." The popular assumption that RKO was in such a state of financial instability that RKO's president, George J. Schaefer, wooed Orson Welles, the boy wonder of stage and radio, to Hollywood in the hope of working wonders for the studio, is one such untruth. In "A History of RKO Radio Pictures, Incorporated, 1928–1942" Richard B. Jewell has shown that in 1940, the year RKO signed Welles, its finances were in good shape.[13] Furthermore, the studio had a tradition of hiring stage personalities such as Katharine Hepburn, George Gershwin, and director Garson Kanin; thus, RKO's hiring Welles was not inconsistent with studio policy, although his being given the right of final cut was inconsistent with Hollywood policy in general.

Although one may never know whose idea it was—Welles's or Herman J. Mankiewicz's—to make a movie based on the life of newspaper tycoon William Randolph Hearst, films about the rise of an entrepreneur from obscurity to renown were not unknown. Since Mankiewicz, who wrote the first two drafts of *Citizen Kane* (which he entitled *American*), had been writing for the movies since 1926, he may well have been influenced by the script Preston Sturges wrote for *The Power and the Glory* (William K. Howard, 1933), which dealt with a Kane-like railroad magnate. Thomas Garner (Spencer Tracy) in *The Power and the Glory* is as enigmatic as the master of Xanadu. Moreover, there are points of contact between both films: the Horatio Alger theme, the flashbacks following the tycoon's death, violations of chronology, and the extremes of admiration and contempt that both men inspired.

Mankiewicz, however, was not wholly responsible for the script of the film that ultimately became *Citizen Kane.* Pauline Kael's "Raising Kane" is in error on this point.[14] In an attempt to refocus attention on

Mankiewicz, whom Welles has eclipsed, Kael downplayed Welles's contribution even to the point of undermining its orginality. What other critics consider Wellesian, she would attribute to Gregg Toland's cinematography. Kael invites us to compare *Kane* with *Mad Love* (Karl Freund, 1935), a Peter Lorre "mad doctor" movie, which Toland photographed and which has certain features in common with *Kane:* gothic sets, a physical resemblance between the bald Lorre and the bald Welles in *Kane's* final scenes, cavernous rooms, and even a white cockatoo.

"Raising Kane," which has occasioned controversy since its publication, has been superceded by what appears to be the definitive work on the subject, Robert L. Carringer's *The Making of Citizen Kane.* Consequently, we now know that "Mankiewicz . . . wrote the first two drafts. His principal contributions were the story frame, a cast of characters, various individual scenes, and a good share of the dialogue. . . . Welles added the narrative brilliance—the visual and verbal wit, the stylistic fluidity, and such stunningly original strokes as the newspaper montages and the breakfast table sequence."[15] Unlike Kael, who exalted Mankiewicz at the expense of Welles, Carringer is perfectly willing to credit Mankiewicz for a contribution of "fundamental importance" but, knowing what he does about the film's genesis, cannot attribute the script solely to him.

Nor can Carringer allow the myth to persist that Gregg Toland determined how *Citizen Kane* would be photographed. Carringer proves that Welles and Toland were in total agreement as to how the film would be shot; it was not to resemble a typical Hollywood movie but rather it would display all the techniques at which Toland excelled (low angles, deep focus, high contrast photography, etc.). Deep focus, long takes, and a paucity of close-ups would also serve Welles's purpose. One must never forget that Welles came from the theatre; hence, deep focus and long takes would be as close as Welles could come to duplicating stage drama. Since stage actors project more forcefully than film actors, a preponderance of close-ups would reveal their lack of film experience. One must also never forget that the leading roles were played by members of Welles's Mercury Theatre. Finally, it should also be remembered that the Mercury Theatre had a weekly radio series, *The Mercury Theatre on the Air,* which Welles hosted and in which he frequently appeared. *Citizen Kane* contains examples of a common radio drama device, the cross fade, in which a character will begin a sentence in one place, and someone else will finish the sentence in another.

Although *Citizen Kane* is not always thought of in terms of RKO, it was an RKO product. As Carringer demonstrates, the glass paper-

The glass paperweight in Kitty Foyle *(Sam Wood, 1940) that probably inspired the one in* Citizen Kane *(Courtesy WCFTR)*

weight that is so crucial to the plot of *Citizen Kane* is not that different from a similar paperweight in an earlier RKO film, *Kitty Foyle*. In both films, the paperweight has a snow motif which conjures up memories of childhood. Since both paperweights were made by the RKO property department, it is unlikely that Mankiewicz or Mankiewicz/Welles hit upon the paperweight idea without some prior knowledge of *Kitty Foyle*.

A knowledge of a film's production history makes it possible to speak authoritatively about the film. Without such knowledge, one runs the risk of crediting the wrong individuals for contributions that others have made.

The *Auteurist*

Like many a first film, *Citizen Kane* contains within it the directors' major themes and preoccupations. Here it is Welles's ambivalence toward wealth and his fascination with corruption. Welles's world is full of potentates, of men larger than life: Kane, Bannister of *The Lady from Shanghai*, Gregori Arkadin of *Mr. Arkadin* (1955), and their alter egos in the director's Shakespearean films (*Macbeth*, 1948; *Othello*, 1952; and *Chimes at Midnight*, 1967).

Wealth assumes various forms in Welles's films: Kane's Xanadu, the Amberson mansion in *The Magnificent Ambersons*, the yacht in *The Lady from Shanghai*, the castle of Dunsinane in *Macbeth*, the castle at San Tirso in *Mr. Arkadin*, and Henry IV's court in *Chimes at Midnight*. Conversely, symbols of squalor also recur: Mary Kane's boarding house, the boarding house to which George and Aunt Fanny retreat in *The Magnificent Ambersons*, the Mexican fleabag in *Touch of Evil*, K's flat in *The Trial* (1963).

There are certain Wellesian artifacts that characterize the rich, the corrupt, and the guilty: mirrors (*Kane, The Lady from Shanghai, Othello*); corridors (*Kane, Macbeth, The Trial*); staircases (*Kane, The Magnificent Ambersons*); chauffeured cars (*Kane*) and private planes (*Mr. Arkadin*).

Another Wellesian theme is the war of the worlds. The extraordinary world encroaches on the ordinary, and the fortuitous and the irrational confront the stable and the orderly. In *Kane,* Susan Alexander gives up a secure but mediocre existence to enter Kane's erratic world in which she clearly does not belong. In Welles's other films the two worlds are reflected in various ways: the automobile confronts the horse and buggy in *The Magnificent Ambersons;* Nazism brings disorder to a quiet Connecticut town in *The Stranger* (1946); an Irish sailor is exposed to the idle but murderous rich in *The Lady from Shanghai;* an ordinary couple is thrown into a nightmarish world of drugs and violence in *Touch of Evil;* the little man is introduced to fascist bureaucracy in *The Trial.* Even in the Shakespearean cycle, worlds collide: Macbeth's and Lady Macbeth's, Macbeth's and Macduff's (*Macbeth*); Othello's and Iago's, Othello's and Desdemona's (*Othello*); Falstaff's and Henry's, Falstaff's and Hal's (*Chimes at Midnight*).

The Wellesian king-figure dies as he lived—in style: Kane's arms solemnly folded on his breast, Othello's bier carried aloft, Henry IV expiring on his throne. Even the Wellesian villain goes out in the grand manner: from the top of a tower (*The Stranger*), in a maze of mirrors (*The Lady from Shanghai*), plunging through space (*Mr. Arkadin*).

As Welles's first film, *Kane* represents the beginning of the Wellesian style that would continue to manifest itself visually (long takes, dichotomy of light and darkness, recurring mirror and snow imagery) and aurally (overlapping dialogue, cross fades) in his later work. The three-minute-long take that begins *Touch of Evil* had its origin in the camera's moving up the gate of Xanadu at the opening of *Citizen Kane* and in the camera's craning up the billboard advertising Susan Alexander Kane's appearance at El Rancho, moving over to the skylight, then shooting down at Susan seated at a table. Kane's multiple image reflected in the panels of the mirrored corridor anticipates the multiple images of Elsa and Bannister in the climax of *The Lady from Shanghai.* Welles's ambiguous attitude toward light (source of knowledge and sign of its absence; symbol of innocence and illusion as well as the glare of reality) runs throughout his films. Susan, a study in white with her blonde hair and gleaming white skin, is a symbol of innocence exploited. The light that floods her face makes her even more pathetic; so does the light that masks the face of the doomed Isabel in *The Magnificent Ambersons.* Conversely, the light that hardens the face of the already hardened (and blonde) Elsa Bannister in *The Lady from Shanghai* mocks the symbol of innocence by its profusion.

Like *Kane*, other Welles films open in darkness or semi-darkness (*The Lady from Shanghai, The Stranger, Macbeth, Touch of Evil*). Darkness can suggest womb-like withdrawal (the dimly lit Xanadu) as well as a universe unilluminated by grace or providence (*The Lady from Shanghai, Touch of Evil*).

For a true appreciation of *Kane*, one must know how, as the first expression of Welles's visual and aural style, it foreshadowed themes and techniques that reappear in his subsequent films.

The Myth Critic

Every leading character in *Citizen Kane* is the incarnation of a mythological figure. Kane himself is a Zeus type. Zeus, who never had a childhood, was whisked off to Crete by his mother so that his wicked father, Cronus, would not devour him as he had done his other children. Charles Foster Kane was also deprived of a normal boyhood. When he was a child, his mother entrusted him to a guardian so that he could have the life she could never give him.

Neither Zeus nor Kane was happily married. Zeus's marriage to Hera may have been made on Olympus but it was not blessed with tranquillity. Kane's marriage to the cool, patrician beauty Emily Norton was no different. A president's niece, Emily was socially superior to her husband and showed it by her demeanor. Thus, Kane looked for love elsewhere, finding it briefly in an aspiring but untalented singer, Susan Alexander. Zeus also sought other women, rarely appearing to them as himself but taking another form (a bull, a swan, a husband away from the war). Kane also conceals himself by diluting his importance when describing his job to Susan, preferring that she love him for himself: "I run a couple of newspapers. How about you?"

When Kane tries to make Susan into an opera star, he steps out of the role of Zeus and into that of Pygmalion. But Kane becomes a Pygmalion in reverse. The sculptor Pygmalion fell in love with his own creation, which miraculously came to life. Welles inverts the myth, making Kane into an anti-Pygmalion who fashions a puppet for himself out of a living woman.

Zeus replaced his father's tyranny with the enlightened rule of the Olympians. Kane must fight his surrogate father (Thatcher, his guardian), who embodies the worst qualities of the privileged class. When Thatcher asks Kane what he would like to have been, Kane replies, "Everything you hate." In fact, Kane is always fighting Cronus in some form: Thatcher, the elderly owner of *The Inquirer* that he takes over, the political boss Jim Gettys. When he is not clashing with Cronus, he is battling Prometheus in the person of

Leland, who sees Kane for what he is: "You don't care about anything except you."

Ultimately, Zeus became another Cronus: authoritarian, misanthropic, vindictive, fearful of having his power usurped, and finally aloof. Kane gradually grows more and more like Thatcher-Cronus; although he wants to benefit humanity, he has become too corrupted by wealth to do so. In the *Iliad*, Zeus, weary of all the infighting among the Olympians, frequently retired to the topmost peak of Mount Ida; Kane, disillusioned by political defeat, broken friendships, and Susan's failure as an opera star, retires to the seclusion of Xanadu.

If it is viewed as myth, *Kane*'s universality is more evident than it would be if the film were studied as a historical artifact or as the work of an *auteur*.

A SOCIAL/ECONOMIC APPROACH

As Machiavelli noted in *The Prince*, half of our affairs are governed by fortune (*fortuna*); the other half, by personal endeavor (*virtù*). It was by pure chance that Mary Kane, a boardinghouse owner, acquired the Colorado Lode. A boarder, unable to pay his rent, gave her a deed to an abandoned mine shaft that turned out to be the world's third richest gold mine. Once *fortuna* places something in our path, *virtù* must take over. Unfortunately, Mary Kane's *virtù* was diseased; married to a failure, she did not want her son Charles to become a replica of his father. Therefore, she entrusted the boy to the care of Walter P. Thatcher, a noted financier; in so doing, she deprived Charles of a normal childhood so that he could enjoy a life befitting a millionaire.

The American dream can become a nightmare. Charles Foster Kane first tries to redeem himself. When he assumes control of the *New York Inquirer*, he begins exposing trusts and slumlords. He tells his guardian: "It is my duty—I'll let you in on a secret—it is also my pleasure—to see to it that decent hard-working people of this community aren't robbed blind by a pack of money-mad pirates!"

Kane is a principled muckraker. He also refuses to run the newspaper as if it were his private enterprise; instead, he delegates authority. He even writes a Declaration of Principles, promising his readers an honest newspaper. However, while he is writing it, his face is shrouded in darkness. Kane is clearly irredeemable.

There is no salvation for Kane because he is heir to his mother's belief that the purchasing power of money is infinite. Just as his mother bought him a privileged life, Kane buys his second wife an operatic career as well as an opera house, forcing her into a role for which she has no talent. Finally, to achieve the seclusion he requires, he buys a pleasure dome on the Florida Gulf Coast.

Who is Charles Foster Kane? After his death, the press called him a plutocrat; his guardian branded him a communist; the Union Square demagogues labeled him a fascist. Then there is Kane's view of himself: "I am, always will be, and always have been one thing: an American."

The popular conception of Kane, confused and contradictory, is no different from the popular conception of America: the republic to which we pledge allegiance, the democracy we claim we are, the empire others perceive us to be. The three faces of America become Kane's three faces. First, he is the republican editor who delegates authority to his representatives; then, he is the democratic leader, promising in his Declaration of Principles to be a champion of human rights; finally, he is the imperialist, bald and gowned, an Oriental potentate living in splendor at Xanadu.

Citizen Kane forces us to watch the transformation of the country through the transformation of one man.

While each interpretation is valid as far as it goes, one could easily write an essay combining all of them by recounting details about the film's production history, showing how *Kane*'s visual style is repeated in Welles's other films, relating its archetypal plot to well-known myths, and noting its ambivalence about a society that encourages "rags-to-riches" optimism that places material values before spiritual ones.

GUIDELINES FOR FILM CRITICISM

There is no one way to criticize film. After a lifetime of reviewing, Dwight Macdonald wondered whether the norms that had once served him were still valid. Since Macdonald's guidelines are among the best that a contemporary critic can offer a student of film, it is worthwhile to repeat them here. They represent ways of approaching film, however, not ironclad laws. Thus, there will be exceptions; some of the guidelines may not be applicable to a particular film, as Macdonald is the first to admit. Still, it is easier to deal with exceptions when one has standards by which to measure them than if one has no standards at all. The following excerpt from Macdonald's work, *Dwight Macdonald on Movies*, summarizes his guidelines succinctly:

> I know something about cinema after forty years, and being a congenital critic, I know what I like and why. But I can't explain the *why* except in terms of the specific work under consideration, on which I'm copious

THE THREE FACES OF KANE
The Republican Kane flanked by Leland, his drama critic (Joseph Cotten), and Bernstein, his managing editor (Everett Sloane). (Courtesy MOMA/ FSA and RKO)

enough. The general theory, the larger view, the gestalt—these have always eluded me. Whether this gap in my critical armor be called an idiosyncracy or, less charitably, a personal failing, it has always been most definitely there.

But people, especially undergraduates hot for certainty, keep asking me what rules, principles or standards I judge movies by—a fair question to which I can never think of an answer. Years ago, some forgotten but evidently sharp stimulus spurred me to put some guidelines down on paper. The result, hitherto unprinted for reasons which will become clear, was:

(1) Are the characters consistent, and in fact are there characters at all?

(2) Is it true to life?

(3) Is the photography cliché, or is it adapted to the particular film and therefore original?

(4) Do the parts go together; do they add up to something; is there a rhythm established so that there is form, shape, climax, building up tension and exploding it?

(5) Is there a mind behind it; is there a feeling that a single intelligence has imposed his own view on the material?

The last two questions rough out some vague sort of meaning, and the third is sound, if truistic. But I can't account for the first two being there at all, let alone in the lead-off place. Many films I admire are not "true to life" unless that stretchable term is strained beyond normal usage: *Broken Blossoms, Children of Paradise, Zéro de Conduite, Caligari, On Approval,* Eisenstein's *Ivan the Terrible*. And some have no "characters" at all, consistent or no: *Potemkin, Arsenal, October, Intolerance, Marienbad, Orpheus, Olympia*. The comedies of Keaton, Chaplin, Lubitsch, the Marx Brothers and W. C. Fields occupy a middle ground. They have "consistent characters" all right, and they are also "true to life." But the consistency is always extreme and sometimes compulsive and obsessed (W. C., Groucho, Buster), and the truth is abstract. In short, they are so highly stylized . . . that they are constantly floating up from terra firma into the empyrean of art, right before my astonished and delighted eyes.[13]

The Democratic Kane as Man of the People. (Courtesy MOMA/FSA and RKO)

The Imperial Kane as Master of Xanadu. (Courtesy MOMA/ FSA and RKO)

If philosophy begins with wonder, as Plato claimed, so too does film criticism—with a sense of amazement that pictures can move, and the desire to explain how the moving picture can be a work of art. Even though you know the pictures do not move miraculously, never lose that childlike sense of wonder that you felt when you saw your first movie. Realize that when you are asked to write about a movie that you are sharing in an ancient art, the art of criticism, that goes back to the fourth century B.C. Although film criticism is in its infancy compared to literary criticism, it works from the same principle: the desire to explain structurally, descriptively, psychologically, or ideologically how a work of art functions. The papers you write will be on limited topics; they always are: "Deep Focus in *Citizen Kane*, "The Chronology of *Citizen Kane*," "Expressionism vs. Realism in *Citizen Kane*." Yet if you peruse scholarly journals such as *Film Criticism, Film Quarterly,* and *Literature/Film Quarterly,* you will discover articles by film scholars that are equally specific. One would have to write a book to articulate a philosophy of film. Still, when you write your papers, at least try to relate your particular topic to the whole film, showing how deep focus figures in the film's overall meaning, how the alternation between expressionism and realism is part of the film's tension, or how the jumbled chronology reflects the film's attitude toward Kane's life and biography in general.

Think of the parts in relation to the whole. This is what *Anatomy of Film* has attempted to do: to proceed from the components of narrative film to the total film and finally to ways of interpreting film. Whether you pursue film criticism professionally or simply as a moviegoer, remember that a work of art possesses integrity or wholeness. A film is a totality; even if it is approached piecemeal, it does not lose its integrity, although that integrity may be hard to discern unless the parts are reassembled.

Alexander Pope has been quoted earlier in this chapter because Pope, who was not even twenty when he wrote *An Essay on Criticism,* formulated principles that are still relevant. As you might expect, he also had something to say about focusing on the whole rather than the parts:

'T is not a lip or eye we beauty call,
But the joint force and full result of all.
   —*An Essay on Criticism, II, 45–46*

No matter what kind of critic you become or what kinds of critics you read, relate your approach and theirs to the film as a whole.

NOTES

[1] Raymond Spottiswoode, *A Grammar of the Film: An Analysis of Film Technique* (Berkeley: University of California Press, 1969), 29.

[2] Rudolf Arnheim, *Film as Art* (Berkeley: University of California Press, 1974), 133.

[3] Ibid., 57.

[4] André Bazin, *What Is Cinema?* Vol. 1, trans. Hugh Gray (Berkeley: University of California Press, 1967), 50.

[5] Siegfried Kracauer, *Theory of Film: The Redemption of Physical Reality* (New York: Oxford University Press/Galaxy Books, 1965), 305.

[6] One of the best general studies of semiotics is Kaja Silverman, *The Subject of Semiotics* (New York: Oxford University Press, 1983); on film semiotics, see J. Dudley Andrew, *The Major Film Theories: An Introduction* (New York: Oxford University Press, 1976), 212–41. Also recommended is the structuralism issue of *College English* (October 1975).

[7] Christian Metz, *Film Language: A Semiotics of the Cinema*, trans. Michael Taylor (New York: Oxford University Press, 1974), 105.

[8] Laura Mulvey, "Visual Pleasure and Narrative Cinema," in *Film Theory and Criticism*, 3rd ed., ed. Gerald Mast and Marshall Cohen (New York: Oxford University Press, 1985), 804.

[9] James Agee, *Agee on Film: Reviews and Comments by James Agee* (New York: Grosset & Dunlap, 1969), 39.

[10] On Crowther's career, see Frank E. Beaver, *Bosley Crowther: Social Critic of the Film* (New York: Arno Press, 1974).

[11] Dwight Macdonald, *Dwight Macdonald on Movies* (Englewood Cliffs, NJ: Prentice-Hall, 1969), 471.

[12] Pauline Kael, *Deeper into Movies* (Boston: Atlantic-Little, Brown, 1974), 378.

[13] Richard B. Jewell, "A History of RKO Radio Pictures, Incorporated, 1928–1924" (Ph.D. diss., University of Southern California Press, 1978).

[14] Pauline Kael, "Raising Kane," *The Citizen Kane Book* (Boston: Little Brown, 1971), 1–84.

[15] Robert L. Carringer, *The Making of Citizen Kane* (Berkeley: University of California Press, 1985), 35.

[16] *Dwight Macdonald on Movies*, ix–x.

Appendix I: Sample Student Paper
Transformation and the Human Condition in Psycho
PAMELA R. BRAUTIGAM

Transformation is a vital part of the horror film, which capitalizes on our fear of change, a change into something foreign to ourselves or to human nature. It can be a change in form, appearance, or character; it can be a change of the familiar to the unfamiliar. Psycho (Alfred Hitchcock, 1960) deals with transformation as well as with the defamiliarization of the familiar; the film also arouses our deepest fears about human nature and change.

Marion Crane (Janet Leigh) undergoes several

kinds of transformation. The film opens with Marion
and her lover, Sam (John Gavin), in a Phoenix hotel
room where they are having a lunch—hour tryst. She
is wearing a white bra and half—slip—the color may
signify innocence although the situation does not.
Marion wants to marry Sam, who is in debt and therefore cannot give her the life he feels she deserves. Later that day, Marion steals $40,000 from
the company for which she works. Before she leaves
Phoenix with the money, she changes her clothes, including her lingerie, which is now black. Perhaps
this is Hitchcock's way of suggesting her new life
as a thief (Naremore 34). At any rate, she has undergone a transformation of character: she has
changed from a trusted employee to a criminal.

Her relatively calm life becomes one of panic.
We next see her leaving town, "driving hard . . .
tormented not so much by conscience as by fear"
(Durgnat 128). At a stop light, she sees her boss,
who also sees her. Marion imagines what will be
said when the money is discovered missing. A "growing paranoia and desperation" (Naremore 37) results
as Marion becomes a fugitive.

Marion stops at the side of the road for the
night and is awakened by a police officer the next
morning. He is wearing glasses that are so dark
they seem opaque. He is suspicious of Marion, but
is really "in the dark" about her situation. After
he lets her go, he seems to follow her, but as
Durgnat points out, perhaps this is an aspect of
her paranoia (128). Marion takes the precautions of
trading in her black car for a white one. The color
change is ironic. After she stole the money, she
changed her lingerie from white to black. Now that
she feels under suspicion, she changes the color of
her car to white, perhaps in an unconscious attempt
to proclaim her innocence.

Eventually, Marion arrives at the Bates Motel,
where she decides to spend the night. Norman Bates
(Anthony Perkins), the proprietor, is a naive young
man who seems to have led a lonely and somewhat peculiar life in the country in contrast to Marion's
lonely but fairly normal life in the city. As they

talk, it becomes clear that both of them are hiding
something. Norman tells Marion that he takes care
of his mother. After all, he remarks, "a boy's best
friend is his mother." Norman appears to be a
quiet, introverted young man who has sacrificed his
life for his mother. However, when Marion suggests
that he institutionalize mother, his tone changes
as "he talks about insane asylums with the glazed
eyes and the angry, intense voice of a man who has
been there" (Naremore 52). The former soft—spoken
Norman has been transformed into something frighten-
ing.

When Marion admits that she is running away to a
"private island," Norman replies that one can never
really run away from anything. When Marion claims
that people sometimes deliberately step into their
private traps, Norman answers that he was born in
his. Marion regards Norman's life as far more mis-
erable than her own. She realizes she has become a
different person, acting against her nature. Thus,
she decides to return to Phoenix and rectify what
she has done. She then goes to her room and proceeds to take a shower, thereby cleansing herself
of her "sin." The bathroom is noticeably white; it
has also been defamiliarized. An ordinary shower becomes a sort of sanctuary, a place where Marion can
cleanse herself of sin and become "clean" again.
She is killed, however, supposedly by Mrs. Bates,
who appears in blurred silhouette. The bathroom,
then, is transformed into a place of death, a
morgue; the shower stall is Marion's coffin.

Norman buries Marion and her car in a swamp near
the house. Here, black and white are again in contrast. Durgnat remarks that the bathroom scene, in
which everything is shining and white until the murder, is in sharp contrast to the scene in which the
car, Marion, and the money disappear into a "black
sticky cesspool" (131). Here we see Norman's transformation on another level. Originally, he had only
undergone a change of character. Throughout the
rest of the film we see a Norman who also undergoes
a transformation in both nature and appearance. He
changes back and forth between Norman and Mother,

for Norman's mother has been dead for ten years. Norman killed her and her lover; to alleviate his guilt, he stole her corpse and preserved her body and her memory. Because of his guilt for having taken her life, he feels obligated to give her half of his, becoming "a little more than a double for his mother's corpse" (Naremore 66). Norman uses his voice to make her talk and act jealous whenever he feels sexually attracted to a woman. Each time he undergoes a transformation into Mother, it results in the murder of the woman to whom he is attracted, as is the case with Marion Crane. Norman dresses in his mother's clothes and actually believes his mother is the culprit. When he reverts to Norman, he is horrified at what Mother has done and must cover up her crime lest she be arrested for murder. After all, he believes Mother did this out of love for him.

Norman's last transformation is complete. After he is caught, Mother takes control. Norman the introvert no longer exists. While his mother was alive, she dominated him and continues to do so even in death. Norman is a split personality, but his dominant personality, Mother, has taken over. It is as if Mother has killed Norman and now inhabits his body (Durgnat 135). Norman has undergone a permanent transformation in nature and character, although he still remains Norman in appearance.

In Psycho, Hitchcock shows the dark side of the human condition through Marion and Norman. Marion is "one of us," a normal person who is a little lonely but capable of becoming a thief in an effort to achieve happiness. She experiences a transformation of which we are all capable. Norman, however, represents our deepest fears and insecurities. He is the hidden darkness in all of us that we may be afraid to admit exists even to ourselves. In Psycho, Hitchcock may be saying that such transformations of appearance, character, and nature are not necessarily nonhuman.

Works Cited

Durgnat, Raymond. "Inside Norman Bates." <u>Focus on Hitchcock</u>. Ed. Albert J. LaValley. Englewood Cliffs: Prentice, 1972. 127–37.

Naremore, James. <u>Filmguide to Psycho</u>. Bloomington: Indiana U P, 1973.

<u>Psycho</u>. Dir. Alfred Hitchcock. With Anthony Perkins and Janet Leigh. Universal, 1960.

Appendix II:
A Basic Film Library

Since film studies entered the college curriculum in the 1960s, the number of books on film has multiplied to such an extent that even film journals have not been able to review all of them. Anyone interested in going beyond the boundaries of an introductory film course is naturally in a quandry. Unable to read, much less own, all the books listed in the standard bibliographies, you want to know which are the essential ones or, to use a distinction made on syllabi, which are required rather than suggested. Since personal preference plays a role in any recommendation, I have chosen to identity certain study areas in which you should be knowledgeable and suggest the best books for acquiring that knowledge.

FILM HISTORY

A basic film library should include a comprehensive history of film. Currently, the most complete one is David Cook, *A History of the Narrative Film* (New York: Norton, 1981). However, you should remember that film history is being made every day; thus, no text can give you the latest information about the industry or tell you about the current status of the studios. If you want up-to-the-minute news about the world of film, you should read *Variety*, the bible of the entertainment industry, which is published weekly and, on the West Coast, daily.

Since Cook's is a mammoth work, you might wish to begin with something briefer. In that case, Arthur Knight, *The Liveliest Art: A Panoramic History of the Movies* (New York: Mentor, 1979) is both informative and, by and large, reliable. The silent era is an area unto itself; the best introduction to the silents is William K. Everson, *American Silent Film* (New York: Oxford University Press, 1978).

FILM CRITICISM

Before even attempting to read the more specialized film studies, familiarize yourself with the major approaches to film criticism. Two books will provide you with the general background you need. The first is Gerald Mast and Marshall Cohen, eds., *Film Theory and Criticism: Introductory Readings,* 3rd ed. (New York: Oxford University Press, 1985). This anthology, which has been cited in this text, contains the major theories arranged in sections, each of which is prefaced by a short introduction. J. Dudley Andrew, *The Major Film Theories: An Introduction* (New York: Oxford University Press, 1976), explains the schools of criticism better than any other book.

Since semiotics has become fashionable in film circles, you might wish to learn more about it. The most readable account of what is really an easy science that has been rendered complex and even obscured by the murky prose of some of its practitioners is Kaja Silverman, *The Subject of Semiotics* (New York: Oxford University Press, 1983). Remember too that Andrew has a good account of semiotics in Chapter Eight of *The Major Film Theories.*

Auteur Studies

Because of its historical significance, Andrew Sarris, *The New American Cinema: Directors and Directions 1929–1968* (New York: E.P. Dutton, 1968) is a book one should own. Unfortunately, it has not yet been revised; thus, Sarris's ranking of a director may not correspond to current critical opinion. If a particular director interests you, you should have at least one book about that director. Twayne Publishers has a book on every major director and quite a few minor ones. If you have taken English courses in which you had to consult a critical study of an author for a paper or a report, reading a critical study of a director will convince you that it is just as possible for a film scholar to discuss a director's films as it is for a literary scholar to discuss a writer's works.

BIOGRAPHIES

A good film biography should include some analysis of the filmmaker's works or the actor's films. One of the most controversial film biographies is Donald Spoto, *The Dark Side of Genius: The Life of Alfred Hitchcock* (Boston: Little, Brown, 1983), which illustrates the similarity between Hitchcock's life and his art. The result is a portrait of a tortured genius who translated the tension between his religious scruples and sexual repression into film art. If you are a Hitchcock admirer, your library will not be complete without one of the most informative interviews ever conducted: Truffaut's with Hitchcock, in François Truffaut with the collaboration of Helen C. Scott, *Hitchcock* (New York: Simon & Schuster, 1967).

AUTOBIOGRAPHIES

Film autobiographies tend to be suspect because they are too frequently a catalogue of love affairs and anecdotes that tells nothing about the medium in which the autobiographer became famous. Two exceptions are Lillian Gish, *The Movies, Mr. Griffith and Me* (Englewood Cliffs: Prentice-Hall, 1969), a charmingly written memoir about the early days of moviemaking; and Frank Capra, *The Name above the Title* (New York: Macmillan, 1971), a moving account of a Sicilian immigrant's rise from obscurity to fame.

STUDIO HISTORY

To understand what is meant by Hollywood's golden age, roughly the years between 1930 and 1950, one should know something about the studios and the men who ran them. These *moguls*, as they were called, provoked ambivalent feelings in those who knew and worked for them. On the one hand, the moguls were parental, treating stars like children in need of protection; on the other hand, they were tyrranical, interfering with the stars' private lives and determining their public image. Most of the great studio heads (Darryl F. Zanuck of Fox, Louis B. Mayer of MGM, Jack L. Warner of Warner Bros., Harry Cohn of Columbia) and legendary producers (Samuel Goldwyn, Hal B. Wallis) have been the subjects of biographies. The most colorful biography is Bob Thomas, *King Cohn: The Life and Times of Harry Cohn* (New York: Putnam, 1967). Unfortunately, *King Cohn* is out of print—although you might come upon a copy in a used book store or at a book sale. Two other out-of-print books you should look for are Norman Zierold, *The Moguls* (New York: Avon, 1972) and Philip French, *The Movie Moguls* (Pelican Books, 1971).

Each of the major studios has been the subject of a coffee table book that offers a year-by-year history of the studio with capsule summaries and stills of the films. *The MGM Story, The United Artists*

Story, The Paramount Story, The Warner Bros. Story, and others have been published by Crown Publishers. They are often found on remainder counters in bookstores or are included among publishers' closeouts. Since they are attractively illustrated and moderately informative, they are worth having. The best studio book is *The RKO Story* (Arlington House, n.d.) by film scholar Richard B. Jewell, who drew on the vast knowledge of Vernon S. Harbin, RKO archivist and Hollywood historian.

REFERENCE WORKS

It is actually possible to purchase inexpensive reference works. Truly indispensible is Leslie Halliwell, *The Filmgoer's Companion,* now in its eighth edition, published by Avon. Alphabetically arranged entries from Bud Abbott to Adolph Zukor provide not only biographical information on stars, writers, directors, and so forth, but also definitions of film terms and descriptions of familiar themes and genres. Georges Sadoul's, *Dictionary of Film Makers* and *Dictionary of Films,* translated, edited, and updated by Peter Morris (Berkeley: University of California Press, 1972) are valuable, although they are the kinds of reference books that need constant updating. If you are vitally interested in contemporary film, you should acquire the updated edition of James Monaco, *Who's Who in American Film Now* (New York: Zoetrope).

The vocabulary of film is relatively stable; however, new terms and expressions will continue to enter it. Thus, no dictionary of film terms can claim to be definitive. Frank E. Beaver, *Dictionary of Film Terms* (New York: McGraw, 1983) is as comprehensive a glossary as one will find.

Eventually you will find yourself adding to your collection in the areas in which you are most interested. You will also begin paying more attention to book ads and reviews in such magazines as *Premiere, Film Comment, American Film and Television, Film Quarterly,* and *Sight and Sound.* At the point you discover you need more shelf space, you will no longer be a student of film but a film scholar.

Index